Advisory in Urban High Schools

Palgrave Studies in Urban Education
Series Editors: Alan R. Sadovnik and Susan F. Semel

Reforming Boston Schools, 1930–2006: Overcoming Corruption and Racial Segregation
By Joseph Marr Cronin (April 2008)

What Mothers Say about Special Education: From the 1960s to the Present
By Jan W. Valle (March 2009)

Charter Schools: From Reform Imagery to Reform Reality
By Jeanne M. Powers (June 2009)

Becoming an Engineer in Public Universities: Pathways for Women and Minorities
Edited by Kathryn M. Borman, Will Tyson, and Rhoda H. Halperin (May 2010)

The Multiracial Urban High School: Fearing Peers and Trusting Friends
Susan Rakosi Rosenbloom (October 2010)

Reforming Boston Schools, 1930 to the Present: Overcoming Corruption and Racial Segregation (updated paperback edition of *Reforming Boston Schools, 1930–2006*)
By Joseph Marr Cronin (August 2011)

The History of "Zero Tolerance" in American Public Schooling
By Judith Kafka (December 2011)

Advisory in Urban High Schools: A Study of Expanded Teacher Roles
By Kate Phillippo (August 2013)

Advisory in Urban High Schools
A Study of Expanded Teacher Roles

Kate Phillippo

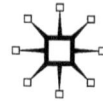

ADVISORY IN URBAN HIGH SCHOOLS
Copyright © Kate Phillippo, 2013.

All rights reserved.

First published in 2013 by
PALGRAVE MACMILLAN®
in the United States—a division of St. Martin's Press LLC,
175 Fifth Avenue, New York, NY 10010.

Where this book is distributed in the UK, Europe and the rest of the world, this is by Palgrave Macmillan, a division of Macmillan Publishers Limited, registered in England, company number 785998, of Houndmills, Basingstoke, Hampshire RG21 6XS.

Palgrave Macmillan is the global academic imprint of the above companies and has companies and representatives throughout the world.

Palgrave® and Macmillan® are registered trademarks in the United States, the United Kingdom, Europe and other countries.

ISBN: 978–1–137–31125–2

Chapter 5, "The Toolbox and How Teachers Used it: Individual Characteristics that Explain Differences in Advisor Role Enactment" is a revision of the article, "Teachers Providing Social and Emotional Support: A Study of Advisor Role Enactment in Small High Schools," which previously appeared in *Teachers College Record*, vol. 112, no. 8 (2010). Republished with permission of *Teachers College Record* through Copyright Clearance Center, Inc.

Library of Congress Cataloging-in-Publication Data

Phillippo, Kate.
    Advisory in urban high schools : a study of expanded teacher roles / Kate Phillippo.
       pages cm.—(Palgrave studies in urban education)
       Includes bibliographical references and index.
       ISBN 978–1–137–31125–2 (alk. paper)
     1. Urban schools—United States. 2. Counseling in secondary education—United States. 3. Teacher participation in educational counseling—United States. I. Title.
LC5131.P49 2013
370.9173′2—dc23   2013004039

A catalogue record of the book is available from the British Library.

Design by Newgen Knowledge Works (P) Ltd., Chennai, India.

First edition: August 2013

10 9 8 7 6 5 4 3 2 1

For Noam

Contents

List of Figures and Tables	ix
Series Editors' Foreword	xi
Acknowledgments	xiii

One	Advisory: A View into Expanded Teacher Roles	1
Two	"Very Nice, but Not Very Helpful": The Education Profession's Divergent Representations of Teachers' Social-Emotional Support Responsibilities, 1892–2011 *With Beth Wright*	21
Three	Advisor Role Structure: How Schools Support or Undermine Expanded Teacher Roles	41
Four	Consistency and Variation in Teachers' Implementation of the Advisor Role	65
Five	The Toolbox and How Teachers Used It: Individual Characteristics That Explain Differences in Advisor Role Enactment	83
Six	Occupational Hazards and Innovation: Teachers' Responses to the Advisor Role	115
Seven	Tying It All Together: Lessons about Formally Expanded Teacher Roles, Teachers Advising Students, and Teachers Providing Social-Emotional Support	141
Appendix A	*Teacher Interview Participants, Sorted by School*	167
Appendix B	*Overview of Research Methods*	169

Notes	175
References	177
Index	195

Figures and Tables

Figures

2.1	Documents' categorization of teachers' social-emotional support role	26
2.2	Frequency of documents that include and exclude teachers' social-emotional support roles, by ten-year period (1892–2011)	27
3.1	The advisor role's structural elements	46
3.2	Alignment of the advisor role's structural elements at King	54
3.3	Alignment of the advisor role's structural elements at Los Robles	55
3.4	Alignment of the advisor role's structural elements at Western	56
4.1	Percentage of advisors engaging in different activities, by school	68
4.2	Number of advisors defining role as concerned with academic support, social-emotional support, or life skills instruction, by school	73
5.1	Conceptual framework illustration: Interaction between teacher-level resources and schemas and school-level resources and schemas	87
6.1	Teacher quadrants used for analysis of between-teacher variation in teacher responses to advisor role	124
7.1	Recommendations for developing teachers' social-emotional support competence	159

Tables

1.1	Participating schools: Select descriptive characteristics	19
2.1	Conceptualizations of teachers' social-support responsibilities: A typology	29

3.1	Structural elements of advisor role	47
3.2	Time allotted for advisory class, by school	48
3.3	The impact of the advisor role's alignment	60
5.1	Teacher-level schemas for the advisor role	90
5.2	Teacher-level advisor role resources	93
5.3	Mean scores and standard deviations for individual teacher characteristics, sorted by teacher quadrant	102
6.1	Teacher responses to the advisor role, sorted by school	120
6.2	Teacher responses to the advisor role, sorted by teacher quadrant	124

Series Editors' Foreword

Kate Phillippo's book *Advisory in Urban High Schools: A Study of Expanded Teacher Roles* is an important addition to research on the changing and expanding roles of teachers in urban high schools, especially those developed as part of the small schools movement of the past three decades. Phillippo provides both a historical and sociological analysis of how urban schools and the roles of urban teachers have expanded and changed in the twentieth century. She provides an important corrective to the literature on teacher roles and the small school movement by acknowledging, as we have pointed out in our own work, that the origins of small, progressive schools with advisory is not a new phenomenon, but must be traced back to the early small progressive schools of the twentieth century, including the Dalton School, the City and Country School, and the Organic School. In fact, one of the three components of Helen Parkhurst's Dalton Plan implemented in 1919 at her school in New York City was House, which was one of the early precursors of advisory; a fact that most small school researchers and advocates fail to point out or simply do not know.

But these schools were all private and served a mostly white and affluent student population, one of the paradoxes of the early progressive schools: that they were "democratic" education for the elite. This book shows how contemporary advisory and small schools have been public, mostly urban, and dedicated to the progressive principles of equity and social justice for low-income students, the majority of whom are students of color. And most importantly, during a period of continuing emphasis on testing and the academic and cognitive domains of schooling, Phillippo reminds us that teachers who provide social and emotional support to their students are more vital than ever.

Phillippo provides a detailed analysis of the ways in which organizational context, school processes, philosophy, and mission affect the ways in which schools function. More importantly, she demonstrates how tensions between mission, capacity, and implementation provide keys to understanding the ways in which teacher roles are defined and the degree to which teachers are able to implement their academic and social goals.

Through detailed and theoretically and methodologically rigorous case studies of three high schools, 47 teachers, and 35 students, Phillippo demonstrates the complexities of expanded teacher roles, especially as advisors. She reminds us that the tensions between the academic and social are significant, with many teachers caught in an ever-expanding set of roles, which contribute to teacher dissatisfaction and burnout. Nonetheless, drawing upon her rich ethnographic insights and powerful stories, she teases out a number of important themes that these schools and teachers have in common. Most importantly, she provides important evidence that despite these tensions teachers as advisors serving the social and emotional needs of students living in challenging situations must be part of urban school reform.

We are at a crucial moment in educational reform, particularly in urban districts. With a continuation of the Obama/Duncan neoliberal reforms through Race to the Top, including the closing of low-performing schools and value-added models of teacher evaluation based on student standardized tests, there is less room than ever for advisory and teacher roles that entail more than test preparation. Policymakers continue to ignore the pernicious effects of poverty on academic achievement. Nonetheless, as Linda Darling-Hammond convincingly points out, teachers and schools can and do make a difference and school-level policy must also be a part of improving urban schools. This book reminds us that teachers who meet the social and emotional needs of their students, not just the academic, are central to urban school reform. It is an important addition to the Palgrave Studies in Urban Education series and the literature on teachers, teaching and teacher roles in particular and urban school reform in general.

ALAN R. SADOVNIK
AND
SUSAN F. SEMEL
February 27, 2013

Acknowledgments

First and foremost, I express my profound appreciation for the teachers, students, and administrators at the schools where I collected the data that inform this book. Their hospitality amidst their jobs' often-spiraling demands was nothing less than inspiring. Their openness, curiosity, and willingness to push my thinking shaped this book in more ways than I can name. May the pages that follow do justice to their efforts and their generosity.

I thank Alan Sadovnik and Susan Semel for their confidence in and commitment to this book project. Having admired their work for years, it was truly an honor to get to work with them and to receive their support as editors. Appreciation to the acquisition editors Burke Gerstenschlager for helping to bring this project to Palgrave Macmillan, and Sarah Nathan for seeing it through to publication. The scholars who anonymously reviewed my proposal provided just the right mix of challenge and encouragement. The opportunity to write a book with so much guidance has strengthened me not only as a writer but also as a thinker.

The mentorship of senior scholars has shaped every stage and step of this book. In particular, Larry Cuban has shepherded this project from its very beginning. He saw a book in this project long before I did. I deeply appreciate his enthusiasm, editing vision (and hard labor), advice, and honesty. He has always struck the right balance between supporting me and nudging me toward greater independence. I could not ask for a better role model as a scholar. I thank the other scholars who guided me as a doctoral student collecting and analyzing the dissertation data that would inform this book: Tony Bryk, Dan McFarland, Linda Darling-Hammond, Susan Stone, David Tyack, Dick Scott, and David Labaree. The abundance, excellence, and diversity of guidance I received were truly a gift.

The Spencer Foundation provided not only invaluable financial support, through a research training grant and a dissertation fellowship, but also intellectual nourishment by connecting me with outstanding peers and senior mentors, particularly Mark Smylie and Jim Spillane, who spirited along this project as well as my growth as a junior scholar.

I also thank Loyola University Chicago's Department of Academic Affairs for awarding me summer research funding, which made it possible for me to conduct the document research and analysis that informed chapter 2 of this book. My appreciation goes to Michael Sedlak, for his contribution (along with Larry Cuban) of reviewing and suggesting additions to the list of documents I analyzed as part of this segment of research.

The editing and revision of this book was truly a team effort, and my team was exceptional. I thank the following scholars for sharing their perspectives and their frank opinions of earlier drafts of chapters: Betsy Levine Brown, Amy Heineke, Annette Hemmings, Leanne Kallemeyn, Michael Kelly, Rachel Lotan, Dan McFarland, Linn Posey-Maddox, Ann Marie Ryan, Martin Scanlan, and Jim Spillane.

Susan Stone made vital contributions to chapter 4 by leading the analysis of teacher survey data, and has my gratitude and admiration for her ever-sharp work. Beth Wright coresearched and cowrote chapter 2 and provided valuable assistance with other aspects of manuscript preparation, and I am grateful for her many contributions.

I appreciate the many ways in which my parents, Ron and Betty Phillippo, have expressed their confidence in me and their excitement about this opportunity from start to finish. My parents- and sister-in-law, Henry, Janet, and Beth Levinsky, have provided their own share of encouragement as well as invaluable help caring for my son during the dog days of writing.

To my husband, David Levinsky, may my appreciation match his countless forms of support. He encouraged me to study more deeply what I already knew well and found fascinating—the intersection of public education and student mental health—when my next career steps were uncertain. He insisted that I accept the golden ticket of a fellowship to attend Stanford University when it looked completely impossible to me. He supported every step of this study, from my days of gathering data in three different cities to helping me scrape together the hours I needed to analyze data and write to celebrating my accomplishments and putting my setbacks in perspective. Having a strong thinker as a partner has been a real asset as well, and I appreciate his often surprising and insightful suggestions.

And I last thank my son, Noam, for his optimism and curiosity about my work, understanding its importance to me, and for sparing me at times when I had still more to do. Noam has truly helped me see firsthand how important it is for young people to have teachers who can really see, appreciate, honor, and support them as they learn and grow.

Chapter One
Advisory: A View into Expanded Teacher Roles

"I don't talk to Ms. Renato[1]," snarled Omar on a December afternoon. In spite of his distaste for talking with her, Omar got a lot of attention from Ms. Renato, the teacher assigned as his advisor, charged with the responsibility of overseeing her 20 advisees' academic progress and addressing any obstacles to it. A 10th-grade student, Omar read at a 4th-grade level, had fallen behind on credits toward graduation due to multiple course failures, and, by his own admission, frequently ran afoul of school rules. Omar told me that Ms. Renato, his mother, and Western Preparatory Academy's principal had met to discuss whether he could even continue at Western.

At the end of the same academic year, Omar remained at Western, was passing his classes, and had had far fewer disciplinary incidents at school. He credited his teachers, including Ms. Renato, for this turnaround. "Even though she's a little grumpy, I'll still work for her, I'll try my best," he explained. Ms. Renato had worked closely with Omar, his other teachers, Western's principal, his psychiatrist outside of school, his mother, and his uncle (who had custody of Omar while his mother was out of the country for several months) to address the obstacles to Omar's academic progress. Although she described her work with Omar as demanding, frustrating ("makes you want to poke things in your eyes"), and puzzling, she also spoke clearly of her sense of her own effectiveness with him over time.

Twenty miles away at Martin Luther King Academy, effectiveness seemed to evade Ms. Li as she attempted to advise Dolores, a soft-spoken 11th grader whose mother had died, who Ms. Li suspected was involved with local gang members, and who ran behind on academic credits. Ms. Li did not know whether Dolores was currently passing her classes, but she did see her as a young woman in need of academic support and counseling. Even though advisory programs attempt to engage teachers in providing these kinds of supports (with help from professional counselors) to their student advisees, Ms. Li and Dolores remained amicably distant from one another. When I asked Dolores to tell me what advisors at her school did, she told me that advisors "get you to open up, and sometimes they become like best friends." When I asked if that had been her experience so far in her three years as Ms. Li's advisee, she replied, "Not really."

What explains the difference between Ms. Renato and Ms. Li as advisors? The research summarized in this book, gathered with 47 teachers serving as advisors at 3 urban high schools, tells us that there is no curriculum, set of skills, personality type, or school management technique that leads to exceptional (or poor) performance of the advisor role. A fuller understanding of how Ms. Renato and Ms. Li performed the advisor role can be gained by considering their individual stores of knowledge, skills, experience, support, and ideas that inform their work, set in professions and schools that provide scaffolding (whether weak and incomplete or substantial and well-developed) for work such as advising. Looking at the advisor role from this perspective, one can see that this role, which requires teachers to add social and emotional support to the list of things they do each day for their students and for their employing schools, is poorly integrated into the profession of teaching and into the organization of schools. As such, teachers such as Ms. Li and Ms. Renato are on their own to figure out how to advise, with some languishing and others flourishing. Adding to teachers' responsibilities with such limited scaffolding often turns out badly, and is effective only by fortunate coincidence. Nevertheless, today's teachers find themselves increasingly required to add unfamiliar tasks to their list of responsibilities, in the absence of substantial support for such expansions of their roles, and under increased professional and public scrutiny.

Expanded Teacher Roles: Increasingly Present as Teachers Face Scrutiny

It is not difficult to imagine how Ms. Renato and Ms. Li would fare in contemporary discussions and debates about teacher quality, teacher effectiveness, and teacher retention. As discussions about education have come to focus increasingly on teachers, emphasizing their central contributions to student progress (Cuban, 2010; Kumashiro, 2012), Ms. Renato and Ms. Li could serve as human talking points. Educators, policymakers, researchers, and concerned citizens have engaged in often-heated discussions about teacher quality, illustrated most recently by the controversial publication of Los Angeles and New York City teachers' individual effectiveness ratings (Freedberg, 2012; Santos & Otterman, 2012; Song, 2010) and disputes over a new teacher evaluation system during the 2012 Chicago teachers' strike (Banchero & Maher, 2012; Rothstein, 2012). Summarizing

America's current stance toward teachers, Thomas and Wingert (2010) asserted, "Nothing, then, is more important than hiring good teachers and firing bad ones." Ms. Li would likely receive criticism, while those same critics would scramble to recruit, train, reward, and retain as many Ms. Renatos as possible.

Amidst these debates and discussions, however, one hears limited consideration of the degree to which teachers are ready for, or supported in, the jobs they must do each day. Valli and Buese (2007) illustrate the tensions that arose when teachers, under pressure to raise student achievement in accordance with No Child Left Behind legislation, faced dramatically more complex and demanding jobs. They argue that teachers in their study, working under conditions of heightened accountability for student outcomes, contended with new tasks (which Valli and Buese called "role increase"), a growing scope of teacher responsibilities (role expansion), and greater responsibility for teaching and learning (role intensification). Consequences of role increase, role expansion, and role intensification, Valli and Buese argue, included deterioration in the quality of instruction, weakened student-teacher relationships, and diminished teacher well-being.

Teachers' roles have formally expanded in new directions under conditions of public and professional scrutiny. From teacher peer mentoring to teacher monitoring of student performance data to an emphasis on differentiated instruction to the instruction of English-language learners (ELLs) in mainstream classrooms, one can see many examples of teacher role expansion that is required, not optional. "That teachers assume a number of roles in their work in schools and classrooms in hardly news," Valli and Buese write (2007, p. 519), reflecting often-unspoken expectations that teachers work beyond their required hours and adapt in whatever way necessary to promote student success. What is news, however, is the formalization of these requirements. By expanded role, then, I refer to formal expansions of teachers' roles.

Expanded teacher roles are ever-present in American schools. As America's ELL population grows, political pressures toward English-only instruction and shrinking budgets have culminated in the reduction of ELL specialist positions and separate classes for ELLs (Cervantes & Hernandez, 2011; Lucas & Grinberg, 2008). Mainstream classroom teachers, then, must instruct their ELL students whether they know how to do so or not. When teachers occupy designated positions as master teachers (Ackerman & Mackenzie, 2007) or teacher coaches (Mangin, 2009), their assumption of an expanded role is not a voluntary extension of their position, but *is* their position. When teachers become advisors, they find themselves implicitly and explicitly required to provide students like Omar and

Dolores with social-emotional support. In my study, such work included developing supportive day-to-day interpersonal relationships with students, informally counseling students experiencing school or personal difficulties (as acute as incarceration, suicidality, unplanned pregnancy, and community violence), and identifying and assisting students who may be experiencing abuse or neglect in their homes. Expanded teacher roles such as the advisor role might seem like just one more thing for a teacher to do, another expansion of an already multifaceted role, one more mouth to feed at the figurative table of hungry children. The research that informs this book, however, tells us that when teachers do "one more thing" by providing social-emotional support, they might experience brilliant results, make no mark at all, or find themselves demoralized and facing a worsening of their students' problems. What made the difference to the teachers discussed in this book was a combination of individual characteristics, professional preparation, and organizational support, the latter two of which were in rare supply but powerful when present. These findings have implications for how teachers provide social-emotional support to their students and for how schools structure and staff advisory programs. This book also contributes new knowledge about the enactment and results of expanded teacher roles. Research strongly supports the idea of teachers taking on some degree of social-emotional support for their students, but the contrasting cases of Ms. Li and Ms. Renato raise important questions.

How much do we ask of our teachers? How much should we ask? Are expanded roles necessarily good for all teachers and, consequently, for their students? What do teachers need to effectively carry out expanded roles? This book pursues answers to these questions by delving deeply into what informs and supports the work of Ms. Renato, Ms. Li, and 45 other teachers who served as advisors. This chapter sets the stage for the book by illustrating more fully the conditions under which Ms. Renato and Ms. Li worked as advisors, both their immediate conditions and the broader organizational and professional contexts in which teachers advise. I then provide an overview of this book, its chapters, and the schools and teachers that tell its story. Before moving on to these portions of the chapter, I briefly consider the value of studying teachers' work as advisors.

Why Study Teachers' Work as Advisors?

Teachers' work as advisors presents four valuable learning opportunities. First, as discussed above, advisory programs represent the formal expansion of traditional teacher roles that has become more familiar in recent years. Teachers have long had the option of voluntarily engaging in a support-oriented relationship with students of their choice. Ingersoll (2003, p. 177) refers to such commitments as "pro-bono," in that teachers donate their time above and beyond their required duties. An assigned advisor role, however, formally adds to teachers' responsibilities. The advisor role provides an opportunity to better understand how teachers adapt and respond to a formal expansion of their role.

Second, advisory programs present a rich opportunity to learn more about student-teacher relationships, particularly the teacher's experience of them. Much of the research on student-teacher relationships (e.g., Crosnoe et al., 2010; Roorda, Koomen, Spilt, & Oort, 2011; Woolley & Bowen, 2007) comes from quantitative analysis of large student data sets. Such studies reveal statistical associations between the quality of student-teacher relationships (usually student-reported) and outcomes such as academic achievement, persistence, and engagement. Qualitative data on student-teacher relationships (e.g., Ancess, 2003; Antrop-González & De Jesús, 2006; Phillippo, 2012; Valenzuela, 1999) illustrates how teacher actions, combined with a school's culture and organizational structures, can promote or discourage student-teacher relationships. This body of work makes it clear that schools and teachers share the responsibility for engendering these relationships. However, these studies provide limited discussion of how teachers navigate and negotiate the work of supporting students or how schools might aid this work, or the sources of teachers' strong (or weak) relational skills. Research on teachers' work as assigned advisors sheds rare light on factors that inform teachers' engagement in relationships with their students.

Third, the advisor role represents a critical and relatively unfamiliar type of role expansion, as it thrusts a range of teachers, not just the *pro-bono* volunteers, into the territory of providing social-emotional support to students. Given recent interest in students' social-emotional learning (Payton et al., 2008), and national attention to social-emotional stressors such as peer harassment and youth homelessness that threaten to disrupt students' academic achievement (Fantuzzo, LeBoeuf, Chen, Rouse, & Culhane, 2012; Miller, 2011; Robinson & Espelage, 2011 & 2012), an empirical exploration of how teachers provide social-emotional support is timely, if not overdue.

Finally, this study's focus on advisor roles in small high schools provides unprecedented data on how teachers fare in small high schools, a schooling model that spread in the late 1990s and early 2000s (Kafka, 2008) and remains in place today across the United States. Most of the research literature on the implementation of the small high school model concerns student performance outcomes (e.g., Bloom & Unterman, 2012; Iatarola, Stiefel, Schwartz, & Chellman, 2008; Sporte & de la Torre, 2010; Vasudeva, Darling-Hammond, Newton, & Montgomery, 2009), with some additional focus on how teacher practice changed (e.g., Kahne, Sporte, Easton, & de la Torre, 2008). The impact of small schools' expectations for expanded teacher responsibility, including, but not limited to, advisory work, has been explored in limited measure (e.g., Johnson & Landman, 2000; Shiller, 2009).

Supporting Students: Two Teachers, Two Stories

Returning to Omar and Dolores, whose stories began this chapter, one can see that their divergent experiences with their advisors make more sense when viewing them through a wider lens that includes their advisors' individual characteristics (knowledge, skills, and ideas about advising) and interlocking professional, organizational, and societal contexts. Ms. Renato, a second-year teacher, came across as having boundless ideas, persistence, and skill. While deeply frustrated with Omar on occasion, she kept up efforts to find and coordinate support for him within and outside of school, to confront him when his behavior sabotaged his progress, and to help him engage with academic work. Her work with Omar exemplified the combination of high expectations and caring that researchers cite as essential to student success (Lee & Smith, 1999; Payne, 2008; Ware, 2006).

Ms. Renato's somewhat unorthodox professional preparation—a bachelor's degree in social work, substantial experience working in and leading a nonprofit youth service organization, and *then* a master's degree in teaching, focused on teaching a diverse population of urban students—prepared her well for this multifaceted work. Even though her school provided very limited formal support to her and her colleagues for their advisory work, Ms. Renato relied on a strong group of immediate colleagues. She belonged to a team of four teachers, who together taught all core-subject courses to a "house," or group of approximately one hundred students. This team supported Ms. Renato's efforts and gave her timely, detailed information about Omar. Like her colleagues, Ms. Renato expressed worry, fatigue, and an occasional sense of ignorance in face of the demands she encountered while advising. Nonetheless, she came across as someone who seemed extremely capable of advising no matter what it entailed, and reported satisfaction with and commitment to her role as an advisor. Professional preparation and workplace support emerged as significant factors in her stance toward her advisory responsibilities.

Ms. Li, Dolores's assigned advisor, approached the advisor role with a fraction of the background experience and support that Ms. Renato enjoyed. She liked the idea of advisory and entertained ideas of using community circle activities or individual check-ins with students as she had seen during her student teaching. None of these activities surfaced in her advisory classroom, however. She used the school's prescribed advisory curriculum, which she described as usually adequate but not exciting. She told me that only a few students were willing to interact with her, and described many of her conversations with them as superficial. Her students corroborated these points, even as they described Ms. Li as "nice."

Relationships in Ms. Li's advisory seemed beyond her range, although she showed great confidence as a fifth-year math teacher who taught multiple courses. "I feel like I'm supposed to be the person that they (advisees) can always come to no matter what, to talk to," Ms. Li said of her role as advisor, but then added, "I don't have that kind of relationship with them." She expressed hope that someone else at her school might connect more meaningfully with her struggling students, but had minimal interactions with colleagues or school-based mental health professionals who might have helped her to develop such connections for students like Dolores. The students' needs and the educator's desire (and sense of duty) were there, but Ms. Li seemed to struggle with doing what she knew she needed to do. Like Ms. Renato, Ms. Li learned very little in her teacher credentialing program about relationship-building, environmental risk, mentoring, or social-emotional support. But unlike Ms. Renato, she had no other experiences or sources of professional preparation or support from which to draw relevant ideas, concrete skills, or perspective. Differences in skills, knowledge, and ideas made a big difference between Ms. Li's and Ms. Renato's performance. The story does not stop there, however.

Supporting Students in Context: Two Teachers, One Story

Ms. Li, Ms. Renato, and the other teachers who informed this book had a diverse range of skills, knowledge, ideas, and informal support that they summoned as they advised students. But while their individual backgrounds varied, the professional, organizational, and social contexts of their work did not. All three schools that participated in this study enrolled significant numbers of lower-socioeconomic status students, had relatively small student populations (less than five hundred students total), and pushed their teachers to personalize school for their students, using advisory programs as a key mechanism toward this end. Also highly consistent across this group was a lack of professional learning experiences to ready them for, and organizational support to help them in, their work as advisors. In spite of a lack of support or guidance for their work, these teachers felt similarly compelled to make their advisees feel cared for by their schools and to provide social-emotional support to them when necessary.

Ms. Li and Ms. Renato tell two parts of the same important story. As will come as no surprise to those interested in school reform, when schools placed unprepared teachers in unfamiliar roles and did not substantially support them in this work, problems could and did occur. Teachers missed, saw but did not act upon, and even evaded crucial opportunities to promote student well-being and achievement. At times, they responded negatively to the role, expressing a sense of overload or plans to leave their positions. Ms. Li cried as she described her work experiences and expressed a sense of having failed her students. "Sometimes it's like maybe I'm doing a disservice and I shouldn't be here," she wondered aloud.

Along with the problems associated with carrying out the advisor role, though, comes a second story. These teachers' near-complete autonomy in performing the unfamiliar, demanding work of advising sometimes turned out very well. In the absence of explicit, substantial teacher professional preparation and organizational support for this work, Ms. Renato and others like her still advised skillfully and avoided becoming overwhelmed by the work, by tapping into their own personal assets. What little school-based support teachers encountered, furthermore, made a substantial difference in the work they did. The Ms. Renatos of this study suggest how organizations that educate and employ teachers might do their work differently to more fully support the work that many of today's schools ask them to do.

Organizational, Professional, and Social Contexts of Advising

Ms. Li and Ms. Renato found themselves in positions where their schools required them to take on tasks, in this case the tasks of caring for, mentoring, and supporting students, for which their teacher certification programs did not prepare them, nor did their employing schools support them. How did this come to be the case? The following section illuminates American schools' varied and complex stance over time toward student-teacher relationships and teachers' social-emotional support of their students. Beginning with a brief history of student-teacher relationships in American schools and working forward to today's schooling and educational policy contexts, evidence shows a winding progression toward an indecisive stance as to whether teachers ought to provide support, beyond academic instruction, to their students.

Student-teacher relationships: From built-in to built-out. A sizeable portion of today's teachers are not required to develop the relationships with their students that include social-emotional support, but this vision of the teacher's role has developed over time. When one-room schoolhouses dominated the US educational landscape, teachers had a connection with students and community that expanded beyond that of subject-matter instruction. They often lived in the same communities where they taught, shared the schoolhouse with community members who used it for other purposes, and knew students and their parents outside of school (Barker & Gump, 1964; Kirkpatrick, 1917). As schools consolidated and grew through increased enrollment, many students traveled longer distances to school, and schools came to be used primarily for teaching and learning. Teachers' roles were constrained to instruction in age-graded classrooms with the advent of bureaucratic school models (Tyack, 1974). Their connections to schools' communities became coincidental and professional rather than natural. When teachers extended themselves beyond professional connections, it was a matter of choice rather than explicit expectation (e.g., Covello, 1958), and sometimes happened in defiance of schools' norms about the scope of teachers' work (e.g., Kohl, 1967; Michie, 2009).

Teachers' social and moral responsibility for their students has also contracted. Until the mid-twentieth century, teachers held socially sanctioned, discretionary authority over students (Grant, 1988; Hurn, 1985). Teachers during this era were widely considered responsible for socializing students, including adolescents, by the means of discipline, manners instruction, moral training, and guidance. Schools, and particularly teachers, experienced a reduction of this scope and exercise of authority during the 1960s and 1970s due to judicial interventions into education and societal shifts away from authoritarian relations between adults and children (Grant, 1988; Hurn, 1985; Mintz, 2006; Sarason, 1996). This narrowing of educators' authority, Hurn asserts, has further restricted teachers' roles to instruction, excluding additional responsibilities.

At the same time, school districts consolidated schools and an increasing proportion of American youth enrolled and stayed in school, rendering secondary schools much larger. Many have questioned the ability of the typical larger US high school to foster the kind of student-teacher relationships known to promote positive educational outcomes. Education scholars (e.g., Bidwell, 1965; Lee, Bryk, & Smith, 1993) have noted how "comprehensive" high schools—larger high schools that enroll upward of 1,000 students, at times approaching or even exceeding 5,000 students (National Center for Education Statistics, 2009)—tend to have organizational environments that do not promote constructive relationships between students and teachers. The comprehensive high school typically serves a large, diverse student population, and attempts to manage this population by sorting students into classes based on age and perceived ability, assigning specialists to oversee programming areas such as school security and student guidance. While these strategies may help schools use money, time, and human resources efficiently, they do not necessarily foster students' academic or personal well-being. Teachers in such circumstances interact daily with numbers of assigned students in the triple digits, rendering sustained personal interactions heroic, if not impossible (Newmann, 1981).

The "human" results of contemporary high school design have been less than encouraging. Research has documented student reactions including alienation and feeling unknown and unfairly treated by adults (Bridgeland, DiIulio, & Morrison, 2006; Fine, 1991; Raywid & Oshiyama, 2000). Some research scholars have found an association between both larger school size and decreased school attachment (Crosnoe, Johnson, & Elder, 2004) and dropout rates (Cotton, 1996; Fry, 2005; Werblow & Duesbery, 2009). Teachers, too, have responded negatively as they have wrestled with the dual tasks of navigating school requirements and attending to 150 or more students per day (Firestone & Rosenblum, 1988; Sizer, 1992). While positive relationships can and do occur in comprehensive high schools (see Hoffman, 1996 and Valenzuela, 1999 for examples), teachers must overcome the constraints of their organizational environments and task demands to connect with students.

Advisory programs: cycling back to a broader teacher role. The advisor role for teachers represents a move back toward a diffuse teacher role that incorporates teachers' knowledge and support of their students. As early as the turn of the twentieth century (Galassi, Gulledge, & Cox, 1997), teachers have engaged in formalized advisor-type roles, with their teaching at times including homeroom and vocational guidance classes. Advisory itself originated in the early twentieth century at the Dalton School, a progressive private school in New York City (Semel, 1992; Semel & Sadovnik, 2008), where students were grouped into houses—one aspect of Helen Parkhurst's Dalton Plan—in which they met four times a week with an assigned teacher. In the late 1960s, reformers in the middle school movement similarly called for teachers to address their students' personal as well as educational needs (Alexander et al., 1968). Advisory programs aimed at developing student-teacher relationships developed and spread, boosted by support in subsequent decades from prominent organizations including the National Middle School Association (1995), the National Association of Secondary School Principals (Alexander & McEwin, 1989), and the Carnegie Council on Adolescent Development (1989). The authors of the Carnegie Council's report, "Turning Points: Preparing American Youth for the 21st Century," asserted that "every student should be well known by at least one adult" (p. 40), and identified advisory as a means to this end. Advisory, the council argued, could improve school environments that they saw as ignoring adolescents' social and emotional needs. Advisory programs expanded teachers' roles into the domains of affective support and guidance, yet did so within the format of the age- and ability-differentiated secondary school by adding advisory classes to existing schedules.

Even amidst concern about their feasibility and their questionable impact upon student learning (e.g., Brown & Anfara, 2001; Galassi, Gulledge, & Cox, 1997), advisory programs have spread beyond middle schools and elite schools to a range of secondary schools. Advisory has factored prominently into small high schools, a model that has promoted student-teacher relationships as an assumed vehicle toward educational achievement, particularly of historically underserved student populations (Ayers, 2000; Nieto, 2000). By intentional, explicit contrast to the comprehensive high school model, the small school model attempts to provide a highly personalized education to students by limiting student enrollment and expanding students' contact with their educators. "In contrast to traditional schools, which presume that knowing students is irrelevant to teaching them," Darling-Hammond (1997) writes of smaller schools, "these schools consciously create strategies aimed at understanding students in order to help them learn" (p. 161). Teachers' regular, close contact with students was positioned as central to small schools' efforts to know students well.

The small school model "rediscovered" the advisory program (Semel & Sadovnik, 2008, p. 1750) and activated it as a key mechanism of personalism. Advisory programs became ubiquitous in small schools (Cushman, 1990; Gewertz, 2007; Tocci & Allen, n.d.). While the advisor role and other efforts to promote personalism in small schools expand teachers' responsibilities, the roles of mental health professionals (who might otherwise fully occupy the "turf" of social-emotional support for students) is somewhat contracted. Small high schools have tended to employ fewer school psychologists, counselors, or social workers than do traditional high schools (Lawrence et al., 2006), and the model minimizes the commitment of resources to nonteaching positions (Darling-Hammond, 1997). Small schools, then, have redistributed part of the responsibility for guidance and social-emotional support to teachers who served as advisors. In small schools, strong student-teacher relationships and teacher support of students are no longer *pro-bono*, but rather part of the job.

This altered job description for teachers spread along with the diffusion of the small schools model and the related small learning communities model (David, 2008; Lee & Ready, 2007; Quint, 2006). These models appeared in many major US school districts, including Austin, Chicago, New York City, and Oakland, which adopted the model in the name of improving student outcomes (Cuban, 2010; Hemphill & Nauer, 2009; Kahne et al., 2008; Vasudeva et al., 2009), and often included advisory programs.

Across school types, implementation support for advisory is mixed, and teachers have responded in kind to advisory with mixed feelings. One can find examples of advisory programs in small high schools that support teachers' expanded roles. The Institute for Student Achievement's (ISA) "Distributed Counseling" model (Allen, Nichols, Tocci, Hochman, & Gross, 2006), for example, supports teacher-advisors' involvement in providing social and emotional support to students through activities such as regularly scheduled collaboration with trained counselors and professional learning experiences geared toward student support and advisory. Such examples, however, seem to be rare. Of the schools where ISA implements Distributed Counseling as part of its reform model, the majority are in the New York City area, where a long-term concentration of small schools provides both more established, "model" schools and a sufficient number of organizations to engage ISA's services. Literature that chronicles teachers' experience with advisory in small high schools is also very limited. Existing literature not only claims advisory's virtues, but also details difficulties with adapting and implementing the model (e.g., Cushman, 1990; Gewertz, 2007; Shiller, 2009), which resemble reported problems with implementing advisory in other kinds of schools. Teachers in these studies often felt uncertain about taking on a guidance role with their students, expressed concern about workload, and felt unprepared to conduct advisory classes. Even though advisory programs have arrived, often by invitation, in secondary schools, teachers do not appear to have what they need to implement it as intended.

Schools and teacher education programs: Limited alignment with teachers' social-emotional support roles. Advisory programs have brought a social-emotional support role to many teachers across the nation, yet it remains unclear how this role expansion works for today's teachers in today's schools. The demand for personalized student-teacher relationships exists in a range of schools, and advisory programs provide a seemingly useful vehicle. Yet most schools remain arranged as they have been since the early twentieth century, with responsibilities for students highly differentiated and carried out by a corresponding array of specialists (Tyack, 1974). Tasks of instructing students fall to teachers, while student-care-related tasks fall to mental health professionals and specialists other than classroom teachers.

The small high school model emphasizes student-teacher relationships, and these schools are in many respects organized differently than more prevalent comprehensive high schools. Strike (2010, p. 96) summarizes small schools' organizational characteristics:

> They are autonomous. They are not bureaucratic. They are flexible. They can be responsive to individual needs. They are collegial. They are more

coherent or more focused. They are less likely to have significant tracking and will have fewer electives.

While these characteristics suggest potential to address teachers' expanded roles, they appear to concern matters of instruction and school-level and classroom-level decision making. These are critical dimensions for reorganization but do not necessarily touch upon scaffolding a significant expansion of the teacher's role into matters of social-emotional support. On this same theme, literature on small schools tends to focus more on broad ideas about advising rather than how to support or carry out the advisor role. For example, *A Simple Justice: The Challenge of Small Schools* (Ayers, Klonsky, & Lyon, 2000), a central text in the exposition and development of the small schools movement, contains no references to advisory in its index. I found this same combination of emphasis on ideas about advising without structures to support it at my study's three sites. "I know what I am supposed to do as an advisor," Ms. Baker, a 26-year-old, third-year teacher told me, adding "I just don't know how to do it." Ideas about supporting students abound, but schools were not organized to support the development or enactment of these ideas. These schools had changed their expectations of teachers without changing *enough* to help teachers meet these expectations.

Research on teacher education suggests that teacher learning doesn't match teachers' social-emotional support role either. Grossman et al. (2007) claim that teaching lags behind other helping professions such as clinical psychology and the clergy with regard to the amount of training that practitioners receive in *relational practice*, the professional practice of engaging with and responding to one's clients (see also McDonald, Bowman & Brayko, 2013). Similarly, scholars concerned with youth mental health have found that teacher education programs do little, if anything, to educate teacher candidates on mental health and wellness issues that their future students will likely confront (Koller & Bertel, 2006; Weston, Anderson-Butcher, & Burke, 2008). These voices add to the chorus of reformers, practitioners, policymakers, and scholars concerned about the fit between teacher education programs and the demands placed on today's teachers.

Other types of expanded teacher roles. This book uses the case of the advisor role in small high schools, but other contemporary examples of expanded teacher roles abound in today's educational landscape. In other examples, such as classroom teachers' work with ELLs and teachers' assumption of school leadership responsibilities, one can see a similar combination of limited organizational support and preservice learning opportunities.

The instruction of ELLs has increasingly become a responsibility of mainstream classroom teachers. Whereas earlier generations of ELLs often began their education in the United States in classrooms that specialized in ELL instruction (or even early instruction in students' native language), this situation has changed due to contributing factors such as an increased presence of ELLs in schools across the United States, political pressure to emphasize English-language instruction in schools, and budget cuts (Cervantes & Hernandez, 2011; Lucas & Grinberg, 2008; Chhandasi, Batalova & McHugh, 2011). Recent federal education policy has required the specification of "highly qualified" teachers' credentials, but state-level implementation of this policy has paid scant attention to teachers' readiness to teach ELLs, and state certification standards' requirements for ELL instruction preparation among general education teachers are considered inconsistent and inadequate (Cadiero-Kaplan & Rodriguez, 2008). Schools, with a decreasing presence of ELL instruction specialists, ask mainstream classroom teachers to take up this responsibility, but have not yet adjusted sufficiently to support teachers' new responsibilities, nor have teacher education programs fully caught up to this daunting and important task.

Similarly, teachers have experienced a rush over the last few decades of opportunities to engage in school-level leadership (Murphy 2005), without accompanying changes in how they are trained or how their schools are organized. Teacher leadership involves tasks of organizational and instructional leadership, specifically for teachers who remain engaged in classroom teaching. These opportunities have not typically met with adequate support. Teachers' limited opportunities for career advancement (Lortie, 1975/2002) appear to operate at cross-purposes to teacher leadership, with teacher leaders' colleagues' mistrusting them or questioning their authority (Smylie & Denny, 1990; Mangin & Stoelinga, 2011). While teacher-leadership-specific programs have begun to emerge in schools of education, educational experiences have not yet sufficiently prepared teachers for these challenges, as leadership is not a substantial focus of generalist teacher education (Murphy, 2005; York-Barr, Sommerness, & Hur, 2008). Bartlett (2004) found significant signs of role overload among teacher leaders, since their other responsibilities did not change sufficiently to allow time for deep engagement in leadership activities (Smylie & Denny, 1990, and Smylie, 1992 report similar findings). Katzenmeyer and Moller (2001, p. 81), sum up the generally unsupportive conditions for teacher leadership in stating, "It is amazing that teacher leadership is possible in schools as they are currently structured."

It is conceptually clear and simple to consider the one-dimensional expansion of teachers' roles, but it is probably more realistic to consider how teachers' roles are simultaneously expanding in multiple directions. Johnson and Landman (2000), describing teachers in nonunion charter and pilot schools, illustrate how teachers' roles in these schools expanded kaleidoscopically:

> Teachers' afternoons were filled with 1 1/2- to 2-hour faculty meetings, grade cluster meetings, school-site council meetings, and professional development sessions. Unscheduled afternoons, evenings, and weekends were devoted to developing original curricula in all disciplines except math, periodically completing 12-page Individualized Learning Plans for each child, selecting and ordering supplies, and collaborating with science and arts specialists. (p. 89)

As policymakers, teacher educators, educational administrators, and citizens contemplate and debate what teachers must to do ensure success for all students, evidence must inform their conversations. Existing evidence strongly suggests that teachers are willing to take on expanded roles that meet contemporary demands, but that the process of assigning and evaluating teacher performance of these expanded roles requires thoughtfulness about who steps into these roles, how they are prepared for and supported in the roles, and how much these roles continue or depart from norms in the teaching profession and in K-12 schools.

One can see, with these examples of the formal expansion of teacher roles, that schools and teacher education programs generally remain oriented toward narrower teacher roles, even as they encourage and at times require teachers to take on broader roles. Ms. Renato, who enjoyed strong collegial support and brought a wealth of advisory-relevant experience to her job, found ways to adjust to a role that was out of sync with the organizations that might otherwise have supported her in it. In a way, Ms. Renato compensated for her school's and her teacher education program's shortcomings related to her advisory responsibilities. Ms. Li, by contrast, appeared to struggle without these critical supports. Her experiences make the lack of an infrastructure for the vital work of supporting students all too apparent, and show how her training and workplace did not match the demands placed on her. This mismatch sends conflicting messages, as described above: student-teacher relationships and teachers' social-emotional support of students are important, but remain relatively invisible in most schools' organizational structures or in the programs that prepare new teachers. Teachers' support of students is simultaneously encouraged and discouraged. We see reasons why teachers may want to work closely with and support students, and equally strong reasons why they so often don't, or can't. This book explores and attempts to define and understand this tension, how teachers go ahead and advise amidst it, and what happens when they do.

Overview of Book and Chapter Descriptions

This book's analytic lens spans from macro- to micro-perspectives on expanded teacher roles, teachers' provision of social-emotional support to their students, and advisory. Its chapters explore the varied contexts of teachers' social-emotional support roles, and also consider how these contexts influenced teachers' work as advisors.

Chapter 2 is the first of two chapters that consider different contexts that frame the formally expanded teacher role. It begins with a discussion of research on the conditions of teaching and teachers' roles in the United States (e.g., Bidwell, 1965; Labaree, 2010; Lortie, 2002; Waller, 1932) that depicts teachers' relationships with students as both essential to teaching and problematic. Using this framework, I report and interpret the results of my analysis of 80 historical documents about education, teaching, and teacher training from the late nineteenth century to present day. This analysis revealed divergent conceptualizations of teachers' social-emotional support roles. This finding suggests that teachers' social-emotional support role not only remains relevant in American education, but also remains an unsettled matter, subject to varied interpretation and subsequent inconsistency in the kind of support that students receive from their teachers. I found that proponents of the small schools movement, which aimed to promote school personalism by encouraging teachers' engagement in students' lives, also left the matter of how teachers might develop relationships with their students open to school and teacher interpretation. Teachers at King, Los Robles, and Western, as a result, received minimal and inconsistent guidance from their profession about how to create and sustain student-teacher relationships or how to provide student support within those relationships.

Chapter 3 shifts attention to how schools support or unintentionally undermine teachers' social-emotional support roles. It begins with a brief review of literature that illustrates the impact of school organization and culture on teacher performance, disposition, and retention. I then analyze King's, Los Robles', and Western's organizational cultures, along with key organizational structures (policies, procedures, and practices) that pertain to their advisory programs and teachers' responsibilities as advisors. At these schools, I found that the nature of cultural or structural features mattered only to a point, and that the alignment of these features with one another and with the school's broader organization were what in fact scaffolded (or failed to scaffold) teachers' work as advisors.

Chapter 4 begins the section of the book focused on teachers' experiences as advisors. In it, I identify how teachers enacted the advisor role along with critical dimensions to consider about the advisor role (and other kinds of expanded teacher roles). I also discuss how these enactments varied across the three participating schools. While these comparisons reveal weak to moderate differences in how schools set up and supported the advisor role, I found highly varied interpretations of the role by individual advisors, both within and across schools.

To make sense of these findings, I turn in chapter 5 to an exploration of what led to variation among teachers in the enactment of the advisor role. After analyzing several individual characteristics (including teacher age, experience, and ethnicity), I propose a typology that uses teachers' knowledge, skills, background experience, support, and ideas about advising to explain this variation. Four advisor minicase studies (including detailed discussion of their work with focal students) illustrate the proposed typology and its connection to role dimensions and contextual factors discussed in earlier chapters.

In chapter 6, I analyze participants' responses to the practical and emotional demands of advisor role through two lenses. These lenses consist of conventional teacher outcomes (e.g., job satisfaction, retention, role overload, and burnout) and "emotional labor" (Hochschild, 2003), meaning work that requires employees to express certain emotions and mute others to create a particular emotional state among their clients, in this case, high school students. Both lenses reveal that teachers with advisory-relevant knowledge, skills, background experience, support, and ideas about advising fared the best among their peers. These data demonstrate that teachers' boundaries upon their work advising students actually helped them to remain productively engaged in the role. I connect these findings back to earlier chapters' discussions of the teaching profession's and schools' support of expanded roles, and make suggestions about the support of teachers in expanded roles to minimize negative teacher outcomes.

In the book's seventh and final chapter, I consolidate my findings and draw implications from them for expanded teacher roles in general, advisory programs' use of teachers, and for teachers' provision of social-emotional support. I highlight findings about how teachers enacted and responded to the advisor role and argue that expanded roles require a combination of strong teachers and supportive organizational and professional contexts, even though the advisor role at King, Los Robles, and Western seemed overly dependent on teacher skill and initiative. I connect these findings to ideas about improving expanded roles' implementation and ultimate results for teachers and students. Connecting back to relevant research literature, I draw explicit implications for school policy and organization, advisory program organization and support, the education preservice and practicing teachers, and teachers' social-emotional support competencies.

Introducing King, Los Robles, and Western

Three high schools, 47 teachers, and 35 students informed this book's empirical portions. Martin Luther King Academy, Los Robles High School, and Western Preparatory Academy—all schools with advisory programs—participated in this study, for which I collected data during the 2006–2007 and 2007–2008 academic years. All teacher participants worked and served as advisors at one of these three urban schools, all located in the Pacific City metropolitan area of California. Twelve of these teachers, representing a range of age, ethnicity, gender, experience, and advisory-related knowledge, skills, support, and ideas, participated in a yearlong series of interviews where we discussed their work with specific advisees (2 to 3 per advisor, 35 in total). These 35 student advisees also participated in interviews that inform this book but are not its main focus (see Phillippo, 2012 for a more detailed discussion of student participants' responses to advisory programs).

Advisory programs were considered de rigeur in the Pacific City metropolitan area's small high schools (part of the movement described on pages 11–13), which arrived in force in the Pacific City metropolitan area in the late 1990s. This movement was furthered by the Coalition of Essential Schools (CES), an organization that supported the development and spread of hundreds of small schools across the United States in an "effort to create an educational system that promotes personalization, equity, and academic challenge for all students" (CES, 2012), as well as the charter school movement that gained steam in California following the Charter Schools Act of 1992 (EdSource, 2012). The policy context during the years of data collection (2006–2008) was one in which state and local funding for formal student social support services such as counseling was extremely limited in all public schools. This situation increased the likelihood of teachers encountering and feeling compelled to respond to demands to provide social-emotional support to their students.

I selected schools (detailed in table 1.1) with similar characteristics (at least 40% low income, at least 65% youth of color, less than 500 students). In all three schools, teacher and student populations differed significantly from one another by ethnicity. Student populations were predominantly students of color, although Western's population, drawing from socioeconomically diverse Pacific City, had about half as many students eligible for free or reduced-price lunch as King and Los Robles did.

These three schools varied somewhat along organizational dimensions, but their students contended with similar issues. King, the result of a district-mandated redesign of the larger South Gate High School due to consistently low student performance, was staffed by unionized, largely

Table 1.1 Participating schools: Select descriptive characteristics

	King	Los Robles	Western
Total student enrollment	354	295	345
Free or reduced-price lunch	69%	82%	40%
Students of color (percent of total enrollment)	97.5%	99%	89%
Total number of teachers serving as advisors	13	24[a]	16
Advisors of color	23%	33%	44%
Years open	7	7	3

Note: [a]Los Robles' number of advisor participants is elevated because my study spanned two academic years there. I included new advisors the second year to compensate for employee attrition.

veteran teachers, while Western was overseen by the charter management organization that opened it, and Los Robles operated in partnership with a local university. Across these schools, students began 9th grade with generally subpar K-8 educational experiences and often performed below grade level. Students also experienced moderate to high levels of social-emotional stress. Faculty and students described student gang activity (including frequent in-school tensions between rival gangs at Los Robles), homelessness, unplanned pregnancies, exposure to community violence and prostitution, and family disruption due to immigration, parents' death, chronic drug use or incarceration, and foster care placement as some of the stresses impacting students. During my school visits, I frequently saw students wearing T-shirts commemorating peers who had died. To support students contending with these stresses, all three schools engaged the services of school-based mental health professionals. These services ranged from one part-time employee at Western to King's full-service medical and mental health clinic, which it shared with other small schools that occupied the same building. Still, teachers at these schools encountered and often took the lead in addressing a wide range of their advisees' personal, behavioral, and academic challenges.

CHAPTER TWO

"VERY NICE, BUT NOT VERY HELPFUL":
THE EDUCATION PROFESSION'S
DIVERGENT REPRESENTATIONS OF
TEACHERS' SOCIAL-EMOTIONAL SUPPORT
RESPONSIBILITIES, 1892–2011

With Beth Wright*

The exploration of the teacher's advisor role continues by taking a very wide view of it, beyond the individual or school level. In this chapter, we provide a broader view of the advisor role by considering the messages that teachers receive from leaders and scholars in their field about how they ought to care for and support their students. In *The First Days of School: How to Be an Effective Teacher* (2005), Wong and Wong advised readers that "the sincerest form of service requires no money, no training, no special clothes, and no college degrees. The sincerest form of service comes from listening, caring, and loving" (pp. 75–76). While this best-selling text showers teachers with pages of detailed advice on procedures and routines for the classroom, it offers no guidance about how teachers might effectively listen to, care for, or love their students. "To say that you are on the side of caring for students is very nice, but not very helpful," Proefriedt (1975, p. 56) writes, 30 years prior, as if anticipating Wong and Wong's statement. "What does such caring mean in terms of the specific behaviors in which you will engage?" (p. 56). Proefriedt's question is particularly relevant to this book's exploration of teachers' work as advisors, in which they encounter expectations to provide social-emotional support to their students by knowing them well, learning about their lives, and intervening when problems arise. But the advisor role presents only one way in which teachers have been assigned these responsibilities. The history of American education contains abundant examples of demands—some subtle, some more explicit—for (and against) teachers to provide social-emotional support. In this chapter, we look at this history by rephrasing Proefriedt's question: What exactly *do* we expect of teachers when it comes to providing social-emotional support to their students?

We pursue an answer to this question by examining discourse about teachers' social-emotional support responsibilities in greater detail, looking at documents about teaching and teacher education from a 120-year period (1892–2011). We specifically consider ideas in the field of education about teachers' social-emotional support responsibilities. What are these ideas? From where have they come? Have they changed over time? Answers to these questions can help us understand how members of the broad field of education—policymakers, teacher educators, textbook authors, scholars, and would-be gurus—develop, or fail to develop, ideas about expanded teacher roles that contribute to the images we hold of how teachers ought to do their work.

In the documents we analyzed, we found multiple, competing representations of how, and even whether, teachers ought to provide social-emotional support to their students. Further, these documents generally provided limited detail on what teachers providing social-emotional support to their students would actually *do*. Readers did not learn what it would look like, for example, for teachers to "detect the social needs of the child," as urban education pioneer Julia Richman (1910) suggested they should. Relevant to this study's three focal schools, we also reviewed a subset of documents (dating from 1992 to 2010) describing the small schools movement. These documents clearly favored teachers providing social-emotional support to students via close student-teacher relationships, and also came up shorthanded on details that would guide teachers' practice. These findings suggest that teachers who serve as advisors, with a role that has expanded into the realm of providing social-emotional support, receive confusing, incomplete guidance from scholarship about teaching as they figure out how to do their jobs.

We approach the framing of teachers' social-emotional support responsibilities from three angles. First, we review research on the conditions of teaching and teachers' roles in the United States that conceptualizes teachers' relationships with students as both essential to teaching and problematic. Second, we report upon the analysis of 80 documents from the years 1892 to 2011, noting chronological trends in our data, differing interpretations of the teacher's role related to the social-emotional support of students, and the degree of specificity in documents that included social-emotional support as a teacher responsibility. Third, we discuss our evaluation (using the same criteria) of a sample of five documents from the small schools movement.

Student-Teacher Relationships: Framed by the Conditions of Teaching

Literature that considers the nature of relationships between American students and their teachers illustrates that these relationships are a necessary part of effective teaching, yet are also problematic. Three themes emerge from this literature: (1) that student-teacher relationships, no matter how authentic, retain an instrumental "bottom line" of academic productivity, (2) that they are inseparable from the school setting, and (3) that they are framed by unclear expectations.

While student-teacher relationships can become quite close and spontaneous, literature underscores that they occur in the service of students' academic performance. Compelled to attend school by laws and social norms, students find themselves required to learn things and behave in ways that others have determined for them. Waller (1932) observes that, under these conditions, teachers must find ways to secure student compliance in order to do their job, or, less delicately stated, "force students to learn" (p. 355). Interpersonal engagement has become one primary way of making this happen (Cusick, 1992; Swidler, 1979). Educational research is replete with books and articles that illustrate the importance of rapport between students and teachers for motivating and engaging students, and for maintaining order in the classroom.

Given this explicit, and often encouraged, connection between student-teacher relationships and learning, Labaree (2010) asserts that any relationship between student and teacher is ultimately instrumental. He claims that the student-teacher relationship has taken on qualities of a primary relationship, which he describes as "an end in itself and not a means to ulterior ends" (p. 142), like relationships that occur between family members or close friends. Student-teacher relationships, by Labaree's definition, also retain qualities of secondary role relationships (like that between cashier and customer), which exist for the sole purpose of getting business done. By these terms, teachers' relationships with their students exist for the sole purpose of producing academic achievement (and other student actions and attitudes believed to support it). To meet this end, however, the student-teacher relationship mixes the two types of relationship together in what Labaree calls a "complicated role environment" (p. 143).

The school as an organizational context also shapes these relationships. Most instructional activities take place within classroom settings (Jackson, 1990), and so a majority of student-teacher relationships transpire within large groups. The development of these individual relationships, then, takes place in a setting that privileges and requires group interactions. Further, student-teacher relationships are constrained temporally by the term of the class period, term of the course (e.g., semester), and academic year. Other constraints are imposed by schools' social positioning of teachers and students, in which teachers possess more power than students do and have a heavier hand in determining which students deserve their care and what teacher care should look like (Stanton-Salazar, 1997 & 2011; Valenzuela, 1999), creating substantial potential for student-teacher relationships involving a power imbalance and uneven distribution across students. Finally, teachers hold responsibilities for evaluating and disciplining students, which not only complicate student-teacher relationships but carry an expectation to treat students in a similar, impartial manner (Waller, 1932). Whether these relationships take place in traditional or alternative schools, qualities of the school's organization exert a substantial influence on how the relationships transpire. These relationships take place in terrain that at best sets parameters upon, and at worst defies, their development. Bidwell (1965) claims, "Paradoxically, to perform adequately in his office the teacher is forced to violate the rules of performance" (p. 979). Teachers must break the written and unwritten rules of how to teach and interact with students to develop relationships with them, in the name of optimal instructional outcomes.

Finally, atop the constraints that student-teacher relationships face, it remains unclear what these relationships should involve or how teachers might develop them. Lortie (2002) and Jackson (1990) famously comment on teachers' isolation from one another and from guidance in terms of day-to-day practice. Under such conditions, teachers experience a high degree of autonomy and receive little direct or indirect guidance about how to do their jobs. Trends of standards-based accountability and teacher coaching have whittled away at teachers' isolation (e.g., Gallucci, Van Lare, Yoon, & Boatright, 2010; Spillane, Pairse & Shererer, 2011), yet teachers' practice with regard to the social-emotional support of their students appears largely untouched. Education researchers have recently described teacher education programs as providing insufficient training in both student mental health (Koller & Bertel, 2006) and the development of student-teacher relationships (Grossman et al., 2007). Further, schools tend to formally differentiate the instruction of students from the social-emotional care of them, putting the former in teachers' hands and the latter in school-based mental health professionals' hands (Lortie, 2002; Phillippo & Stone, 2011), rendering teachers who provide social-emotional support out of their organizationally prescribed (or supported) range. Franklin and associates' finding, that teachers take part in a substantial portion of school-based mental health intervention (Franklin, Kim, Ryan, Kelly, & Montgomery, 2012), suggests to us, then, a misalignment between expected practice and available training and support. Labaree (2010) claims that "teachers are usually left alone to work out a way to teach effectively" (p. 149). Such conditions appear particularly pronounced when it comes to social-emotional support, since teachers receive limited guidance on the matter, schools outsource social-emotional support away from the classroom, and teachers are left to navigate these practice demands on their own.

While student-teacher relationships, and the social-emotional support that teachers provide within these relationships, are often portrayed as desirable and instrumental, American teachers face multiple constraints with regard to how they might carry out these relationships. This situation creates a catch-22, in which teachers are on their own to figure out how to do something that is essential to their job performance. The literature below that highlights this state draws from nearly a century of education research, which suggests a stable conceptualization of teachers' social-emotional support roles, even as schools and what we expect of them have changed dramatically over this time period.

Historic Document Analysis

How unique is the contemporary situation, in which American teachers are implicitly and explicitly encouraged to provide social-emotional support to their students? More specifically, to what extent are social-emotional support expectations of teachers specified and articulated within the US existing educational system, and what are these expectations? To answer these questions, we analyzed a sample of 80 documents about education in grades kindergarten through twelve (K-12) and teacher education in America.

While an exhaustive review of educational literature that meets the above description could involve a near-infinite amount of literature, our sample includes a focused, purposive sample of reports, books, textbooks for teacher candidates, educational policies, school reform programs, teacher education program descriptions, and philosophical discussions about education and teaching. We considered documents dating back to 1892, as the progressive movement gained momentum in American education, prompting educators to consider how students' social and family situations supported or impinged upon their academic learning. Using secondary sources concerning the history of American education (e.g., Fraser, 2007; Herbst, 1989; Labaree, 2008; Rury, 2008; Sedlak, 2008; Tyack, 1974), we identified 80 primary source documents that attempted to influence teachers' work in a variety of ways such as instruction, direct recommendations, critique of contemporary teaching practice, statement of policy requirements, and the description of practices considered effective or ideal by their authors.[1]

To describe the extent to which our documents specified and articulated expectations that teachers provide social-emotional support to their students, we defined social-emotional support as teachers' (1) establishing a relationship beyond that minimally necessary to impart curriculum and measure student progress, (2) assisting a student with a personal situation beyond the scope of curricular content (such as peer relationships, mental health, medical health, or housing), or (3) directly intervening in a student crisis (for example in familial violence or suicidal situations). We sorted documents according to the extent to which they included these activities as part of teachers' responsibilities. We considered documents *inclusive and teacher-specific* if they included social-emotional support of students as a specific teacher responsibility. The *inclusive and not teacher-specific* category was comprised of documents that included social-emotional support of students as schools' or educators' responsibility, but did not specifically assign this responsibility to teachers. Documents in the *explicitly exclusive* category overtly excluded social-emotional support from teachers' responsibilities. The *omission* category included documents that do not mention, either favorably or unfavorably, teachers' or schools' social-emotional support responsibilities.[2]

Mixed, Shifting Messages about Social-Emotional Support as a Teacher Responsibility

These 80 documents told a story of mixed messages about teachers' social-emotional support responsibilities (see figure 2.1). Just under half of

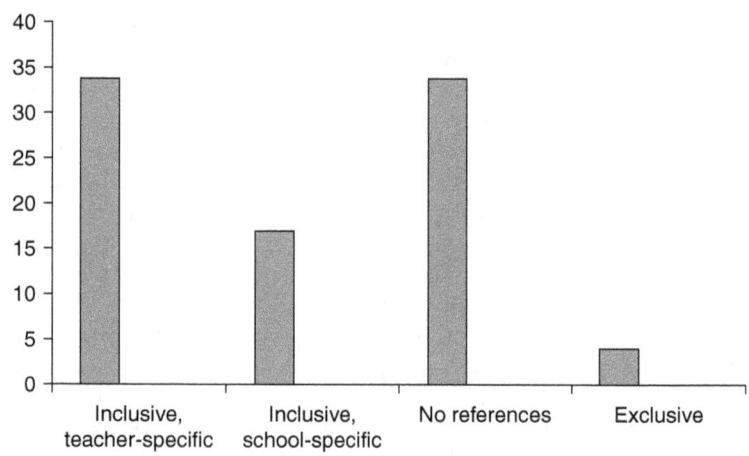

Figure 2.1 Documents' categorization of teachers' social-emotional support role.

the sample (34 documents) included an identification of teachers' social-emotional support role, with 17 more describing schools (but not specifically teachers) providing social-emotional support to students. Twelve documents described social-emotional support in both teacher-specific and not teacher-specific ways. Four documents explicitly stated that it was not the teacher's role to provide social-emotional support to students, while 35 documents did not mention social-emotional support at all, instead emphasizing other aspects of teaching and learning.

We also considered the distribution of different teacher role depictions over time and found signs of chronological trends. Using figure 2.2, we demonstrate the distribution of documents that included and excluded the teachers' social-emotional support role. We left the "Inclusive, but not teacher-specific" category out of figure 2.2 in order to focus on specific inclusion or exclusion of teachers' social-emotional support responsibilities. The "exclusive" category includes both documents that explicitly excluded social-emotional support from teachers' responsibilities and those that made no mention of social-emotional support. We note that our sample is somewhat weighted toward recent documents (26% were published after 2000, although four of those documents are later editions of texts published prior to 2000). While the frequency of documents goes up for these years, it does so for both "inclusive" and "exclusive" documents, resonating with earlier years' distinction between these two categories.

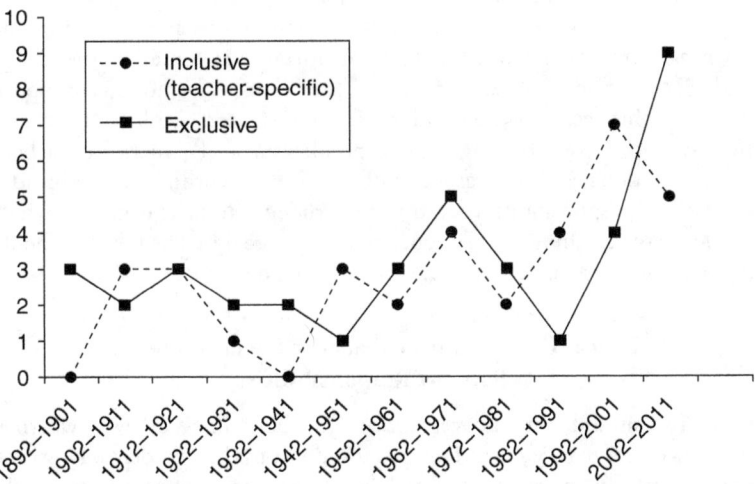

Figure 2.2 Frequency of documents that include and exclude teachers' social-emotional support roles, by ten-year period (1892–2011).

From the 1890s to the present, educational documents have more often excluded teachers' social-emotional support role. However, the reverse was true at specific points in time, particularly the first decade of the 1900s, the 1940s, and the 1980s–1990s, which saw moderate peaks in the number of documents depicting social-emotional support as teachers' responsibility. Those peaks were concurrent with trends that promoted social-emotional support as part of educational movements that considered how social-emotional support might boost student engagement, well-being, and performance, such as the late nineteenth and early twentieth century's social progressivism, life adjustment education (popularized in the 1940s and early 1950s), and education models from the late 1960s and forward that specifically targeted lower-income students. Documents released since 2002 more frequently omit or exclude social-emotional support from the teacher's role (as we illustrate in figure 2.2). Even though a clear majority of the more recent texts exclude social-emotional support from the teacher's role, arguments for and descriptions of a more inclusive role continue. We draw particular attention to how neither inclusive nor exclusive documents have gone away during this 120-year period. These signals about teachers' responsibilities have fluctuated, but both have persisted.

Investigating what underlies the differences between these clusters of documents, we considered recurrent themes in these documents, framed by the literature that we reviewed earlier in this chapter (e.g., Bidwell, 1965; Labaree, 2010; Lortie, 2002; Waller, 1932). We explored the degree to which sample documents' descriptions of teachers' social-emotional support responsibilities (1) related to curriculum-oriented teaching and learning, (2) were integrated with the organizational context of the school, and (3) specified how teachers would provide social-emotional support. Through this second wave of analysis, we identified two key dimensions that synthesize our findings. Conceptualizations of American teachers' social-emotional support responsibilities varied according to the breadth of teachers' responsibilities toward their students and the degree to which teachers' social-emotional support role was integrated with the school's systems for the social-emotional support of students.

Critical Dimensions of Teachers' Social-Emotional Support Responsibilities

Our analysis did not uncover agreement about how, or even whether, teachers ought to give social-emotional support to their students. However, two critical dimensions of teachers' social-emotional support responsibilities emerged from the study's sample documents' diverse arguments, as illustrated in table 2.1. These dimensions involve the breadth of teachers'

Table 2.1 Conceptualizations of teachers' social-support responsibilities: A typology

		Breadth of teachers' responsibilities	
		Narrow	Wide
Degree of teachers' social-emotional support role integration within school systems for student support	Low	Teacher as academic specialist	Teacher as individual agent
	High	Teacher as system component	Teacher as team member

responsibilities toward students—spanning from strictly academic to a more "whole child" orientation—and the degree to which those responsibilities were integrated with teachers' employing schools' efforts to provide student support. When combined with one another, these two dimensions produce four distinct clusters of how educators, policymakers, and others interested in shaping American K-12 education have envisioned the teacher's responsibility for providing social-emotional support to students. These clusters comprise a typology of different conceptualizations of the teacher, relative to the teachers' social-emotional support role.

Teacher as Academic Specialist

This category is largely informed by the "omission" and "exclusion" findings discussed above, in which the teacher's role is defined primarily as that of providing academic instruction and nothing more, with no consideration of either the teacher's or school's responsibilities for providing social-emotional support. Such texts make recommendations for specific curricula or teaching methods, or discuss teacher certification and training, often with a primary focus on the teacher as a specialist in instruction and subject matter. Stepping a bit beyond this range, Evenden's summary of a national teacher survey (1933) advocated that teacher education programs help candidates develop "a sympathetic understanding of the physical, mental and social characteristics of the children or adults to be taught" (p. 93). He described coursework of this nature, though, as rare and did not connect this kind of work to his recommendations to change the content and structure of America's teacher education programs. Instead, like other documents in this cluster, he focused exclusively on teachers' academic responsibilities.

Other documents explicitly conceptualized social-emotional support as antithetical to teachers' and schools' instructional role. Bestor, in *The Restoration Of Learning: A Program For Redeeming The Unfulfilled Promise*

Of American Education (1955), reacted against life adjustment education, which broadened the teacher's role relative to students into the realms of personal guidance and student support. He claimed, "there is one particular need that schools—and only schools—are peculiarly adapted to satisfy. That is the need for intellectual training" (p. 120). Bestor criticized schools' efforts to address other perceived student needs, asserting that "the fact that psychiatric help may be needed by many students does not mean that schoolteachers or administrators have any business undertaking the practice of psychiatry themselves" (p. 31). *A Nation at Risk* (1983), the document often credited with fueling America's standards-based accountability movement, similarly asserted that nonacademic endeavors undermined schools' academic integrity. Schools, the authors claimed,

> are routinely called on to provide solutions to personal, social, and political problems that the home and other institutions either will not or cannot resolve. We must understand that these demands on our schools and colleges often exact an educational cost as well as a financial one.

Interestingly, both documents were written during time periods (the 1940s and 1980s) that our analysis identified as high in references to teachers' social-emotional support responsibilities. These documents seemed to react against these trends, though, and minced no words in asserting that teachers' responsibilities should be primarily, if not exclusively, instructional.

Teacher as System Component

Another subset of our sample documents' authors characterizes teachers as components within differentiated schools or school systems. Tyack (1974) highlights how American schools and school districts tend to differentiate tasks and roles by dividing the work of education into spheres such as management, clerical work, and instructional and noninstructional support of students, in the name of maximum efficiency and precision of worker skill. Teachers, by this arrangement, function largely as academic specialists with others, such as school psychologists and social workers, doing the work of providing social-emotional support to students. As an illustration of this depiction of the teacher, we use the widely replicated Success For All (SFA) school reform program. SFA focuses largely on raising students' academic achievement, and involves a family support team to this end. This team consists of social workers, parent liaisons, and counselors, and gives "assistance when there are indications that students are not working up to their full potential because of problems at home" (Slavin, 1994, p. 642). In discussing a program that focuses on student academic achievement, teacher professional development, and students' social-emotional needs, Slavin and colleagues never intermingled teachers' work (or learning experiences) with matters related to student social-emotional support. These entities existed in separate spheres, even though they served the same children. Similarly, Dryfoos and associates (2005), describing the community schools model, often characterized teachers as a group of professionals that contributed to the model's success, but largely enlisted teachers as sources of service referrals to community partners who then provide social-emotional support services to their students. This trend is magnified in recent initiatives, such as the US Department of Education's (2010) Elementary and Secondary Education Act reauthorization, which emphasized the role of community partners (rather than teachers) as addressing out-of-school obstacles to academic achievement.

Relevant to the matter of student social-emotional support, a few authors criticized school differentiation and specialization as forces that negatively impact student-teacher relationships. "The teachers have abdicated their personal role to specialist counselors and administrators," Goodman wrote in *Compulsory Mis-education* (1964, p. 81), "so that confiding and guidance tend to occur only in extreme situations. One must be 'deviant' to be attended to as a human being." This cluster of documents describes schools as organizations that provide social-emotional support, but does not depict teachers as engaged in this work.

Teacher as Individual Agent

In contrast to the more constrained teacher roles described above, another group of authors presents the teacher as an individual agent, a figurative virtuoso in the concert hall of a classroom, calling the tune in order to make the music of education. This teacher does "whatever it takes" (Kopp, 2001, p. 167) to educate students, and social-emotional support is but one aspect of that work. Individual agent teachers connected effectively with their students and seemed to intervene in their personal lives as a matter of course. Gregory Michie, author of *Holler if You Hear Me: The Education of a Teacher and His Students* (2009), a now second-edition book that has sold over 60,000 copies, recounted interactions with a number of his 6th-grade students where he took such actions. When his student, Mayra, gave him a note in which she disclosed personal and family distress ("Once there was a helping hand that was guiding me out of the mist but the hand let go, and I was taken back into the middle, lost in the depths of mist once again," p. 118), Michie continued the conversation. Mayra disclosed a history of sexual abuse, a desire to run away from home, and uncertainty about whether she should continue to attend school. Michie responded calmly, thoroughly, and attentively, even assuring Mayra that he would check the next day to see that she'd made it to school. Covello (1958) also describes intervening in his students' lives, such as making home visit to counsel a student's father against continuing the use of physical discipline with his son. This home visit, Covello noted, was not a rarity but a matter of course: "There were so many others in those days that sometimes it seems as if I spent almost as much time in the homes of my students as I did at the school" (Covello, 1958, p. 134). Teachers in these documents handle emergent social-emotional issues with expertise and attunement.

A striking characteristic of this characterization of teachers is the limited connection made between the teacher's provision of social-emotional support and the workings of the surrounding school. In these accounts, colleagues, administrators, or school-based mental health specialists factored scarcely into the support that teachers provide directly to their students. No components or cogs in any machine, this group of teachers operated on their own and did so effectively, often outside of the parameters of the classroom or even the school day. If outside support providers were involved, teachers had a hand in it, as illustrated by Teach for America (TFA) founder Wendy Kopp: "When they (TFA corps members) discover that health issues or family problems are holding their students back, they find social services that can help" (Kopp, 2001, p. 167). Herbert Kohl, in *36 Children* (1967), spent significant time with his students outside of school hours (before the morning bell, on out-of-state trips, and when they visited his home). He portrayed colleagues and administrators as either not understanding the purpose of these interactions with his students or as obstacles to them. The *Commonwealth Teacher-Training Study* (1929), which assessed the nature of activities undertaken by teachers, listed activities that addressed social-emotional issues (e.g., "performing parental functions for pupils," p. 508, "conversing with needy pupils to determine exact needs," p. 509), with no mention of collaboration with colleagues, administrators, or mental health professionals. In these documents, individual teachers worked on their own, and, in all of our sample documents (except for the Commonwealth study, which does not contain data describing teachers' work in detail), did so with apparent success. In several instances, this group of authors portrays schools and the educational system as flawed, thus making the individual teacher's actions key to student well-being and success. This depiction of teachers is both, as this chapter's title suggests, "nice," in that it shows us examples of strong teachers providing social and emotional support to students who appear to benefit from it, and "not very helpful." Readers get clear representations of teachers enacting and even embracing the social-emotional support role, but do not get a clear sense of how teachers carry this work out in the organizational environment of the school, whether or how others support their work, or how they came to possess these skills in the first place.

Teacher as Team Member

Another set of documents characterizes teachers as integral members of a student support team. On this literal or figurative team, teachers take on direct social-emotional support responsibilities as part of a schoolwide system for student support. While the "teacher as system component" depiction frames teachers as specialists who count on others to provide social-emotional support to their students, this group of teachers is characterized as substantially involved in student support along with others. This cluster of documents' emphasis ranges from student mental health to more general kinds of student support. Comer's description of the School Development Program (SDP) school reform model (1995) detailed diffuse social-emotional support responsibilities across the school, delivered by mental health specialists, teachers, and other school staff. "The application of social and behavioral science principles to every aspect of the school program," Comer wrote, "will improve the climate of relationships among all involved and will facilitate significant academic and social growth of students" (p. 60). Throughout SDP schools, adults supported students' academic progress and social-emotional well-being. Teachers who engaged this work, per Comer's description, were connected with mental health professionals for the sake of guidance and referral. Similarly, Ravitz argued in *Education in Depressed Areas* (1963) that social support implemented throughout the school was associated with good teaching for lower-income students. She wrote, "Although social work ordinarily does not cut to the root of social problems, better coordinated social work activity is an important adjunct of successful teaching" (p. 17). In these cases, teachers provided social-emotional support in coordinated tandem with professionals with related, but distinct, skill sets.

Other authors conceived of teachers *as* a social support system, providing the bulk of social-emotional support to students with limited input from school- or community-based mental health providers. "Team members take on the hyphenated role of teacher-counselor," writes the National Commission on Teaching & America's Future (1996, p. 58), illustrating this point as they describe what they consider model practices. Proponents of the life adjustment education movement similarly described the teacher as a "significant counselor" (US Office of Education, 1948, p. 38) and later asserted that "most of our guidance should be done in the classes, clubs, teams and social units of the schools, not in the offices of deans, personnel directors, and counselors" (Rosecrance as cited in US Office of

Education, 1948, p. 57). Mathews (2009) describes Knowledge Is Power Program (KIPP) charter school network founder Dave Levin as an individual agent-style provider of social-emotional support ("It was made clear [by Levin's employing school before he founded KIPP] that young white teachers should not be wandering into the neighborhoods served by Bastian Elementary. Levin didn't care," p. 26). However, Mathews depicts KIPP network schools as systems in which all teachers provide whatever support students need, working side-by-side to address the personal, family, and social issues that threaten their students' school performance. In these depictions, teachers provide social-emotional support as a (if not *the*) central part of a system of support for students.

Small Schools: A System of Individual Agents

Since this book focuses on the advisor role and explores its enactment in small high schools, we conducted an analysis (identical to that described above) of five texts that publicized and explained the small schools movement, which gained steam in the 1990s and continues today through small schools opened in recent years in many US cities. All five texts (Ayers, Klonsky, & Lyon, 2000; Cotton, 2001; Meier, 2002; Sizer, 1992; Strike, 2010) portrayed the social-emotional support of students as a specific teacher responsibility as well as the broader school's responsibility. Interestingly, these depictions are of a school model in which every teacher takes on the function of an individual agent providing social-emotional support, the staff a team of individual agents.

All five texts emphasized student-teacher relationships as central to small school communities. Most importantly, the authors stressed the importance of teachers knowing their students well in order to teach them effectively, to diffuse negative behavior and to help build trust. Strike (2010) emphasizes that all of the small school's endeavors, not just student-teacher relationships, must combine to create and sustain the school's community. The other authors, however, focused more intently on the central role of student-teacher relationships in supporting student achievement. Mohr, in Ayers, Klonsky, and Lyon's text (2000), states, "Staff members know how and why each student learns best, they know the students' histories, they see the students grow over time, and they are a part of the process" (p. 152). Two texts (Ayers Klonsky, & Lyon, 2000; Strike, 2010) portray teachers in small schools as knowing students well enough to identify the potential for and prevent violent student acts (both texts use the 1999 Columbine school shooting as a point of reference). "Can't educators really get to know kids to the degree that the seeds of violent, antisocial behavior can be detected well in advance and dissipated?," Klonsky (2000, in Ayers

Klonsky, & Lyon, 2000, p. 25) asks. In addition, Theodore Sizer (1992) described these relationships as involving direct student guidance. He asserted that "good teachers are good counselors...students turn to them for help, whether or not their titles identify them as 'guidance' people" (Sizer, 1992, p. 137), and later describes teachers' multiple obligations as "teacher-manager-counselor" (p. 227). Portraying the systemic quality of strong student-teacher relationships, Deborah Meier wrote, "every adult in the school feels responsible for every kid" (2002, p. 111). By this description, teachers are not specialized components of a system, but rather *comprise* a system of individual agents expected to thoroughly know, support, and teach all of their students. Mental health professionals were present in these depictions, but teachers substantially shared social-emotional support responsibilities with them.

Despite this consistent emphasis on strong student-teacher relationships that include direct intervention and social-emotional support, however, none of these texts specify how teachers might develop such relationships. Sizer (1992) commented that "staff members who are well trained in counseling and testing skills can support the teachers in each small academic unit" (p. 137), but readers do not learn what training or support teachers might expect. Reviewing a range of literature about small schools, Cotton (2001) states that teachers "can become knowledgeable about students' learning strengths and needs and identify ways to respond to them in a way that is not possible in the typical large high school" (p. 29), but does not go on to discuss what those ways are. The index to Ayers and associates' book (2000), which compiles the work many of the small schools' movement's strongest and most well-known advocates, contains no references to advisory or to specific strategies for growing the relationships that are so central to the movement's approach to educating young people. The inclusion of the social-emotional support as a school and teacher responsibility is paired with a lack of specificity about how teachers might carry out such a responsibility. This theme is echoed in the larger set of documents that we analyzed for this chapter.

Lack of Detail about Broader Teacher Roles

Documents that conceptualized the teacher's role as broader (whether as an individual agent or as an integral part of support systems) varied with regard to the level of detail they provided about how teachers might go about carrying out these roles. While Comer's SDP (described above, 1995) specified what teachers do (as well as the structures and colleagues that scaffold their work) in providing social-emotional support, most documents that included references to teachers providing social-emotional support did not offer this high level of detail. We rated, on a 5-point scale, each document's specificity about the sorts of activities teachers would perform, how those activities related to student needs, or schools' broader efforts to meet those needs. Only 28 percent scored 4 or 5 points, indicating that the majority ranged from not specified at all to moderately specified. The modal document scored 2.6 points, indicating that its level of specification was less than moderate.

Armstrong, Henson, and Savage's *Education: An Introduction* (1993), exemplifies this group of documents' limited specificity. The authors discuss teachers' "counseling function" (p. 147) but provide limited additional detail on how to carry out this function. Most strikingly, this introductory text presented a vignette in which a teacher (Laura) learns that a student of hers (Sarah) was about to initiate a sexual relationship with a boyfriend. The authors raised important questions about the teachers' social-emotional support role:

> What should Laura do? Should she talk to Sarah's parents?...Should she take it upon herself to provide birth control information to Sarah? Should she counsel Sarah about the need to avoid a physical relationship? Should she involve the school counseling staff?...What kinds of actions can be taken that will resolve the problem and still maintain confidentiality? What would you do in this situation? (Armstrong, Henson, & Savage, 1993, pp. 177–178)

The authors, however, did not answer any of these questions themselves. After encouraging the teacher's involvement in her student's personal life, and raising implicit questions about the advisability of different courses of action, they left the reader (most likely a teacher candidate) hanging as to how a teacher might answer these questions for herself. The inclusion or exclusion of teachers' social-emotional support responsibilities is one matter worth considering; the other is how much guidance teachers receive about taking on responsibilities that lie outside of the conventionally understood teacher role. When authors broadened this role, they most often did not support this breadth with sufficient detail about how it might unfold in a teacher's classroom or a school.

Conclusion and Implications

This chapter demonstrates persistently divergent expectations about how, and whether, teachers ought to provide their students with social and emotional support. We see teachers characterized as needing to focus on academic instruction alone, to serve as mechanisms for connecting students to support services, to function independently as hyphenated teacher-counselors, and to operate as part of a larger system that meets students' needs. Across these divergent characterizations, we identify a persistent signal about teachers' social-emotional support responsibilities. There is something about teachers providing social-emotional support that American educators and those who write to, for, and about them, just can't (or don't want to) shake.

However, even when authors advocate teachers taking on social-emotional support responsibilities, their messages are most often underspecified. Most of the descriptions reviewed above stop short, usually quite short, of going into detail about how teachers might provide social-emotional support in the classroom setting. The conflicting, incomplete messages teachers receive accompany them into professional contexts that compound their potential confusion. Divergent, underspecified conceptualizations of teachers' social-emotional support roles come alongside (1) an emphasis on the role's importance and (2) a lack of support by schools as organizations and by teachers' formal and informal professional learning opportunities, as discussed in this chapter's early pages. One can hardly expect teachers to succeed in this aspect of their work, given this maddening setup. That some teachers succeed anyway comes as a curious surprise.

These conditions are, as the next chapter indicates, magnified in the small schools that we studied, and the documents on small schools that we analyzed suggest an explanation. These documents, which described and advocated for the small schools model, consistently contained descriptions of a teacher role expanded into the realm of social-emotional support alongside limited detail about how teachers would carry out the role. Teachers in schools that overtly encouraged them to engage more deeply in their students' lives, often as much or more so than school-based mental health professionals, would find the same lack of guidance that other teachers did.

Given that 120 years of data on this topic reveals so little coherent or specific guidance for teachers, we would have been surprised to see a dramatic shift in the small schools model with regard to how teachers' roles were depicted or supported. Nonetheless, we must conclude that teachers at King, Los Robles, and Western—this book's focal schools—were exposed to a persistently inconsistent, undeveloped discourse about their social-emotional support responsibilities, both as American educators and as educators working in small schools. The discourse that we review in this chapter offered little to guide them as they encountered their workplaces' demands to advise and provide social-emotional support to their students.

While social-emotional support by teachers—such as that provided by teachers who take on the advisor role—has a clear (if somewhat shaky) place in American schools, this place requires additional groundwork if it is to be actualized. Involved parties have not reached agreement about how or even whether teachers ought to take part in the social-emotional support of their students. We propose drawing more stakeholders—including students, parents, teachers, school leaders, school-based mental health professionals, and policymakers—into this conversation and connecting it more directly to teachers' practice in schools. A dialogue among these stakeholders, taking into account evidence of the persistent, conflicting, and unclear messages reported above, as well as the organizational constraints that schools place on student-teacher relationships, could contribute to greater clarity. In this conversation, stakeholders could more explicitly address the range of students' social-emotional matters that today's teachers encounter, what support tasks fall to them (in accord with or in defiance of formal job descriptions), and how stakeholders would like to see teachers respond.

Such expectations would need to be accompanied by clear guidance about how teachers would go about providing social-emotional support to their students. Our analysis highlights the minimal detail that many writings for and about teachers provided in this area. Teacher education (both traditional and alternative) has a number of footholds where such learning experiences might take place, or in fact already do. These include courses, course modules, or other kinds of learning opportunities in classroom management, child and adolescent development, and teaching K-12 students of diverse cultures, linguistic backgrounds, and learning styles. Further study about how teacher education programs already address social-emotional support related issues could inform such work. Given that student social-emotional matters vary by school and by community, as well as over time, school-based determination of teachers' learning needs, as well as on-site professional development tailored to these needs, might also provide relevant learning opportunities.

K-12 educators, policymakers, scholars, and teacher educators may not necessarily or quickly buck the 120-year trend of conflicting, poorly defined expectations about teachers' social-emotional support responsibilities. If this trend continues, however, we anticipate that America would continue to produce teachers who range from having nothing to everything to do with the social-emotional support of students, which is indeed what occurred at King, Los Robles, and Western (as described in chapter 4). With teachers interpreting and enacting social-emotional support responsibilities in such divergent ways (as one can only expect they would), students would in turn receive inconsistent support, varying from teacher to teacher, and school to school.

These findings and implications illustrate how expanded teacher roles do not simply drop out of the sky into schools ready to receive them.

Instead, they more likely represent a culmination of earlier, more informal expectations of teachers—expectations that may have gone over well, poorly, or both, that may have vacillated over time. Expectations that generalist teachers instruct English-language learners, for example, have had a long and winding history preceding current emphasis on this aspect of teachers' responsibilities (MacDonald, 2004). An understanding of how such expectations fared over time should help invested parties (such as school and district administrators) understand what to anticipate when putting expanded teacher roles into action. Further, it is important to remember that school contexts may not necessarily offer fertile ground for expanded teacher roles. The example of teachers' social-emotional support roles highlights how these roles are largely incompatible with the ways in which schools are set up. The next chapter builds upon these findings by shifting the focus to the school context for expanded teacher roles. It explores King, Los Robles, and Western as organizations and analyzes the ways in which these schools scaffolded the advisor role.

Chapter Three
Advisor Role Structure: How Schools Support or Undermine Expanded Teacher Roles

Policymakers and researchers have recently focused on schools' contributions to the quality of teachers' work as well as student outcomes. This fascination has manifest itself in standards-based accountability policies' emphasis on schools' average achievement (Jennings & Rentner, 2006; Valli, Croninger, Chambliss, Graever, & Buese, 2008), controversy about the existence and prevalence of "high flying" schools where students meet high performance standards despite economic and educational disadvantages (Baeder, 2011; Harris, 2006; Rothstein, 2004), and research that connects school-level factors to student achievement (e.g., Bryk, Sebring, Allensworth, Luppescu, & Easton, 2010) and teacher retention (Ingersoll & Perda, 2010; Johnson & Kardos, 2008). To continue the study of the advisor role's context that began in chapter 2, I focus here on the school's influence on the work of advising, and how the school contributes to the implementation of expanded teacher roles such as the advisor role.

The cases of Ms. Li and Ms. Renato, introduced in chapter 1, illustrate that schools can support or undermine expanded teacher roles such as the advisor role, or do both at the same time. Both Ms. Li and Ms. Renato had access to their advisees through advisory class meeting time, but their experiences diverged from there. King, Ms. Li's employing school, set up a limited advisor role. Ms. Li went as long as three weeks without seeing her advisees, since King also used advisory class meeting periods to administer standardized testing and to hold schoolwide events. Support for Ms. Li's work as an advisor was also scarce. Formal support took the shape of voluntary, periodic all-faculty meetings (scheduled during teachers' lunch periods) to discuss advisees and plan advisory class as a grade level. Like many of her colleagues, Ms. Li did not always attend these meetings, so teachers had limited opportunities to collaborate with a full set of colleagues about their shared students. Nor could Ms. Li easily connect with her advisees' classroom teachers outside of these occasional meetings, since her planning period did not coincide with theirs. She referred a few advisees to King's guidance counselor and mental health professionals for support, but heard little about what actions were taken, and got no guidance about her subsequent work with students whom she had referred. With an advisor role undercut by weak, limited infrastructure, Ms. Li described her influence on her advisees as "a small drop."

In contrast, Ms. Renato experienced far more consistent structural support for her work of advising students. Western used a *house* plan to organize its assignment of students and teachers (Oxley & McCabe, 1990), and paired groups of approximately one hundred students to a group of four core-subject teachers who also served as these students' advisors.[1] As a result, Ms. Renato saw her advisees at least once a day, between advisory class meetings (four a week) and her content-area classes, in which each of her advisees was enrolled. The house's teaching team held weekly meetings, during which six members layered information about shared students and diverse perspectives on supporting adolescents. Ms. Renato coordinated her advisees' parent-teacher conferences, graded their capstone student projects, and facilitated meetings between faculty, parents, and students when problems arose. While she readily identified places where the advisor role needed additional development and support, Ms. Renato described advisory as integral to Western's ability to serve its students. The advisor role, as Western's administrators set it up, seemed to sit at the center of the school.

The contrast between Ms. Li's and Ms. Renato's experiences illustrates that the advisor role required a certain amount of support from the school to work as intended. It also illustrates that schools' acts of creating an advisory program and dedicating instructional time to it were not in themselves sufficient to truly support the role's enactment. When the advisor role's different elements—what I describe below as the role's *resources, procedures,* and *cultural dimensions*—existed in sufficient amount and aligned with one another, they tended to reinforce one another and to support teachers' practice. When these elements diverged from one another, they seemed unable to help teachers organize and carry out their advisor-role-related tasks. The degree of alignment between the advisor role and other school structures also seemed to weaken or reinforce the advisor role, to make it seem like it furthered the school's efforts or that it contradicted, or worse, competed against them.

This chapter continues with a brief review of literature about structures (such as the advisor role) in schools, distinguishing school structures' three elements (resources, procedures, and cultural dimensions) and then considering how these elements align with one another. From there, I use empirical data from King, Los Robles, and Western to illustrate the advisor role's structure, describing its structural elements at the three sites and how those elements aligned with one another. I next consider alignment between the advisor role and other school structures, particularly instructional and student support structures. I conclude that while it is possible and optimal to have both conditions present, King, Los Robles, and Western were simply not set up—apart from conditions arising on two of Western's house-based teacher teams—in ways that supported the advisor role. This body of evidence suggests that schools can design expanded roles in ways that support implementation, but that optimal design requires attention to multiple aspects of the role.

Structures in Schools

Observable practices in schools are a mixture of formal and informal, concrete and indefinite, intended and spontaneous, necessary and ideal. These strands all come into play when schools create expanded teacher roles such as the advisor role, and when teachers then enact them. Giddens (1984) and Sewell (2005) offer useful tools for reckoning with and learning from these different strands in their scholarship on structures. Giddens asserts that social systems (such as schools) are made up of different practices, which can come to be systematically carried out and largely consistent across time and space. Under such conditions, practices take on structural properties, particularly the power to orient and focus human behavior. Giddens (1984) calls those properties "structures" for short. The organization of secondary teachers' work into academic departments—replicated and recognizable across a variety of schools over time, even as each department will vary to some extent from the virtual template—serves as one example of a practice that has become a structure. Sewell (2005) contends that structures not only shape practice, but are in turn also shaped *by* practice, as individuals interpret them in different ways. I approach the advisor role as a structure that both shapes and is shaped by teachers' practice of it.

Both Giddens and Sewell break the concept of structures down into more specific components, which helps to clarify how they work. Drawing heavily from Giddens' work, Sewell (2005) claims that structures are made up of combined *resources* and *schemas*. He defines resources as either human (e.g., knowledge) or nonhuman (e.g., land) matter "that can be used to enhance or maintain power" (p. 133). Sewell defines schemas as "generalizable procedures applied in the enactment/reproduction of social life" (p. 131). By this definition, schemas guide individuals' behavior, both their thoughts and their actions. Sewell uses the image of a building to illustrate the concept of the structure and its components. He likens schemas to the blueprints that guide the construction of the building, and resources to the bricks that form the building. The saying, "you can't have one without the other" applies to the relationship between the two. Without bricks, blueprints would remain just designs. Without blueprints to guide construction, a pile of bricks could not form a building. Further, neither takes precedence. The blueprints specify an arrangement for the bricks, but the condition and volume of bricks can limit and transform what the blueprint will ultimately accomplish. Similarly, neither schemas nor resources take precedence over one another, but rather interact with and influence one another. Expanded teacher roles such as the advisor role also consist of different elements—these roles are neither bricks nor blueprints alone.

Elements of School Structures: Resources, Procedures, and Cultural Elements

The structure of the advisor role has specific elements. Here, I discuss resources and then consider schemas, including both formalized procedures and their less-formal cultural dimensions. A broad array of *resources*—different kinds of bricks—underpins school structures. Cohen, Raudenbush, and Ball (2003) take a wide view of resources. Rather focusing narrowly on resources as "money or the things that money buys" (p. 119), such as facilities, instructional materials, and staff salaries, they expand the notion of resources to include personal resources (such as educators' knowledge and skills) and environmental and social resources (such as professional leadership and family involvement). Recent research has focused on how school resources—such as school and class size (Biddle & Berliner, 2002; Crosnoe et al., 2004; Lee & Smith, 1997; Whitehurst & Chingos, 2011), leadership and teacher stability (as opposed to turnover) (Allensworth, Ponisciak, & Mazzeo, 2009; Ingersoll, 2001; Holme & Rangel, 2012), and social networks within and spanning beyond schools (Coburn & Russell, 2008; Reagans, 2011)—contribute to desired outcomes such as student achievement, teacher collaboration, and schools' ability to effectively engage in reform activities. Continuing with the example of the academic department as a school structure, a department would make use of resources such as meeting time, department member skills and knowledge, curriculum materials, and relationships with one another and with others within and beyond the school.

Formalized *procedures* in schools specify expectations and requirements of individuals including students, faculty, leadership, and parents. Such procedures are examples of schemas (Sewell, 2005) that are codified and visible to members of a school community, much like a viewable blueprint. These might include teacher union contracts, student graduation requirements, or organizational flow charts that specify a chain of command. Along these lines, Spillane, Pairse, and Sherer (2011) report evidence of schools' organizational routines that served "as a broad script for the staff" (p. 591), which guided teachers' actions according to state performance standards. Such routines included regularly scheduled student performance assessments (geared to state performance standards), which teachers used to guide adaption of instruction to help students meet standards. School leaders specified processes for administering these assessments, as well as for teachers' and administrators' use of their results, with expectations that individuals would comply. Returning to the example of the secondary school academic department, its procedures might involve delineation of the department chairperson's duties and authority as well as tasks required of department members.

Many individuals who work in schools will recognize that they also encounter unwritten, often unspoken, expectations from colleagues, students, parents, administrators, and community members. Even though these expectations do not take the shape of visible, codified procedures, they can be expressed and enforced with the same intensity and assumption of compliance. To return to the blueprint analogy, these expectations would guide construction without taking official or physical form. Our same figurative academic department might have traditions and unwritten rules of conduct that conflict with the formal procedures, or a member who wields more power than the designated chairperson. A range of customs, norms, routines, and expectations are not formally codified or officially required in schools, but nonetheless can be described as schemas that guide and justify individuals' behavior. These kinds of schemas hang together as school structures' *cultural dimensions*. This concept derives from research on organizational and school culture (e.g., Firestone & Louis, 1999; Sarason, 1996), beginning with Schein's definition (1992) of organizational culture as

> a pattern of shared basic assumptions that the group learned as it solved its problems of external adaptation and internal integration, that has worked well enough to be considered valid and, therefore to be taught to new members as the correct way to perceive, think, and feel in relation to those problems. (p. 12)

Assumptions and understandings about how schools ought to work clearly develop within schools, but also originate in educators' professions (such as teaching, administration or guidance counseling) and among policymakers (Mawhinney & Smrekar,1996). Just as organizations have culture, school structures have cultural dimensions to them as well. Structures' cultural dimensions involve ideas about how the structure should (and should not) work, norms and patterns of how the structure is used, and why it exists in the first place, even if formal policies or written rules do not reflect these things. Martin (1992) notes that organizational culture, while pervasive and potentially powerful, can be coherent or fragmented across organization members, with a range of perspectives on "correct" ways to approach one's work. Likewise, a structure's cultural dimensions can be a topic of agreement or conflict. Bolman and Deal (2008), for example, describe school faculty members' conflicting norms and expectations about academic department chairpersons' span of authority that devolved into verbal conflict and physical threats.

In this discussion, I distinguish structures' different elements from one another. Schemas have both formal and informal elements, with informal elements less accessible through official channels such as written policy. Formal schemas, however, do not in and of themselves fully account for the norms, patterns, and expectations that guide behavior. In contrast with both kinds of schemas, resources do not guide so much as they serve as the raw material necessary to bring schemas to life. Next, I discuss how school structures' distinct elements relate to one another.

Alignment of a Structure's Elements

While my depiction of school structures extends the understanding of school structures from two (resources and schemas) to three elements (resources, procedures, and cultural dimensions), the same notion persists: the elements relate to one another. The quality of that relationship can vary, particularly with three elements in play. But Giddens and Sewell contend that structures' elements depend on and reinforce one another. Extending

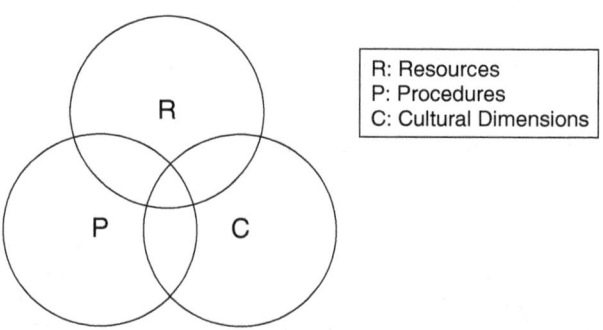

Figure 3.1 The advisor role's structural elements.

their work, I assert that alignment among these three elements—in other words, interdependence—is optimal to the enactment of the advisor role. Education policy research supports this contention. Cohen et al. (2003) call attention to the importance of matching educational resources to goals rather than haphazardly allocating resources. Similarly, Newmann, Smith, Allensworth, and Bryk (2001) discuss instructional program coherence, which they say occurs when a school's common instructional framework (which guides curriculum, teaching practice, and learning climate) is paired with staff working conditions and adequate resources that support the framework's implementation. In both conceptualizations, ideas and expectations preferably work hand-in-hand with sufficient resources. If they do not, Newmann et al. (2001) assert, educators' efforts become fragmented and inconsistent from classroom to classroom and grade to grade, impairing student achievement. Tying these ideas together, Elmore (2004) discusses alignment, specifically in reference to how school norms and teacher practice relate to accountability mechanisms. He uses overlapping circles to illustrate the alignment among the three entities, which he describes as referring to "the consistency and strength of agreement inside the school, not the subject of that agreement" (p. 142). I adapt Elmore's visual representation to the advisor role's structural elements, as shown in figure 3.1.

Having considered these three structural elements and how they might align with one another, I now turn to evidence of the elements of the advisor role in action at King, Los Robles, and Western.

Structural Elements of the Advisor Role

The advisor role's structural elements (as summarized in table 3.1) were readily apparent at King, Los Robles, and Western. Analyses revealed that

Table 3.1 Structural elements of advisor role

Structural element	*Examples*
Resources	Time for advising (during and out of advisory class)
	Instructional materials for advisory class
	Advisor skill
	Support for advisors
Formalized procedures	For activities in advisory class
	For out-of-class tasks assigned to advisor (e.g., disciplinary oversight, parent-teacher conferences)
Cultural Dimensions	Expectations of advisor role scope and effort
	Norms regarding the extent of advisor outreach

(1) resources largely concerned time but were overall insufficient relative to expectations, (2) procedures tended to be weakly specified, and (3) cultural dimensions concerned expectations about effort and the scope of advisors' work, and seemed more pronounced than formalized procedures.

Advisor Role Resources

The most notable resource for advising was time, which was, in different ways, both overabundant and lacking. King, Los Robles, and Western all dedicated time for advisory class meetings, as indicated in table 3.2. As I discuss in greater detail in chapter 4, advisory class meetings tended to involve independent work on assignments from other classes, whole-group activities, and consultation in the classroom between individual students and their advisor. At Los Robles and Western, teachers had enough time to conduct these activities in advisory class. In fact, some teachers reported that they had more time than they needed and felt that they had to scramble to fill the advisory class period. Mr. Bell, whose junior-senior advisory class often included engaging discussions and time dedicated to college planning, acknowledged that he and his colleagues at Western often faced advisory period with little in the way of plans. "I, like many others, spend lunch figuring out what I'm going to do for advisory because that's the only time in the day that I have time to do it," he explained. In some advisory classes, teachers left students to use the time as they saw fit, which occasionally included activities such as chatting in small groups, sleeping, covertly sending text messages, and applying makeup.

King's teachers spent from one-third to one-half as much time as other schools' teachers did with their advisees. While some felt that this time was sufficient (Ms. Baca quipped that any more time allotted to advisory would have resulted in her showing movies), others saw it as constraining what they could do. At King, the lack of time to conduct out-of-class advisor role tasks was further compounded by frequent cancellation of advisory class due to other activities, such as standardized testing, schoolwide assemblies,

Table 3.2 Time allotted for advisory class, by school

School	Minutes per week allotted for advisory class
King	80
Los Robles	245
Western	160 (9th–10th grades)
	190 (11th–12th grades)

and make-up time from shortened school days. King's advisory curriculum required multiple individual contacts between teachers and advisees in which they discussed advisees' academic progress, but limited and interrupted time for advisory class made this task difficult. Ms. Williams broke the task down this way:

> I only see these kids twice a week for 40 minutes, so I'll get through maybe three kids a day. It will take me a whole year to get through the class! It is so unrealistic to the point of like, you didn't even think this through! This is impossible!

Questions arose at all three schools about how to manage a classroom while meeting individually with one advisee. "How do you focus on one kid for five minutes while the rest of the class is setting the drapes on fire?" Ms. Baca asked, summarizing many other teachers' sentiments. Mr. Westerberg had similar concerns about the kind of time available to him:

> I have very little time during actual advisory class to sit down and address the individual needs of individual students, to have those serious conversations... First of all you're in a public room and second there are the management issues attached with keeping a group together.

While complaints about insufficient time for myriad tasks are endemic to the work of teaching (Jackson, 1990), time seemed to be a particularly complicated issue for teachers who carried advisory classes.

Advisory class time did not provide teachers the time they needed for planning class sessions or for the more intensive individual contact with advisees, their parents, teachers, and other support providers (at the school or community agencies) that schools expected from advisors. Most left such tasks to their planning periods, while Ms. Sosa used the class period for some of these tasks (her advisees worked independently). She called a student's mother during advisory class, leaving a message indicating that the student had left school for a doctor's appointment earlier in the day but had not returned yet. "I'm worried that she's telling you one thing, and me another," Ms. Sosa said on the message. This call was easily audible to all of Ms. Sosa's other advisees, raising questions about student privacy in the semipublic space of the classroom.[2] When teachers relegated advisory-related tasks to their planning periods, however, those tasked faced stiff competition for their attention. Teachers in these small schools were likely to teach multiple courses (instead of multiple sections of the same class, which is common at high schools with larger enrollments and larger faculties), and often had responsibility for developing curriculum (not just for implementing it). Teacher planning periods, then, were strained even without the additional demands generated by the advisor role. If teachers could not connect with advisees, parents, or other teachers during their planning period, they either rolled these tasks over into before or after school hours (like Ms. Bruce, who told me she had programmed her colleagues' phone numbers into her phone for this purpose), squeezed these tasks (uncomfortably for students) into advisory class time, or chose not to do them at all.

Advisor role resources in consistently shorter supply included instructional materials for advisory class, teacher skill, and support for student behavioral or mental health issues. Only King had formal, written advisory curricula, one for each grade level. Western had two advisory program coordinators for grades 9 and 10, who designed activities for advisory class. One resigned midyear, which ultimately resulted in the coordinators' duties being reassigned to those grades' teaching team leaders, one of whom did not perform the duties. Many teachers at Western and Los Robles stated a desire to have activities to conduct with their advisees (rather than feeling compelled to fill up the advisory class time), such as Ms. Little, who simply stated, "I need a curriculum to use in advisory. Something planned out, on topics, but not totally telling us exactly what to do." At King, many teachers welcomed the curriculum as material they could modify ("Tweaking is a lot easier than saying 'Oh my God, what am I gonna do?'"), but most teachers described existing curricula and activities as incomplete, insufficient for the time period allotted to advisory class, and poorly attuned to student interests and needs. Ms. Hamilton, at King, wished that the curriculum for her grade level was "more ninth grade," describing it as "more upper level, boring, just not entertaining, not well put together." Some teachers welcomed the opportunity to tweak or supplement the curriculum to better fit their students (Ms. Hamilton dedicated part of class to reading aloud from a young adult novel series), while others rejected it out of hand and developed other activities or simply held study hall or gave students free time during advisory class. "They play their music and I don't even yell at them for that because...why should I be sitting here yelling at them for having music on when there's no curriculum anyway?" Ms. Sobotka shared. In all of these cases, advisors found themselves on their own to effectively fill the class time allotted to advisory class meetings.

The advisor role demanded diverse skills of its occupants, but schools rarely attempted to build these skills. Teachers and advisees alike told me of the importance of advisors' skills in the areas of relationship building, academic guidance, social-emotional intervention (with issues such as depression, physical danger, and loss coming up frequently) and advocacy. These skills varied substantially across teachers, from quite developed ("There wasn't anything that really shocked me or made me feel inept.") to extremely limited ("I don't know what to do!"), as I discuss in greater detail in chapter 5. Formal teacher professional development in areas such as these did not occur during the time I spent at the three schools. During a previous academic year, a number of Los Robles' teachers attended an on-site training, conducted by the school's psychologist, about understanding and responding to adolescent crises. Mr. Hart, a second-year teacher, who said the training helped him deal with specific advisees, reported also learning about "listening and talking to people," adding "I don't know that you can get real professional development in this area." While training and literature on developing interpersonal skills is widely available (an Internet search for the term "interpersonal skills training" yielded over 13 million results), Mr. Hart's statement reflects the distance of such learning opportunities from his day-to-day work. Teachers often found informal learning opportunities in their consultations with school-based mental health professionals about their advisees. These consultations, however, depended on both parties' initiative (and time), and so did not impact teachers whose advisees were not engaged in mental health services or teachers who did not consult with their schools' mental health professionals.

Formalized Procedures

In general, teachers felt that there were few specific procedures that guided their steps as advisors. "I wish I knew exactly what I should be doing but it's up in the clouds," Ms. Janus, an advisor at Western, said of her work advising students. "There are ideas of what we should be doing but nothing is concrete." Only King provided written advisory curricula. Western's 9th and 10th grades designated a focus for the advisory period meetings (e.g., one day focused on advisor-advisee consultation, another on a themed discussion) and, for part of the data collection period, provided advisory class activities that specified what they would do during advisory class meetings. Similarly, Western's 11th and 12th grades focused advisory on preparing for a required internship, the college admissions process, and graduate portfolio completion. Even while working with this division's orientation to these goals, though, Ms. Sathe still felt at sea: "We've gotten a lot of guidance on, like do this-this-this but others [activities] are more open ended and I'm struggling because... I don't feel that I'm the best person to be helping them with all this stuff." Aside from classroom-activity-focused guidance (when it was offered), clearly articulated procedures were limited across all three schools. Teachers did not generally encounter written guidelines for the advisor role. Instead, they often learned via word of mouth about tasks—such as overseeing advisees' preparation of major assignments, facilitating parent-teacher conferences and arranging necessary support services—that they were expected to accomplish.

For example, teachers at Los Robles encountered particularly detailed procedures related to their role addressing advisees' disciplinary issues, but these procedures did not fully account for the work related to discipline that teachers found themselves doing. Los Robles required teachers to coordinate the school's response to their advisees' disciplinary issues, and to implement a color-coded card system of progressive consequences and teacher interventions. The school clearly stated, in writing, which tasks (e.g., require that an advisee get a brief written behavior rating from every teacher every day for a week, call home) corresponded with which color cards. However, this procedural clarity dropped off with regard to what to do beyond administering the color-coded cards. If a teacher ran through all the required steps and advisee misbehavior persisted, for example, steps were not spelled out (informally or formally), even though the teacher still retained chief responsibility for addressing advisee disciplinary issues. Similarly, at Western, Mr. Bennett said there was no guidance beyond early disciplinary steps (the advisor's responsibility): "Once the advisors have exhausted their options, there's no second level to go to." In these cases, teachers had to independently figure out what to do next, and often had to advocate for administrators to assist them. In agreement with Mr. Bennett's critical assessment, Western's principal more affirmatively stated, "Everything is going to be the advisor's job, ultimately." In contrast, King's procedures regarding advisory generally involved either following the curriculum or referring students for intervention by others (administrators, guidance counselors, or mental health providers). These procedures did not specify teachers' responsibilities after the initial referral. Even when procedures existed to specify teachers' responsibilities and tasks related to the advisor role, much remained undefined.

Cultural Dimensions of the Advisor Role

King, Los Robles, and Western had a more ample supply of informal norms, customs, values, and ideas about the advisor role. These cultural dimensions concerned the advisor role's scope more so than specific actions, which gave teachers something to work with, but again did not spell out precisely what they needed to do. Teachers who advised at Western and Los Robles were generally expected to take a whatever-it-takes approach to their work. A number of teachers voiced an understanding that their advisees' success depended primarily upon them. From disciplinary oversight to college planning to advocacy with other teachers to social-emotional intervention, teachers at Los Robles understood that, in founding teacher Ms. Goodman's words, "Doing all of these different things is the advisor's job. Who else is going to do it?" Persistently high, expansive expectations pinned to the advisor role, however, were paired with a tacit tolerance of colleagues who did *not* do whatever it took to ensure their advisees' success. Teachers who did not meet, or who ignored, their responsibilities spoke of occasional peer pressure to do more. Still, they rarely experienced direct peer or supervisor attempts to change how they advised. When Ms. Saenz, who had inconsistently followed Los Robles' disciplinary procedures for her advisees, learned that her principal expected her to provide evidence of behavioral intervention for an advisee, her response reflected the request's unusual nature. "I knew that it [the card system] didn't work, that it wasn't really being followed. So all of a sudden now, I'm supposed to have been following this to the T?," she commented. An acknowledgment of the advisor role's importance seemed to go hand-in-hand with unspoken acceptance that not all advisors carried the role out to its full extent.

At King, the advisor role's cultural dimensions connected more explicitly to an understanding of the role's potentially excessive demands. Ms. Moré, a founding teacher, told me that when she and her colleagues designed King, they "wanted to do school right," which included creating teaching positions that, in her words, "treated teachers respectfully" without overwhelming them. This approach translated into a shared view of the advisor role as a responsibility that should never overshadow teachers' instructional or personal responsibilities. Ms. Carbonell, another of King's founding teachers, readily acknowledged that she limited what she did as an advisor, even as her students' support needs were pressing. When I compared her approach to that of advisors across the three schools who felt pushed to identify and meet all of their advisees' learning needs and used planning and personal time to do the work, she referred back to Ms. Moré: "When she [Ms. Moré] hears you start doing that stuff, she will calm you back down and say. 'Look, it doesn't help anybody if you wear yourself out.'" Advisor role culture at King favored limited expectations of teachers' efforts and the role's scope, in which teachers could, but did not have to, expend more effort. "A lot of people are just, 'Do your best,'" Ms. Williams said as she shrugged her shoulders, explaining norms about advising at King. Whether reinforcing a narrow or inclusive definition of the advisor role, cultural dimensions of the role were relatively apparent to advisors.

Internal Alignment among the Advisor Role's Structural Elements

The advisor role's structural elements had varying degrees of alignment with one another, or what I will call "internal alignment." In this section, illustrations of internal alignment represent both elements' relation and proportionality to one another.

54 / ADVISORY IN URBAN HIGH SCHOOLS

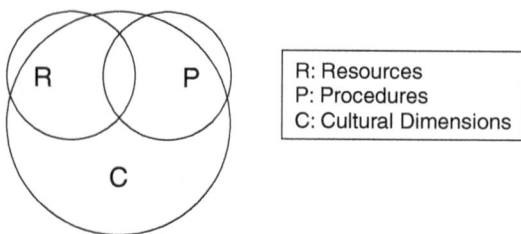

Figure 3.2 Alignment of the advisor role's structural elements at King.

King: Alignment on a Limited Scale

Elements of King's advisor role align with one another to a modest degree. Figure 3.2 illustrates this, using circles whose size represent the amount of structural elements and whose degree of overlap represents alignment. King provided grade level-specific advisory curricula and 80 minutes a week for advisory (sometimes preempted by other activities). Teachers' actions during advisory class were guided to some extent by the curricula, although, as noted above, many advisors said that they still found themselves having to customize or completely replace the activities recommended by the curriculum they used. Teachers' work with advisees beyond the classroom, which was very limited in the first place, was guided by referral procedures that funneled students to other school-based providers (such as guidance counselors, mental health professionals, and administrators).

While advisor role resources and procedures did not align substantially with one another, these role elements were effectively framed by the advisor role's cultural dimensions, which specified the role's narrow scope and placed limited demands upon advisors. The cultural dimensions circle, larger than and largely encompassing the rest, illustrates how the role's cultural dimensions explain the limited nature and alignment of resources and procedures. Expectations for a narrow role commanded only minimal resources and procedures. These elements' alignment with one another was not as important as their ability to support the role as designed.

Los Robles: Limited Alignment

Like King, Los Robles had limited advisor role resources and procedures, with comparably limited alignment among the two. Unlike King, however, the nature of these two structural elements had limited alignment with the advisor role's cultural dimensions. Los Robles faculty considered the advisor role central to teachers' work and to the school's functioning, as illustrated by Ms. Coltrane's dry comment, "Advisors are pretty much in charge of everything." Teachers described by their peers as "good" at the advisor role conducted home visits, worked with advisees who were behind on their work to ensure that they caught up or made up work in order to pass their classes, collaborated with Los Robles' social worker and psychologist on shared students, and knew their students' academic and personal lives extremely well. Expectations of advisors were expansive. Ms. Bruce was irritated, but not surprised, to find out that advisors would likely be the ones to implement Los Robles' initiative to introduce physical fitness activities to students (since Los Robles had no gym class). "Oh, for the love of God, is there anything else we could possibly do as advisors? I mean, would you like me to change the kid's diaper?" she exclaimed.

Los Robles' all-encompassing ideas about advisory, however, scarcely aligned with the role's resources and procedures, as suggested by the limited overlap of circles in figure 3.3. Even though teachers spent over 6 hours each week in class with their advisees, the school did not allot out-of-class time for teachers to conduct the individualized interventions that they were expected to provide. Teachers' planning periods did not align with those of others who advised students in the same grade (for common planning purposes) or with those of the content-area teachers who taught their advisees, rendering collaboration between advisors and content-area teachers literally extracurricular. Johnson (2004, p. 108), similarly described "haphazardly assigned" planning periods. Aside from ideas that traveled around the school via word of mouth, teachers received limited guidance regarding what to do with advisory class time or how to conduct the out-of-class tasks deemed essential to effective advising at Los Robles. If teachers used their planning or personal time to figure out this work, they could compensate for a poorly aligned advisor role, but they were on their own to do so.

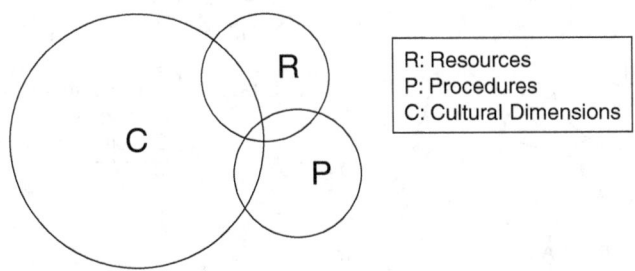

Figure 3.3 Alignment of the advisor role's structural elements at Los Robles.

Western: Alignment by Team

Strive Public Schools, the charter management organization that ran Western, centered its instructional and organizational plans on the house model, which grouped students and teachers together for instruction and advisory. I found that alignment among the advisor role elements varied across the teacher teams that served each house, as illustrated by the contrast between 9th- and 10th-grade house teacher teams A and B (see figure 3.4), two of the four teacher teams at Western.

In comparison to team B, team A had less developed structural elements and more limited alignment among them. Both teams met weekly during the school day, with content-area teachers assigned to teach the same students that they advised: a substantial difference from King and Los Robles. Team-level resources, procedures, and culture, however, differed across teams. Team A consisted of two newer teachers (with one and three years experience), two more senior teachers (with over five years' experience), an assistant principal, and a special education resource teacher. Mr. Bennett, one of the newer teachers, served as an advisory program co-coordinator and drove Team A's discussion of advisory-related issues (both class session planning as well as shared students) on these meetings, while the team's designated lead teacher cooperated with but did not initiate such conversations. In an interview, he expressed that he felt forced into a team leadership role that he would have preferred not to take as the team's second-most junior team member. Mr. Bennett's midyear resignation from Western left a gap that revealed team A's overall weak culture, limited human resources, and lack of procedures related to the advisor role. Team A teachers often missed team meetings. These meetings had a limited agenda, and seemed to only focus on individual students when they experienced significant behavioral or academic problems.

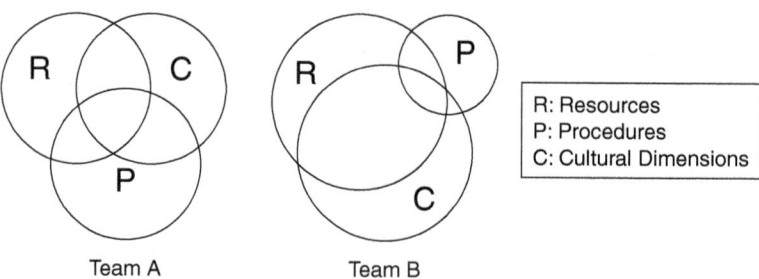

Figure 3.4 Alignment of the advisor role's structural elements at Western.

Team B, by contrast, used and extended the team model in a way that enhanced the advisor role for its members. This team consisted of four teachers (two of whom had taught for less than two years), an administrator, and a special education resource teacher. While chapter 5 addresses in detail individual teachers' assets such as knowledge, skills, experience, and ideas related to advising, I note here that team B possessed exceptional amounts of such assets. Ms. Renato, the team's leader, brought a degree in social work and experience with youth development and program administration from her previous career, and was joined on this team by two other career-changers who brought rich perspective to the generally unscripted work of advising at Western. Ms. Elba (team B's special education teacher) brought significant knowledge of Pacific City's social service offerings from a previous position.

Team B's culture was one of collaboration, mutual support, and receptiveness to new ideas, and this culture permeated the advisor role's cultural dimensions as well. Teachers assigned as advisors were considered "lead" for their advisees but received substantial support from other team members, all of whom taught each others' advisees. This team made use of the time provided by Western and of each other's perspectives as it strove to support teachers and individual students. It did not develop formalized structures but provided significant support to teachers regarding the use of advisory class time and work with individual students. During team meetings, I observed team B members collaboratively planning advisory class activities, exchanging information and suggestions about individual students, and delegating support tasks to members most suited to them. These conversations, in turn, nuanced and reinforced the team's culture of what teachers were expected to do within the advisor role. When visiting multiple advisory classes on the same day, I saw nearly identical activities occurring across multiple Team B classes. Ms. Reinhardt, a novice teacher, described her team as a source of vast information and support for her work as an advisor: "Once you combine our creative powers we inspire each other enough to be even better than we were as individuals. It's beautiful!" Team B's wealth of teacher skill and perspective combined with a strong team culture to expand on Western's existing advisor role structure.

Alignment between the Advisor Role and Other School Structures

The advisor role did not exist in a vacuum at these schools. It connected to other school structures. The nature of this connection, particularly the alignment between the advisor role and other structures, or external alignment, influenced how the advisor role worked. This section focuses on school instructional and student support structures' relationships to the advisor role. Qualities of these relationships further illustrate how alignment can support or unintentionally undermine the advisor role.

The Advisor Role's Alignment with Instructional Structures

All three schools had instructional structures such as academic departments and curricula. The contrast between Western and Los Robles illustrates how instructional structures can reinforce or conflict with the advisor role. As discussed above, Western grouped teachers into houses, where teachers worked across core subject-matter areas (math, literacy, science, and social studies) to coordinate instruction and student support. Subject area teachers doubled as advisors within the same pool of students, so their departmental grouping aligned with the advisor role's demands upon teachers to oversee and support students' academic progress. Teachers could easily communicate with their colleagues about advisee progress, and also saw this progress firsthand in content-area classes.

At Los Robles, however, subject-matter-driven departmentalization seemed to work against the advisor role. Teachers had extensive planning time with subject-matter peers (e.g., all mathematics teachers, grades 9–12), which they used frequently and easily to coordinate instruction. Los Robles did not allot similar time for advisory-related collaboration within or across grades, nor were assignments of advisees done in any way to consolidate groups of advisees within subsets of Los Robles' faculty. An attempt to dedicate faculty meeting time to group grade-level advisors together with their advisees' teachers, for the purposes of planning and consultation, consumed hours. Tellingly, the assembled groups could not meet concurrently because each advisory discussion group (one for each grade level) included nearly every faculty member. Teachers and students at Los Robles were grouped for instructional purposes alone. This arrangement worked well for subject-matter instruction but did not align effectively with the advisor role. As a result, instructional structures and the advisor role did not support one another.

The advisor role's alignment with student support structures
Student support professionals (such as psychologists, counselors, and social workers) seem like a natural support for advisors, who had varying degrees of responsibility to provide academic and social-emotional support to advisees. The structures that organized these professionals' work, however, had almost nothing to do with the advisor role. This misalignment existed at all three schools but was particularly pronounced at King, which shared (with three other small schools in the same building) an on-site student clinic

that provided 30 hours of mental health services a week. Most of King's advisors referred advisees to the clinic, but few had a sense of how the clinic's staff worked with their advisees, and none received guidance from clinic staff about the day-to-day work of advising, even though many advisors expressed interest. Mental health providers' confidentiality guidelines constrained the exchange of information about students to a degree, but King's teaching and clinic staff, their buildings separated by a 50-yard-long sidewalk, rarely visited each others' work areas for any purpose. Clinic staff worked to maximize their billable hours by seeing as many students as feasible during school hours, which further detracted from collaboration with educators through informal meetings or attendance at faculty meetings. A similar situation existed at Los Robles, where highly regarded mental health professionals worked tirelessly with students but had very limited access to advisors, and vice versa. Many of the teachers who worked closely with mental health professionals did so before or after school, or communicated via email or evening telephone calls. Mental health and advisor role structures simply did not overlap.

Ms. Cruz, Western's part-time counseling psychologist, contended with similar challenges, as did Western's teachers, many of whom expressed strong interest in gaining more information about shared students as well as guidance about how to effectively support their advisees in general. She strained to serve Western's student mental health needs with her limited hours and often struggled to preserve student confidentiality when advisors and teachers expressed great interest in collaborating with her. Teachers serving as advisors also felt this strain. "I kind of feel detached," Ms. Janus told me about her communication with Ms. Cruz about shared students, "because there is not a huge communication between what she is dealing with when she sees them [advisees], and what I should be doing when I see them."

At Western, though, the house structure provided some opportunity to align mental health structures with the advisor role. Ms. Cruz participated on one of Western's house teacher teams (Team C), as she carried her own advisory class as part of the *house* of students served by team C. This team made extensive use of her professional perspective and knowledge of students (within the bounds of Ms. Cruz's ethical code for her profession) as it determined courses of action, often carried out by advisors, for individual students. Ms. Cruz, for example, gave team members guidance regarding accommodations to make for a student whose trauma history appeared to interfere with an assignment that required a live performance in front of her peers, and later facilitated a meeting between this student and her teachers when she had gotten behind on assignments. The house team structure aligned Ms. Cruz's skills and perspective with the work that teachers did as advisors. This fruitful occurrence, while confined to Team C, suggests that external alignment of the advisor role is possible but was rare at King, Los Robles, and Western.

Impact of Alignment

Above, I have highlighted different kinds and degrees of alignment related to the advisor role. How does alignment matter to schools and teachers? I provide different answers to this question (see table 3.3) by weaving together the effects of the two kinds of alignment discussed above: internal alignment (the alignment among the advisor role's resources, procedures, and cultural dimensions), and external alignment (the alignment between the advisor role and other school structures).

Quadrant 1 depicts an advisor role that has poorly aligned, mismatched structural elements, and that does not align with other school structures. Ms. Powers, an advisor at Los Robles, summarized this kind of alignment at her school: "Here's a bunch of kids. Get them to the end. Good luck." A weak advisor role structure had marooned her, leaving her on her own to figure out how to advise. Ms. Powers encountered pressure to perform, a lack of procedures helping her know how to fulfill her role, and a relative scarcity of resources that she might employ along the way, with other school structures doing little to make up the difference. In such a situation, whatever energy or resources the school commits to the advisor role stand a good chance of dissipating rather than making impact. Los Robles had dedicated a significant portion of the school day to advisory, but that time was not matched by other needed resources and procedures that could have

Table 3.3 The impact of the advisor role's alignment

		Extent of internal alignment (among advisor role elements: resources, procedures, and cultural dimensions)	
		Limited	*Full*
Extent of external alignment (between advisor role and other school structures)	Limited	Quadrant 1 Advisors "marooned" by weak, unsupported role structure	Quadrant 2 Advisor role competes against other school demands
	Full	Quadrant 3 Other school structures partially compensate for weak advisor role structure	Quadrant 4 School structures work in tandem with advisor role

reinforced the advisor role and helped teachers to carry it out. As a result, time dedicated to advisory could accomplish very little.

When the advisor role's structural elements aligned with one another, but not with other school structures, as is represented by quadrant 2, teachers found themselves working with a more defined, supported role. However, they still faced competing demands for their time and energy. This happened at King, where the advisor role was moderately aligned, but did not align particularly well with other school structures such as structures for student support. Teachers at King, already taxed for time, had no reason to prioritize their advisor role when it competed for their time against other demands that the school supported more effectively. If they chose to prioritize their advisor role, they did so with the understanding that they exceeded expectations as well as available supports. Under these circumstances, the advisor role's effective implementation was again threatened by its weak compatibility with other school structures.

If, on the other hand, school structures aligned with the advisor role (as in quadrant 3), those structures could support it, even if the role itself was somewhat lacking in its definition and internal alignment. This was the case at Western, where the advisor role placed a lot of demands upon teachers in the absence of substantial resources or procedures to guide their work. The grouping of teachers into house teams made it possible, although not completely certain, that teachers could use team meetings and the within-house assignment of shared students to develop a more coherent approach to advising. Team B, Ms. Renato's team, capitalized on this opportunity while Team A, steps away along the same corridor, did not. Similarly, Western's team structure regularly brought Team C together with Western's mental health provider, creating productive overlap among the advisor role and mental health structures. Such structures' compensatory powers gave the teams space to sort out advising and to try out different arrangements and approaches that could become part of the advisor role's formal structure once better understood. These powers, however, did not extend to the entire school.

Western's Teams B and C came the closest to demonstrating alignment both *among* the advisor role's structural elements and *between* the advisor role and other school structures (represented by quadrant 4). Under such circumstances, the advisor role extended what the school could do, while the school's other structures supported advisors' work. The convergence of the advisor role and other school structures, however, did not exist across all of Western's teams. For this reason, Western was not a quadrant 4 *school* with regard to how it structured the advisor role. An advisor role that, schoolwide, had strong internal alignment and that aligned well with other school structures would stand in the position to enhance, and be enhanced by, its host school.

Conclusion and Implications

Examining the advisor role through the lens of structure (Giddens, 1984; Sewell, 2005), I demonstrate how a school's structuring of the role significantly impacts what advisors do in that role. In this chapter, I break down the advisor role structure into three elements: resources, formalized procedures, and cultural dimensions. This detailed exploration of the advisor role's structure shows that these elements must not only be present when implementing the advisor role, but that they must also be ideally aligned—both related and proportionate to one another. The more alignment of the elements (what I have called internal alignment), the more these elements support one another and, ultimately, the teacher asked to carry out the role. I also found alignment between the advisor role and other school structures critical to the advisor role's implementation, in that school structures could optimally support and be supported by the advisor role, or could compete for teacher and school priority. This line of research further substantiates and extends existing research on program coherence (Newmann et al., 2001) and alignment (Elmore, 2004).

Most of this chapter's findings, interestingly, lean toward negative confirmation of alignment's importance to expanded teacher roles. Los Robles came up short with regard to both the advisor role's internal alignment (of the various elements) as well as the role's alignment with other school structures. King, by contrast, had greater alignment of the role's elements, but managed to align them by keeping the role narrow and requiring little of teachers who advised, which limited the role's alignment with other school structures. Interestingly, two teacher teams at Western managed to show uncharacteristically strong alignment within the advisor role as well as between the role and other school structures. The presence of alignment on these teams suggests that the team had the potential to extend the structure that the school provided, and to also compensate for what the school did not provide.

These findings lead to two conclusions about the advisor role as implemented at King, Los Robles, and Western. First, it seems entirely possible, but not a given, to support the advisor role with sufficient organizational structure. The act of simply dedicating school hours for advisory class to the role's implementation proved insufficient to ensure effective implementation, but a more thorough structuring appeared to support even novice teachers as they took on the advisor role, or to provide what Johnson (2004) calls organized support. More common at these schools, however, was an incompletely structured role, with either a combination of insufficient resources and procedures that could have helped bring ideas about advising to fruition (at Los Robles, and on Western's team A), or a reduction of expectations about advising (at King) in order to match limited resources and procedures.

Second, in the relative absence of school-level structures to support the advisor role, teachers found themselves on their own to figure out this unfamiliar role. Consistent with the findings from chapter 2, ideas abounded at the three schools about providing support to students, but resources and procedures to scaffold those ideas and bring them to fruition were in much shorter supply (except at King, where teachers had ample support for a limited role, but found little support for addressing student issues that emerged from their work with advisees). Western's Teams B and C, which more effectively developed the advisor role's structure, did so on members' own initiative, making use of the resources (particularly collaborative planning time) that the school provided. Team C's use of Ms. Cruz, the school's counseling psychologist, as a team member reflects the potential for school-based mental health professionals to support teachers' work as advisors by building teacher knowledge and by extending the limited social-emotional support that teachers provide. This potential contribution, however, was more of a missed opportunity across King, Los Robles, and Western.

These conclusions imply that if expanded teacher roles are to work well, they demand sufficient structuring and alignment with other school structures. Without such arrangements, resources expended may dissipate rather than reach their intended ends. This structuring appears to take work that, at least in this study's limited sample, schools did not always do. Looking forward, these findings and conclusions lead next to a consideration of what teachers do when required to advise under conditions of (1) mixed, limited guidance from the teaching profession (as discussed in chapter 2) and (2) generally inadequate organizational support (this chapter's focus). Given this setup, what did teachers do with the advisor role, and how did it turn out? Subsequent chapters explore these questions, addressing how teachers interpreted and conducted the advisor role (chapters 4 and 5), judged their own performance, and coped with its pragmatic and emotional demands (chapter 6).

CHAPTER FOUR

CONSISTENCY AND VARIATION IN
TEACHERS' IMPLEMENTATION OF
THE ADVISOR ROLE

"Today is consultancy day," Ms. Renato said to her advisory class of 19 Western Preparatory Academy students as they settled into their seats. "We're going to do a quick go-around. What are you working on? Please take out your planners." As students took out their school-issued planning calendars, books, and written work, each student in the rectangle-shaped desk arrangement took a turn saying what work they would do. Since all of Ms. Renato's advisees had the same instructors, many mentioned the same English assignment. "What stage are you at?," Ms. Renato asked the group. "Typing." "Pictures." "Reading." "Revising." When each student had shared an update, Ms. Renato directed the class to begin working on their tasks, and handed out computers to students who had requested them. "Remember, this is individual work time," she tells the group. She met in the hallway with a student who had arrived late to class, brought to the door by one of Western's paraprofessional staff members who handled school discipline. Occasionally, Ms. Renato would lean into the doorway to remind students to stay on task.

A few weeks later, I returned Ms. Renato's advisory to find her advisees seated in a loosely arranged circle, taking turns reading aloud from a newspaper article about the merger between Western and another of Strive Public Schools' charter schools. Wallace, a 10th-grade student, facilitated the group. He read the norms for Socratic seminar at Western, in which students discussed and explored a topic selected by the advisor (Copeland, 2005, describes Socratic seminar methods in great detail), and explained the activity's next steps. Students then discussed the experience of their schools merger, guided by the questions Wallace occasionally posed ("Did students from the two schools have stereotypes of each other at the beginning of the year?"). Ms. Renato stepped in when multiple students spoke at once or to give clarification about the activity. As the discussion continued, she shared with me the written plan she had created for it. It included discussion objectives, a warm-up activity, links to the material to be discussed, explicit questions that framed the discussion, and guidelines for advisors on structuring the activity itself (for example, "YOU MUST DEBRIEF!!! Make sure that you end the seminar early enough to do a debrief session on what was said and how the seminar went."). On the same day, I visited two other advisory classes led by members of Ms. Renato's teaching team. Each advisor used and followed the same written plan.

Martin Luther King Academy's 11th-grade advisory curriculum guided Ms. Li's work with her advisory class. Yet she told me she felt like she wasn't reaching the advisees who seemed to need her support, including students who ran behind on credits and missed classes frequently, others who expressed interest in attending college, and others in the midst of personal difficulties. To begin an advisory class in December, she read school announcements as directed by the advisory curriculum. "You're talking but no one's listening," Kim said loudly (and accurately) as Ms. Li read announcements for 12 minutes. Ms. Li concluded with a final announcement as students continued to enter and leave her classroom: "If any of you are interested in transferring to another high school, see the guidance counselor. The deadline is January 15. If you don't make the change before then, you are pretty much stuck here for the rest of the year." Ms. Li then introduced a quiz that checked students' knowledge of King's previous words of the week (known by the acronym "WOW"), in which advisors introduced, defined, and then led brief activities about vocabulary words. "Some of you are down to sixty-something on your WOW quizzes," Ms. Li said as she passed out quizzes, which contained write-in items such as follows: "To speak out against, to condemn. Starts with the letter D." As students completed the quiz, 25 minutes after advisory class had begun, Ms. Li transitioned the group to work on their "brag sheets," in which they wrote about different skills, accomplishments, and interests in preparation for writing resumes. After introducing the activity, she circulated around the room, working with individual students. I excused myself, and briefly joined Ms. Byrd's 11th-grade advisory down the hall. Three students worked independently while others talked quietly or listened to music on headphones. "We're all done with the activities for today," Ms. Byrd told me, waving me into the room. "I gave them an extra worksheet with information on the world's population, and they are on their own now."

Just as Ms. Byrd's advisory class was on its own after quickly completing its curricular activities, Ms. Li found herself on her own to make her school's curriculum work for her students. By contrast, Ms. Renato and her teaching team colleagues engaged in more structured activities that came with clear guidance, sufficient materials, and a teaching team culture that included expectations that all team members would conduct similar, although not necessarily identical, advisory classes. One can also see in Ms. Li's and Ms. Renato's work a range of advisory class activities, including whole-group instruction, individual guidance, academic work supervision, college exposure, and community-building. These examples illustrate this chapter's key finding that most advisors in this study found themselves on their own to define and carry out their work as advisors, and figured that work out in a variety of ways, some of which did not appear to engage or serve students. Those who encountered a more developed role that worked in tandem with other school structures—as described in chapter 3—found themselves a good deal less isolated, and conducted advisory class in ways that were more consistent with one another. Teachers' differing interpretations of the advisor role come as little surprise, given this book's findings so far—that the teaching profession has given mixed, incomplete messages about teachers' social-emotional support responsibilities and that this study's three participating schools most often provided insufficient structure for the advisor role. Schools' formal expansion of the teacher role left much to the teacher to figure out. This freedom from a more prescriptive role inspired and facilitated innovation among some, but not all, teachers, suggesting that not all teachers can productively make use of open-ended, expanded teacher roles.

What Advisors Did: The Data

I learned of teachers' activities as advisors through direct observation of advisory classes as well as individual interviews, in which I asked, "What are you trying to accomplish as an advisor with your group of students?" Through these experiences, I identified nine activities in which advisors engaged (illustrated in figure 4.1), although no advisor did all nine. *Academically oriented activities* included academic guidance regarding student progress, exemplified by King's advisors' periodic conversations with students about their progress toward graduation, and academic work supervision, such as "study hall" time, support completing major projects and state standardized test preparation. Advisors at Los Robles, and, to a lesser degree, Western, had *discipline responsibilities*, in which they worked with advisees to address emergent issues. Social-emotional support interactions involved *social–emotional guidance*, such as discussions with advisees about personal issues or advisors' efforts to address these issues, as well as *referral or collaboration with support providers* such as school psychologists or community service providers. Future-oriented activities included *college guidance*—the identification of college programs as well as help with college and financial aid applications—and *workplace readiness activities*

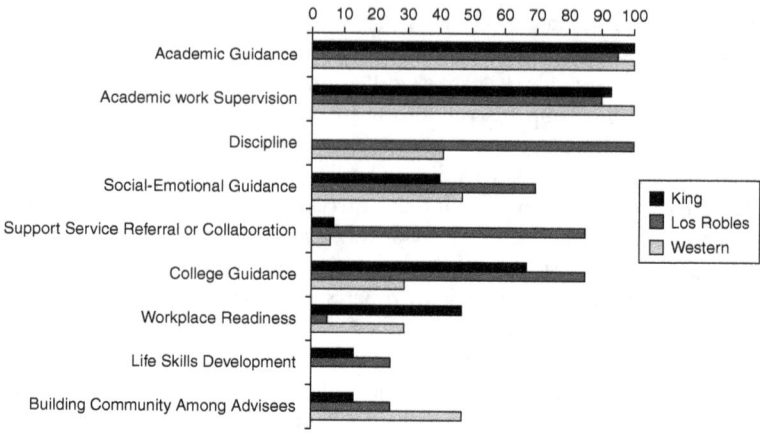

Figure 4.1 Percentage of advisors engaging in different activities, by school.

that developed students' awareness and understanding of different career options. Finally, some advisors focused on personal and interpersonal skills, including *life skills* (such as collaboration, financial management, and independence) and *building community* among advisory class members through shared activities and experiences. Individual teachers had both areas of consistency with and variation from one another in terms of their practice as advisors.

Consistency in Advising Practice among Teachers

Teachers engaged most consistently—within and between schools—in academically oriented activities with their advisees. This happened for two primary reasons: these activities were often the most structured aspects of teachers' work as advisors, and also served as a default choice for teachers uncertain about how to use advisory class time.

While schools generally provided insufficient structure for the advisor role (as discussed in chapter 3), the most structure they did provide for it often concerned advisees' academic work. King's advisory curriculum, for example, included a "Personalized Learning Plan" (PLP) that advisors were to review individually with each advisee, in order to promote advisees' awareness of their grades during and at the end of marking periods, as well as credit-by-credit progress toward graduation. While a number of King's teachers described the PLP as poorly developed, most used some version of it with their advisees. Ms. Hamilton, for example, rolled her eyes and laughed when I asked her if she used the PLP with her 9th-grade students.

"I did it on my own, made up my own format," she said, explaining that the existing PLP "didn't really fit" her students. She asked students to analyze their grades and predict future grades, considering different data including their attendance rate. While she found the curricular activities requiring reflection on grades unhelpful, she still guided her students through reflection on their academic performance. Likewise, Mr. Carmichael did not use the PLP form but focused with his 10th-grade students on interpreting transcripts, grade-point averages, class rank, and on measuring their progress against course credit requirements for advancing grade levels. King explicitly framed its advisory program as academic in nature, so it comes as little surprise that some advisors rejected specific curricular activities but nevertheless followed suit with other academically oriented activities.

Similarly, Western provided structure to the advisor role around academic activities. One of Western's weekly activities in 9th- and 10th-grade advisory classes was consultancy day, in which advisors and students alike knew that students were to work in class on academic material, receiving individual assistance as needed. Although not all teachers organized consultancy day as clearly as Ms. Renato did in this chapter's opening paragraph, they generally knew what to do on consultancy day. Western's 11th- and 12th-grade advisory program was, in fact, called "academic seminar," giving at a minimum an impression of an academic focus. As noted in chapter 3, academic seminar focused on three specific products, one of which was the academic portfolio required for graduation. It followed from this requirement, then, that teachers would oversee their advisees' progress toward completing this portfolio.

At Los Robles, where expectations of teachers' work as advisors outstripped available resources or procedures that could inform or support that work, teachers encountered the most structuring of the advisor role around academics (in addition to discipline, also reported as an activity by 100% of Los Robles' teachers serving as advisors). Teachers graded their advisees' student exhibitions (oral presentations of multiweek, interdisciplinary projects) and were expected to address advisees' deficiencies in credits toward graduation. Teachers used advisory class time, then, to address these topics through both individual advisee guidance and the supervision of advisees' independent work time. In addition, Los Robles' lead teachers and administrators conveyed to teachers that they should all begin advisory with a 20-minute period in which advisees stayed in their advisory classrooms and worked silently. Silent students in a classroom had little to do besides seat work (unless, as occurred in a few classes, advisees did no work but instead simply sat quietly or slept). Although not all teachers complied with this expectation, most did, and many advisory classes continued silent work after the 20 minutes had passed.

Some teachers defaulted to academic work when they felt unable or unwilling to do anything else with the advisor role, or with the time designated for advisory class. "I would provide more structure for the kids aside from (holding) a study hall," Ms. Reynaldo told me about her advisory class, but she felt that Los Robles did not provide enough support for her to do more than that. When explaining her decision to limit advisory ("At some point I decided, you know, I'm not going to kill myself."), Ms. Reynaldo said she did not have sufficient school resources to help her take students on trips to colleges or museums, or to plan lessons that she would use with advisees. Without those resources from her school, she either had to dedicate personal time and money to the work or, in her words, "put people out" by asking them to help her.

Other teachers emphasized the "study hall" aspect of advisory because they did not want to, or felt unable to, develop other aspects of the advisory program. After school at King, Mr. Perrales had a classroom filled with students who attended his tutoring program, where they received academic help, personal attention, and at times, a place to spend the after school hours ("Tutoring doesn't mean that you have to come for help, it might mean that you just need a desk to sit on," Mr. Perrales explained). In spite of his commitment to support his tutoring and content-area students, however, he did not appreciate King's assigning him students to advise and tasks to perform with them. "In advisory, you're forcing these kids to come in here. This doesn't fit my personality," he claimed. Mr. Perrales never used the advisory curriculum for his class but instead reengineered his advisory classroom to focus on building his advisees' math and writing skills. In cases like these, teachers who did not carry out advisory as intended, and in fact rejected their administrators' and colleagues' expectations, still reframed it in academic terms.

Within-School Pockets of Consistency at Western

Teacher teams at Western also provided for consistency in advisor role implementation. As discussed in chapter 3, two of Western's house-based teacher teams, Teams B and C, provided a substantial amount of structure to the advisor role that I did not see on Western's Team A. I looked within these teams to determine the level of practice consistency and found much higher levels than what figure 4.1 suggests.

On Team C, which served the school's 11th and 12th grades, all five teachers whom I interviewed reported that they engaged in college guidance and workplace readiness activities during advisory class, and within-team structure seemed to account for this consistency. Team C's academic seminar had particular foci (the graduation portfolio, the student internship, and college admissions), and its teacher team used team meeting time to coordinate work on the portfolio and internship. During one team meeting, Mr. Bell, team C's leader, asked individual team members, by name, whether they had worked on resumes. When Ms. Sathe said that she had not, Mr. Bell provided suggestions and offered her copies of materials to use. In these actions, Mr. Bell not only communicated an expectation that Ms. Sathe (and, implicitly, others on the team) do the work related to academic seminar's products, but also offered materials to help her meet those expectations. The school's college counselor provided all of the college admissions process curricula, which made up about half of academic seminar's total curriculum, also providing for within-team consistency.

As with Team C, Team B had consistency in practice that appears related to structures that promoted and disseminated ideas about teachers' work as advisors. Team B had levels of participation that exceeded school figures in three activities. Eighty-three percent of Team B's teachers reported providing social-emotional guidance, and 67 percent reported that they addressed school discipline issues with advisees and also that they engaged their advisory classes in community-building. As discussed earlier in this chapter and in chapter 3, team B's teacher meetings provided an opportunity for members to communicate expectations and norms about each other's work advising, as well as an opportunity to collectively work toward meeting those expectations. During conversations about their shared students, team B teachers learned how their peers addressed advisees' discipline situations, which reinforced the advisor's role in doing so. Team B teachers also often used these meetings to collaboratively plan advisory class meetings, with shared planning contributing to practice consistency across team members. On both Teams B and C at Western, scheduled time for collegial interaction about advising contributed to a further structuring of advisors' work, and in turn to greater consistency in practice across advisors.

Variation across Teachers

While I identified areas of consistency in advising practice across teachers—most of which I attribute to a prevalence of academic interpretations of the advisor role and, in a few instances, to the presence of structures that guided teachers' work—advisors' work varied from advisor to advisor at least as much. This finding makes sense, given the generally limited structuring of the advisor role at all three schools. Differences existed between schools, as well as between the group of advisors at the three schools, in how teachers interpreted and carried out the advisor role.

Variation between schools. Between-school variation concerned activities other than academic guidance and academic work supervision. All three schools engaged in some college guidance, but this ranged from 29 percent at Western (and took place only in the 11th- and 12th-grade advisory classes) to 85 percent at King (whose advisory curriculum built in college awareness activities at all grade levels). Discipline, a universal, required advisor activity at Los Robles, factored into 40 percent of Western's advisors' activities. It factored into none of King's advisors' activities, since administrators there handled student discipline. Social-emotional support referrals and collaboration, in which most of Los Robles' advisors (85%) engaged, came up among only 6 percent of Western's and 7 percent of King's advisors' work. Western offered very limited in-house student support services, which may explain its teachers' limited amount of collaboration and referral, but similar numbers at King, which had a full-service student clinic, tell a different story. I heard frequently from King's teachers about their interactions with students about serious personal and family concerns, but these students were teachers' content-area students rather than advisees. Mr. Carmichael, when asked whether he encountered different student issues such as child abuse, homelessness, or community violence among his advisees, answered, "It's not more likely that I'll figure it (the presence of student issues) out through my advisory than it is during my other classes," explaining that "I'm not the adult that that student (an advisee) sees the most." This pattern repeated with most of the advisors at King, reflecting the limited scope of King's advisor role. In contrast, teachers at Los Robles frequently collaborated about their advisees with in-school as well as community-based providers, reflecting their high degree of assigned responsibility for addressing advisees' social-emotional issues.

The range of teachers' activities as advisors also varied across schools. At Western and King, only two activities (academic guidance and work supervision) were performed by 80 percent or more of advisors. In comparison, Los Robles had three additional activities of this type (college guidance, discipline, and social-emotional support referrals or collaboration), for a total of five advisor activities performed by 80 percent or more of a school's advisors. This finding matches numbers to Los Robles teachers' descriptions of the advisor role as all-encompassing, such as "the advisor is like the glue to hold it all together," "I'm like a pseudo-parent," and "It's to keep students from falling through the cracks." Most teachers at Los Robles simply did more things than advisors at King and Western did.

Variation in individual interpretations of the advisor role.
"I went out and talked to a lot of teachers, 'What do you do in advisory?' I took a kind of informal poll to get some ideas. Everybody told me

something different. So that's why I decided to do my own thing. I thought, okay, I see where this is going, I need to decide what I want advisory to be."—Ms. Powers, Teacher and Advisor, Los Robles

"There's been a sub for one group, and those kids are screwed. They're just not getting very much advisory. And Mr. Rico is holding on by a thread. We've tried not to put a lot on him. So Ms. Carbonell and I are going in our own different directions."—Ms. Hamilton, Teacher and Advisor, King

Ms. Powers's and Ms. Hamilton's descriptions of how teachers at their schools went about the work of advising each reflect substantial person-to-person variation in interpretation and enactment of the advisor role. Exploratory factor analysis of teachers' survey responses (see Appendix B for a description of methods used) revealed that their individual interpretations of the advisor role clustered into three groups, in which they focused on academics, social-emotional support, or life skills development with their advisees (illustrated in figure 4.2).[1] Some advisors (24.4%) focused on more than one of these areas.

Academic interpretation of the advisor role. Consistent with other findings reported earlier in this chapter, 75.6 percent of the advisor survey respondents (34 out of a total 45) defined their role and responsibilities

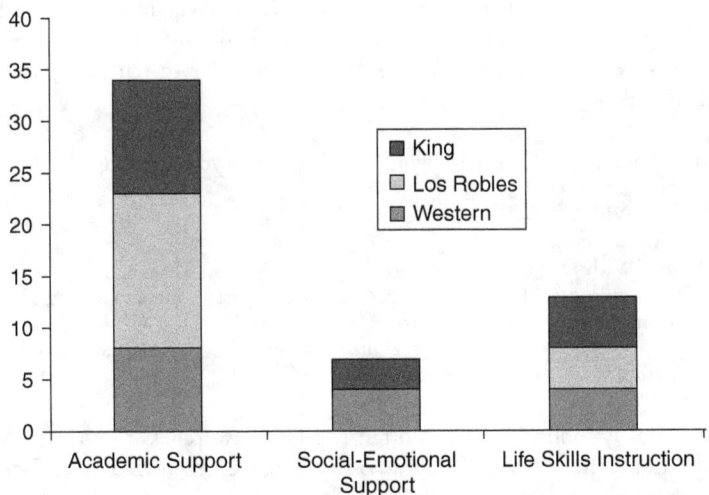

Figure 4.2 Number of advisors defining role as concerned with academic support, social-emotional support, or life skills instruction, by school. N=45.

Note: Categories are not mutually exclusive, although 34 advisors (75.6%) identified only one category.

as academic in nature. On the survey, they agreed with statements such as "I see advisory as a place where students should focus on academics," "The academic and social support of students are separate, distinct activities," and "I see advisory as a place where students should be prepared for college and/or career." On my visits to their classrooms, I found academically inclined advisors interacting with students about issues such as assignments in process, progress toward graduation, and college awareness. "What I try to do is create the dining room table that a lot of middle class students have at home," Ms. Mitchell (Los Robles) told me of her approach. "I try to help, proofread if they need it...And I refer them to summer programs, monitor their work, follow up with them when I get notices they haven't done something, help, especially, keep-up with longer-term projects," she explained. Similarly, Mr. Carmichael, who described frequent interactions with his content-area students at King about social-emotional difficulties, defined his advisor role as entirely academic: "I want my students to be more serious about school. I'm trying to get them to look at their habits, what they actually do and connect it to their performance." I observed Mr. Carmichael as he circulated through his classroom, briefly discussing students' grades with them as they reviewed and wrote a reflection on them (guided by questions he provided). "Do you do your homework for that class?," he asked one student, as he read over his reflection form. In a longer conversation with Jorge, an advisee, Mr. Carmichael helped him navigate to connect his current grades to his future plans as Jorge had laid out in an exercise the previous week that asked students to develop a five-to-ten year plan for their lives:

> Mr. Carmichael: "This is showing how many units you signed up for. Will you get the credits? Yes."
> Jorge: "With C's?"
> Mr. Carmichael: "Yes."
> Jorge: "With D's?"
> Mr. Carmichael: "Yes. You can get into a four-year college. Getting D's won't help. You need 2 years of Spanish, and at least C's to get into a four-year college. You'll get into a better college if you have higher grades."

Academically inclined advisors often expressed awareness that their peers focused on other things during advisory, but seemed to see other foci as areas where they lacked the skill to advise effectively, as well as distractions from academics. Ms. Carbonell, the lead architect of King's advisory program, said that she tried not to get "too involved" in students' personal lives, explaining that "I don't feel prepped or inspired to do it (discuss personal issues). I don't have solutions for them on that. I have solutions for them around graduating and doing well on tests." Also opting for an academic focus, Mr. Bell (Western) saw social-emotional intervention as potentially weakening his academic message to both advisees and content-area students:

> I kind of act as an intellectual role model, in terms of this way of being and thinking that shows them a possibility for the life of the mind...I have good relationships with them (students) but I'm not the teacher where someone is going to come up and talk to me about a breakup with a girlfriend or boyfriend...I think for me to try to be both would be to weaken one and/or the other.

Mr. Bell, like other teachers who defined their advisor role as academic in nature, seemed to define their role in terms of what it would include (academic content) and exclude (nonacademic content).

Social-emotional support interpretation of advisor role. Given this book's focus on teachers' responses to expectations that they provide social-emotional support to their students, one may find it surprising that the topic arises as a secondary finding on advisor role enactment. As discussed in previous chapters, literature and rhetoric about advisory envisions teachers' engagement in students' lives as spanning beyond academic matters. And indeed, 15.6 percent of teachers—7 out of 45 surveyed—defined their role in such a way, agreeing with statements such as "I see advisory as a place where students should get whatever kind of support they need to make it through school" and "I believe I must be both a teacher and a counselor to my students." Still, these teachers' interpretations of their role were in the minority.

Teachers whose survey responses revealed a focus on social-emotional support saw themselves as occupying a pivotal position in students' lives, and felt expected by supervisors and colleagues to step into this position. Ms. Reinhardt, in her first year at Western, encountered these expectations head-on in her interview for her position:

> Mr. St. Charles (principal) said, "We are really looking for a teacher who can be a good advisor and can also be a good teacher, but our main focus in on someone who is going to be a good advisor," and so that to me sent the message: If you can help these kids with their mental health, that's what we really want you for.

Ms. Reinhardt was also part of Western's teacher team B, in which three of four core-subject teachers also defined their advisor role (according to survey responses and interviews) as including social-emotional support.

She received messages encouraging social-emotional support not only from her principal but also from her immediate colleagues.

Other teachers, however, saw social-emotional support as intertwined with and driven by their responsibilities to provide academic support as advisors. Ms. Aron (Los Robles) described her rationale for addressing student social-emotional issues, even when she saw her primary responsibility as academic support:

> When I speak to a student individually about why the grades are low, usually I see a pattern across all classes if it's a socio-emotional thing... Then I talk to a student about how we can problem solve. Could you study at home? No. Can you tell me more about why you can't study at home? You go down the road. If they (students) don't follow you, you don't keep going. If they do, you do. Then, because I went in to solve the academic problem, what's gotten in the way is some sort of issue outside of school.

Similarly, Mr. Colvin devoted most of his advisory class time to academically and vocationally oriented activities, but his overarching view of advisory was one in which academics worked in tandem with strong student-teacher relationships. "I thoroughly believe that advisory is not a purely academic thing. You get the binder, but part of it has to be to get close to the students," he elaborated. Many of his advisees ate lunch with him in his classroom, and he found opportunities then and during advisory class to talk with advisees about their personal and academic concerns.

The approach to advising that involved a social-emotional support role but framed it as secondary to academic support was particularly striking at Los Robles, where no teachers described their advisor role as solely concerned with social-emotional support. Ms. Pozo ran an advisory class at Los Robles that blended academic support with social-emotional support, as illustrated by her insistence on academic work completion during advisory class alongside dedicated time during and outside of this class to work individually with advisees to address emergent social-emotional difficulties. When I asked Ms. Pozo about how she defined the purpose of her advisory class, she replied, "It's threefold. One is helping them with their academics, the second is helping them with their behaviors, and the third is the social-emotional part, kind of supporting the whole student." Social-emotional support was present in her work as an advisor, as illustrated by her detailed descriptions of the guidance she provided students and the collaboration she did with Los Robles' mental health professionals, but did not dominate her work with her advisees. Similarly, Mr. Hart, who spent significant time addressing his advisees' social-emotional matters through individual conferences, parent contact, and collaboration with community social service providers, described his role as primarily academic:

> Even if I'm providing social or emotional support, it usually gets framed within an academic context... When I meet with Delonda, who is due to give birth in 3 weeks, our conversations are about how she's going to support her baby, where she's going to live, what her plan is, but it's always framed in the context of her independent study that she's going do starting in May, how she's going to get her senior exhibition done, and what her plan is to transition back into college after that.

Academics provided a reason for teachers to talk with advisees about their personal lives, and many teachers appeared to keep this academic rationale in the foreground as they engaged in these conversations.

Life skills instruction interpretation of the advisor role. Twenty percent of the participating advisors saw their role as one of imparting life skills to their advisees. "These are 12th graders. Next year they're adults," explained Ms. Brice, a teacher at King, of her decision to take her advisory group in this direction. "My whole idea with advisory was to teach kids how to balance a checkbook, how to write a check, how to save money, how not to apply for credit cards that have high interest." Similarly, Ms. Powers took Los Robles' limited specification of the advisor role as an opportunity to decide what to do with her advisees. She organized her students into a kickball team as a way to teach them to work together as they challenged other advisory classes to games (which a few academically inclined advisors described to me in negative terms), and worked with a local outdoor education nonprofit to help the students learn camping and problem-solving skills that they tested on an overnight camping trip. Ms. Powers's advisees engaged in substantial academic work, including extensive work on their exhibition projects and an independent study program geared to state standardized testing, but Ms. Powers related these activities to students' life plans rather than a strictly academic rationale:

> I am the Sherpa guide. It's up to me to coach them to get to where they want to go. I have students that tell me, "I don't want to go to college." That's okay, you will be college ready but it has to be your dream, not mine. So my goal is for them to formalize what they think they want to do after high school and be the best at that, how can I help them get those skills or contacts or whatever they need... coaching to get them where they need to be so that they can have their happy life.

Interestingly, factor analysis of the teacher surveys found that teachers who agreed with the statement, "I see advisory as a place where students should develop life skills" also agreed with the statements, "The advisor role is a central part of my job" and "I have a 'big picture' plan for my advisory class." Those who saw themselves as imparting life skills to their advisees seemed to have a vision for their work and used the leeway given them by their schools to carry out this vision.

Minimal implementation of the advisor role. The factor analysis that revealed different approaches to advising suggests that individual teachers affirmatively interpreted the advisor role and pursued a direction (or multiple directions) with it. This assumption proved true with a number of teachers. But I also saw, in my observations of advisory classes, interviews, and survey data, evidence of minimal interpretation and implementation of the role, in which teachers did very little with the advisor role. For example, the difference highlighted by Ms. Renato's and Ms. Li's advising practice in this chapter's early pages carries out in their survey responses. While Ms. Renato's responses reflect her strong identification with all three interpretations of the advisor role (academic, life skills, and social-emotional support), Ms. Li's responses reflect that she weakly identified with each, in effect choosing none. Some teachers in this group objected to the requirement that they advise, while others said they felt poorly prepared for or supported in this work. Unlike their peers who improvised when facing similar issues, however, this group attended scarcely to the advisor role or the advisory class period.

Mr. Carver, a 9th- and 10th-grade advisor at Western, showed minimal interpretation of the advisor role as he supervised a large-group discussion on bullying that Western's advisory coordinators had designed for all advisors. Allowing, by the activity's design, students to facilitate the discussion, he sat by as the group disintegrated into a collection of paired discussions (some on topic, some off, one concerning a student's upcoming *Quinceañera* party) and did not designate a replacement for the large group facilitator when she left the classroom. He exclaimed, "We couldn't keep it together without you!" when this student returned several minutes later. Mr. Carver accurately understood what Western expected from its advisory program, saying:

> It (advisory) is supposed to be a place where students can support each other and help each other be successful...and it's supposed to be a place where I can get to know students better and they can get to know me beyond the classroom subject area interaction...where I can help guide them through the two years they are with me.

Despite this understanding, he described his own work as an advisor in an apologetic, lackluster fashion. This perspective was pervasive in

Mr. Carver's advising, from parent contact ("I'm not good at calling parents and that's what an advisor is supposed to do.") to working with Western's advisory class plans ("Even finding the time to read the plans and prepare the plans that are given to us, I find that I'm not planning the time to do that.") to running advisory class on the days where the school provided no plan for advisory ("It wasn't a productive day and I felt bad about it, but this is where it was.") to holding individual conversations with students ("I should probably be more like getting involved by...talking to them one on one, but there is no real time built in where you can do that."). He saw things that needed to be done, but did not do those things.

Mr. Carver, along with other teachers who minimally interpreted the advisor role, struggled alongside colleagues with their schools' limited, poorly aligned advisor role structure as described in chapter 3. Ms. Sobotka found King's advisory curriculum wanting, as many of her colleagues did, but made no moves to replace it with other activities. She told me of one lesson from the curriculum that she found helpful, but said that most often, "I'll look in the binder and there'll be nothing in the binder and I'm like, 'Well what do I do today? I don't know, I'm not going to do anything.'" On days like those, Ms. Sobotka said that she allowed students free time for the entire class period. Mr. Palmieri encountered and responded to pressure from colleagues and administrators at Los Robles to address his advisees' discipline situations (one area in which Los Robles assigned tangible responsibilities to advisors). Otherwise, he described himself as peripheral to what happened in his advisory class. "I let them talk to each other and hope that the principal won't step in," he said. "On other days, when they have deadlines on their work, they'll sit and regulate themselves." Like their colleagues, advisors who minimally implemented their role expressed a sense of confusion about the role, but this group seemed to stay lost rather than taking the role in any particular direction. This group of teachers revealed an important aspect of variation in advisor role interpretation: that while some teachers went off in different directions, others chose no direction in particular.

Variation and Teacher Demographic Characteristics

In this discussion of teachers' varying individual interpretations of the advisor role, it is important to consider sources of variation. I was particularly interested in whether advisor role interpretation varied across teachers by gender or race and ethnicity, given scholars' attention to gender- and race and ethnicity-based differences in teacher caring (Antrop-González and De Jesús, 2006; Beauboeuf-Lafontant, 2002; Garza, 2009; James, 2010; Payne, 2008; Rolón-Dow, 2005; Thompson, 1998; Valenzuela, 1999), a construct that relates substantially to the advisor's responsibility to mentor and support students. However, I found almost no evidence of advisor role interpretation (i.e., academic, life skills instruction, social-emotional support interpretations as well as minimal implementation) varying by race and ethnicity or by gender. I simply found too much variation within gender and race and ethnicity groups (of both teachers and students) with regard to how teachers made sense of the advisor role.

Survey results confirmed a lack of difference by race and ethnicity or by gender in teachers' interpretation of the advisor role. Analysis of the variance between ethnic and gender groups found, with only one exception, no statistically significant differences in group members' role interpretation. The one exception, which concerned how teachers of different ethnic groups saw the advisor's academic support role, is slight and reveals limitations in drawing distinctions between groups. The academic support interpretation variable ranged from 4 to 12 possible points. All five groups (Asian/Pacific Islander, African-American, Latino, White, and Mixed) had average scores that ranged from 6.7 to 10 points. The group with the lowest average, the mixed race and ethnicity group, fell 1.7 points below the total participant average (all other groups' averages fell between 8 and 10 points), and consisted of participants of a variety of racial and ethnic identifies, further weakening any argument that any particular racial or ethnic identity impacted their interpretation of the advisor role.

Conclusion and Implications

This chapter lays out the different ways in which teachers carried out the advisor role. In it, one can see a range of activities—including life skills instruction, social-emotional support, oversight of students' academic work, and college guidance—that teachers undertook in their work as advisors. On a surface level, this range of activities simply helps us to understand what teachers did with advisory class time. A deeper look, however, reveals patterns of consistency and variation in their different activities that clarify the importance of adequately structuring and supporting expanded teacher roles.

Consistency across teachers' advising practice, both within and between schools, related to schools' structuring of the advisor role as well as to teachers' tendency to interpret the advisor role in academic terms. Where schools provided an aligned advisor role structure (meaning that schools provided resources, procedures, and norms that were both sufficient and proportionate to one another), individual teachers' advising practice tended to resemble that of their peers. I particularly noted such consistency at Western, where house-based teacher teams marshaled resources and framed expectations (both formally and informally) to support teachers' work as advisors. In addition, although many teachers at King felt dissatisfied with aspects of its advisory curriculum, such as the PLP form they were to complete and update with each advisee, most (but not all) adapted the existing curriculum or replaced it with a version they felt was better, rather than reject it altogether. Still, even when teachers encountered an advisor role that their schools had insufficiently structured, their work tended to drift toward an academic interpretation of the role, whether they worked with, improvised upon, or rejected their school's expectations for advisors. These findings suggest that most teachers can and will implement an expanded role in accordance with a well-structured role. They also suggest that teachers will most likely implement this role in a way that focuses on students' academic performance, which is understandable given teachers' primary responsibilities and their desire to see their students—whether content-area students or advisees—do well in school. Also, considering policy-driven pressure upon schools and teachers over the last decade to improve measurable student performance, advisors' emphasis on academics comes as little surprise.

The drift toward teachers' academic interpretation of the advisor role, even when schools did not emphasize academics in their advisory programs, also suggests that this group of teachers had substantial (and at times, too much) latitude with regard to how they carried out this expanded role. This finding has pragmatic as well as theoretical implications. First, educators and policymakers concerned with expanded teacher roles can note that teachers left on their own to figure out expanded roles are likely to head off in different directions. Architects of the advisor role—both nationally and at Los Robles and Western—envisioned the role as one that would provide not only academic, but also social and emotional support to advisees. But while just over one-tenth of participating teachers defined the advisor role in a manner consistent with this vision, most did not, and none did at Los Robles. Where administrators did not sufficiently structure an advisor role that included social-emotional support, most teachers did not incorporate social-emotional support into their definition of their advisor role responsibilities, even though they often, but not always, carried out social-emotional support tasks when they felt that they had to. Just as teachers tended to follow and draw ideas from a more structured advisor role, they often could not and did not follow a path that their schools had not clearly created for them. Some teachers serving as advisors did as little as they could manage to do, another result of the insufficient structuring of expanded teacher roles. Whether school administrators and policymakers *want* teachers to improvise and diverge when assigned an expanded role is a matter worth considering. If they want individual interpretation and improvisation, a loose structure leaves plenty of room. If, however, administrators and policymakers want expanded role occupants to carry out particular actions toward specified ends, then a more developed and aligned expanded role structure, as described in chapter 3, would be necessary.

Theoretical implications of teachers' varied interpretations of the advisor role connect back to a central tension in role theory over whether the role or the role occupant determines the nature of role occupants' work. Neither King, Los Robles, nor Western used a heavy hand in determining what teachers did as advisors. The role as a prescriptive, normative script for role occupants, as early role theorists (e.g., Bates & Harvey, 1975; Linton, 1936; Parsons, 1951) described the role, existed weakly, if at all, in these schools. But the role as a script was not replaced by a role that empowered all teachers to construct and reconstruct their roles, as recent role theory would suggest. Some teachers figuratively ran with the advisor role, using it as a license to carry out their own visions for supporting and mentoring students. This response to an expanded role is consistent with scholarship that depicts the professional role as a "resource for action" (Piliavin, Grube, & Callero, 2002, p. 471) that the role occupant can negotiate, claim, use, and reshape (Ashforth, Kreinder, & Fugate, 2000; Baker & Faulkner, 1991; Bechky, 2006; Biddle, 1997; Burke & Stets, 2009; Turner, 1990). Still, other teachers' advisor roles went unclaimed when minimal implementers did little in or with the role. Teachers seemed free to minimally enact the advisor role, and sometimes did, but this type of role interpretation or enactment does not evoke an image of the expanded role as a resource for action. The expanded teacher role was, in this case, neither universally prescriptive nor universally empowering; the absence of the former did not engender the latter. Neither role theorists nor school administrators should regard a nonprescriptive role as a universal vehicle for innovation or coherent job performance.

What leads one teacher to appoint herself her advisees' life skills Sherpa, while her colleagues down the hall focus on college readiness, social-emotional support, or not much at all in their work as advisors? Chapter 5 pursues this question, considering what individual teachers bring to bear on the work of advising. In particular, I explore individual teachers' characteristics—their ideas, knowledge, skills, experience, and support that informed their work as advisors—that seemed to influence who claimed and used the expanded role and who neglected it.

CHAPTER FIVE

THE TOOLBOX AND HOW TEACHERS USED IT: INDIVIDUAL CHARACTERISTICS THAT EXPLAIN DIFFERENCES IN ADVISOR ROLE ENACTMENT

King's, Los Robles', and Western's teachers' interpretations of the advisor role tell a clear story: When left on their own by their profession and their schools to navigate this unfamiliar, expanded role, teachers pushed forward and figured it out, and did so in a multitude of ways. But how did they figure it out? Ms. Li's and Ms. Renato's work with their advisees—in particular, with students who struggled with personal and academic challenges—offers a view of the different ways in which teachers figured out advising and how their work varied as a result.

On the occasions when I visited Ms. Li's 11th-grade advisory class, Randy was rarely present. Over the course of the school year, he dropped from a full schedule at King (six classes) to four classes to two. He planned to leave King and attend a GED program, but had not told Ms. Li, other teachers, or King's guidance counselor of his plans, and none of his teachers had asked him about his declining attendance. "They're not stopping me from what I'm doing," he said, summarizing their response to him. I asked Randy if he thought his teachers should stop him. "Yeah, sometimes," he replied, then elaborating that if teachers saw their students slipping away from them, he thought they "need to get them (students), sit them down to talk to them. Tell them what they need to do, to stop doing what they do."

Ms. Li, aware that Randy was slipping away from King, seemed unsure of what to do, and responded minimally. "I really hope that there is someone that he does have a break-through with," she said about Randy as she described his academic problems, such as poor attendance and a 0.3 grade-point average. She followed King's advisory curriculum, and described ideas she had about getting to know her advisees better and collaborating with teachers to support students, but did not use these ideas with Randy or her other advisees. She knew that Randy was in his uncle's custody, had transferred in to King during the school year, and had knee problems leading him to use crutches, but had not learned any more about these issues. "I feel like it's definitely something other than academics that he needs to talk about," she told me, but had not referred him to King's guidance counselor or mental health providers for support, and had exchanged information about Randy only once with a colleague who taught Randy, and did not take action as a result of this exchange. In spite of her view of advisory as a place to provide academic support and to hold individual advisor-advisee conversations about advisees' progress, she remembered few details about conversations with Randy: "The only thing I recall is more like, come to class, just be here, do something." (Randy could not recall details of his conversations with Ms. Li, either.) She reported no experience or training that helped prepare her to work with Randy, and spoke of her work with him in tentative, uncertain terms, using words such as "should," "unsure," "kind of," "hope," "maybe," and "somehow." Left on her own to figure out how to advise, Ms. Li seemed to come up with little that was helpful to Randy.

There was nothing tentative about Ms. Renato's work with Essie, an advisee she'd known over the course of two school years. Essie had seen her share of adults attempting to intervene in her life, between a stint in juvenile hall, her father's violent death, and occasional scrapes with Western's administrators when she showed up to school intoxicated. She was not interested in a deep relationship with Ms. Renato, even though she described her advisor as attentive, helpful, and caring. "I don't like to share a lot of personal stuff at school," Essie explained to me. While Ms. Renato noticed and respected this distance, and found it challenging given her responsibility to support Essie, she persevered with thought-out efforts to advise her. Ms. Renato described herself as having primary responsibility for advisees, the adult at school who should take action when school arrangements for her advisees weren't working. She convened meetings with Essie's mother when Essie's problems spiraled, involved herself in administrators' decisions regarding Essie, and used her regular contact with Essie as an opportunity to stay on her about her academic progress. Ms. Renato's educational and work history—including a bachelor's degree in social work and years of experience running programs for youth-serving nonprofits—gave her knowledge about adolescent development, mental health issues and collaborating with service providers. Her previous jobs familiarized her with trying new ideas, acknowledging when they didn't work, and adjusting her plans. These experiences proved useful as Ms. Renato strived to support Essie. She also drew in support from colleagues in her attempts to address Essie's chain of difficulties. Administrators backed up the expectations Ms. Renato placed on Essie, and colleagues informed her of Essie's work in other classes. Ms. Renato also enlisted a school discipline paraprofessional to provide immediate help as well as perspective on Essie's neighborhood and family, both of which he knew more closely than Ms. Renato did. Compared to Ms. Li, Ms. Renato came across as highly responsive, persistent, and innovative in her role. The within-school support network that she activated, as well as her studies and work prior to teaching, underpinned her dynamic practice.

Ms. Renato and Ms. Li showed different ways of taking up and enacting the advisor role, far beyond the activities they used in advisory class or their preference for advisory's focus on academics, social-emotional support, or life skills development (as discussed in chapter 4). In this chapter, I explore the sources of those teacher-to-teacher differences. I found that teachers relied upon their own ideas, knowledge, skills, experience, and support related to the work of mentoring and supporting young people, as if using their own individual advisor role toolboxes. In the face of advisees whose circumstances suggested an urgent need for support, Ms. Renato drew liberally and frequently from her well-stocked toolbox, while Ms. Li's sparsely supplied toolbox offered her little of use. As their respective experiences with Essie and Randy reveal, different advisor role toolboxes contributed to consequentially different experiences with advisory for teachers and students alike. Teachers' individual toolboxes were particularly powerful in circumstances where schools did not augment those toolboxes by providing guidance or support to teachers' work as advisors.

In the remainder of this chapter, I use structuration theory (introduced in chapter 3) to frame how I describe the ideas, knowledge, skills, experience, and support that formed teachers' advisor role toolboxes, and consider how these different individual attributes informed teachers' work as advisors. Policy implementation research has illustrated how educators make sense of policy directives as they carry them out (Coburn, 2001 & 2005; Jennings, 2010; Spillane, 2004); in this chapter, I look further into which individual attributes guided this process for teachers grappling with the advisor role. Teachers' highly autonomous, varied work as advisors provides, on one hand, discouraging evidence about the advisor role's limitations: teachers like Ms. Li tried to advise, but often fell short due to a combination of limited individual readiness for the role and limited organizational and professional support. On the other hand, though, teachers like Ms. Renato showed encouraging evidence of success in spite of limited school-level support by activating their own advisor role toolboxes. If teachers experienced school-level support, as teachers on two teacher teams did at Western, all the better for them—this support anchored their often innovative work. Together, these strands of evidence illuminate needed and possible pathways of teacher learning, support, and recruitment related to expanded teacher roles.

Structuration Theory: A Framework for Identifying Teacher Attributes that Inform Advisor Role Enactment

Schools set up the advisor role structure in different ways and to varying degrees of effectiveness (please see chapter 3 for an extensive discussion of this topic). This structure, I argue, consists of the advisor role's resources, formalized procedures, and cultural dimensions. I derived this three-pronged framework from structuration theory (Giddens, 1984; Sewell, 1992, 2005). Advisor role *resources*, which Sewell likens to the bricks that make up a building, provide the goods necessary to carry out the role, and can be either human (such as skills, knowledge, or social networks) or nonhuman (such as facilities, instructional materials, salaries, or time). *Formalized procedures*, as represented in written policies and curricula, specify expectations and requirements of individuals involved with the advisor role, particularly students and advisors. The advisor role's *cultural dimensions* are not codified like formalized procedures, but still convey assumptions, expectations, and norms about the role. Formalized procedures and cultural assumptions, in my interpretation of structuration theory, are two varieties of what Sewell (1992, 2005) calls *schemas,* defining them as "generalizable procedures applied in the enactment/reproduction of social life" (p. 131). Schemas guide individuals' thoughts and their actions. As resources serve as the bricks to Sewell's figurative building, schemas are the blueprints that specify how to construct the building. Advisor role schemas (both formalized procedures and the role's cultural dimensions) interact with advisor role resources, and the two depend on and mutually shape one another. The advisor role requires well-developed schemas to guide its enactment, but cannot not function without necessary resources to underpin advisors' work. Nor can the allotment of resources, without sufficient schemas to guide their use, sufficiently support the advisor role.

To consider how individual teachers enacted the advisor role, I extend structuration theory, usually applied to macro-social and organizational units, to the individual level. Teachers bring their own personal schemas and resources, their own blueprints and bricks, to their work with students, whether this work is related to the advisor role or one of the many other activities of teaching. Individual teachers possess unique combinations of resources (referred to in figure 5.1 as *teacher-level resources*), such as knowledge, experience, and time, that inform how they carry out the advisor role. While I distinguish the advisor role's formalized procedures from its more informal cultural elements in chapter 3, I now blend the two back together, emphasizing the principles, beliefs, and ideas that individual teachers hold that influence how they do their work (referred to in figure 5.1 as *teacher-level schemas*). A view of individual teachers' varied use of this role follows consistently from recent role theory scholarship (discussed in chapter 4) that considers individual role occupants as interpreting, claiming, and using their roles rather than mindlessly fulfilling roles as if carrying out orders.

Advisor role resources and schemas at the teacher level exist in active relation to one another as well as to school-level advisor role resources and schemas. Teacher-level resources and schemas influence and depend upon one another, as illustrated by the circular arrows in figure 5.1, bricks-and-blueprints style, just as school-level resources and schemas do. A two-way relationship also exists between school-level schemas and resources and teacher-level schemas and resources (see the dotted arrows in figure 5.1). Schools have the potential to augment teachers' resources such as experience and skill, and can influence how teachers think about the advisor role. Likewise, individual teachers' resources and schemas potentially contribute to and shape the school's overall structuring of the advisor role. For example, one teacher and one principal at Western (both of whom served as

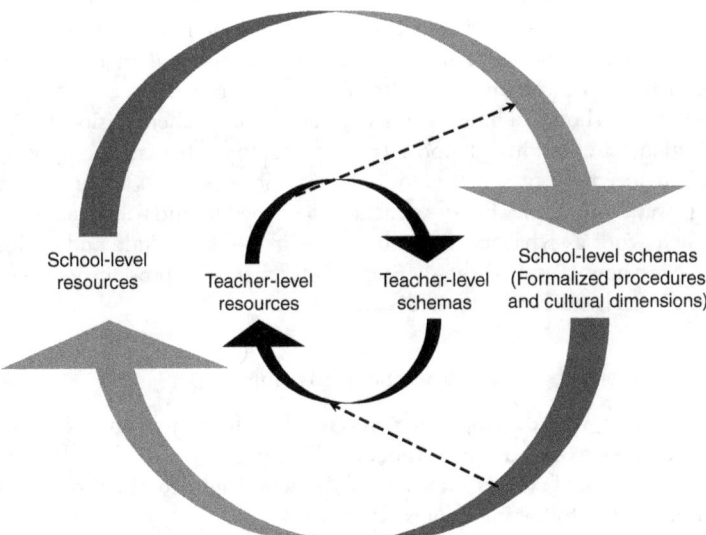

Figure 5.1 Conceptual framework illustration: Interaction between teacher-level resources and schemas and school-level resources and schemas.

advisors) had advised in previous positions at other schools. Each brought ideas about how the advisor role should and should not work (schemas), as well as specific skills that they learned through their practice (resources), to their work as advisors at Western. When schools insufficiently structured the advisor role (as occurred across all three schools participating in this study), individual teachers' schemas and resources stood to contribute substantially to how they carried out the advisor role.

Teacher-Level Schemas Related to the Advisor Role

Just as teachers interpreted the advisor role in different ways (academic, social-emotional support, and life skills instruction), they also had their own sets of ideas, guiding principles, and procedures related to their work advising students, consistent with description of schemas that come from structuration theory, as discussed above. These schemas ranged from undeveloped to well-developed.

Based on pilot interviews with a range of teachers serving with advisors, I developed criteria in order to identify and evaluate participants' schemas for advising. First, advisors had, however developed or undeveloped, an underlying vision for advising their students. This vision concerns the role's pragmatic aspects (how to conduct advisory class) as well as what they hoped to accomplish in their role as advisor. I also considered how teachers—whether explicitly expected to do so or not—addressed their advisees' social-emotional needs, since social-emotional matters such as personal, family, and mental health difficulties came up in advisors' work at all three schools. These included evidence of teachers' vision for providing social-emotional support to students and schemas about how to respond to emergent social-emotional situations, such as a student running away from home. Finally, teachers described boundaries that they set on their work as advisors, regarding what it should include and exclude. I describe how I applied these criteria to teachers and produced a schema score for each teacher in appendix B.

Ideas about Advising

Teachers with well-developed schemas for the advisor role saw a clear purpose to their work advising students. This purpose varied significantly across advisors. Teachers' advisor role schemas guided their work with advisees, as the following quotes illustrate:

- My main role is to get them into college, if that's what they want, and then everything else falls under that.

- What is going to benefit these kids? I try to think of real life. These are 12th graders, next year they're adults. They're going to have to learn how to be responsible. So I try to think of things that really apply to the real world. That's what I think advisory is good for. I do a lot of talking about jobs.
- I want my kids to want to come in here because they know they are loved and cared about, by me and their fellow advisees... What I see advisory as providing is the personal, social, interpersonal stuff that goes along with learning information.

Teachers with less developed advisor role schemas did not state their sense of advisory's purpose so clearly or fluently. They often expressed uncertainty about what their administrators and colleagues expected them to accomplish with their advisees, and expressed frustration at this lack of clarity. They also voiced a limited sense of their own purposes for advising students. Whether or not teachers had access to advisory curriculum from their school (as was the case at King), advisory period with this group of teachers more often included unstructured free time in which they interacted minimally with their advisees. Any absence of curriculum—due to it not existing (at Los Robles), temporary gaps in programming (at Western), or insufficient materials in the curriculum binder (at King)—was felt strongly by teachers with less developed advisor role schemas.

When faced with similar circumstances, teachers with stronger advisor role schemas at all three schools also expressed frustration, but then developed their own frameworks and plans. Ms. Powers, an experienced teacher with strong advisor role schemas, concluded, "I need to decide what I want advisory to be," when she began at Los Robles and saw no consistent school-level plan for advisory at Los Robles. Ms. Powers described a number of units she developed for her advisory class, as well as a plan for how her advisees' work as juniors would connect to her plans for advisory for their senior year. This group of teachers capitalized upon the autonomy their schools (intentionally or unintentionally) granted them. In fact, teachers in this group used the advisor role as a vehicle to intervene with advisees according to their own vision for supporting students.

Schemas for Social-Emotional Support

Not all teachers envisioned the advisor role as one in which they wanted to provide social-emotional support to advisees, yet they all encountered some degree of student social-emotional issues in their work with advisees. Schemas for this aspect of their work (as illustrated in figure 5.1) did not reflect particular expertise regarding social-emotional support (which very

Table 5.1 Teacher-level schemas for the advisor role (N=45)

Schemas	Score Range	Composite Score Mean (S.D.)
1. Vision for advising students	1–3	12.11 (3.71)
2. Ideas of one's own about how to conduct advisory class	1–3	α = 0.7
3. Vision for providing social-emotional support to students	1–3	
4. Sense of how to respond to emergent student situations	1–3	
5. Role boundaries that concern student needs	1–3	
6. Role boundaries that concern one's own professional needs	1–3	
Possible range of total points	6–18	

Note: The score range spans from 1, which represents an undeveloped schema, to 3, which represents a well-developed schema.

few had), but rather clear ideas about how they would go about doing the work. Teachers with more developed social-emotional support schemas usually had a clear sense of procedures to follow for addressing students' social-emotional needs, whether it involved working with school procedures for accessing mental health services or administrative support, customizing school procedures (e.g., talking with a mental health provider rather than filling out the referral form as required) or procedures that they (teachers) developed themselves, such as Ms. Goodman's individual conferences with advisees (table 5.1).

Teachers with well-developed social-emotional support schemas accepted that they did not always know exactly how to respond to emergent situations. They responded in a spontaneous manner that demonstrated attentiveness to the student and a general sense of how to proceed, even when they lacked specific knowledge of the issue at hand. Ms. Aron loved when junior colleagues sought her out for guidance about their work with advisees: "It's great, because then I can say, 'I have no idea what to do. Let's think out loud about this, so it gives me a chance to make explicit my process.'" While she did not have exact knowledge of how to respond, her stance toward what she *didn't* know guided her work with advisees. When Mr. Bennett, a teacher in his mid-twenties, learned from an advisee that she was pregnant, he gave a thought-out response despite an admitted lack of knowledge about teen pregnancy and schooling:

> It came down to getting the resources she would need. I had no idea what she would need! I'm a young teacher, I knew there was going to be a lot that I wasn't prepared for. This one went a little bit above all that, but there

wasn't anything that really shocked me or made me feel inept. I felt like I was learning on the job. I was growing.

Not knowing exactly how to respond didn't stop Mr. Bennett, but rather set him in motion as he collaborated with colleagues and sought out information in order to support his advisee.

Unlike Mr. Bennett, teachers with less developed social-emotional support schemas appeared less sure of how to respond to emergent student needs, and expressed a dislike of being in this position. Their response to student situations—such as inappropriate behavior, disclosure of personal crises, or academic disengagement—was often one of distancing from the student. This distancing occurred through teachers' not pursuing the student's comments, framing the situation as a disciplinary situation rather than a social-emotional one, or making an immediate referral to a counselor or administrator rather than responding to the student in the moment.

Two teachers' responses to the same student, Vida, reflect differing schemas for providing social and emotional support (interestingly, neither teacher was Vida's advisor, but both independently mentioned her when discussing their work with students' social-emotional matters). Ms. Gutierrez, a respected veteran teacher, recounted a frustrating series of incidents with Vida, who had experienced significant family disruption and whose in-school behavior had deteriorated. Vida, whom she viewed as highly intelligent, suddenly began to act out at school, skipped classes, and behaved in uncharacteristically disrespectful ways toward Ms. Gutierrez. Eventually, Ms. Gutierrez, who had previously praised this student's resiliency, asked to have Vida removed from her class. Mr. Chavez, who had strong schemas for his social-emotional support role, also knew Vida well. He learned from her that she had been the victim of a violent crime just before her behavior deteriorated. Based on this knowledge, which Mr. Chavez gained when Vida sought him out during a personal crisis, he discussed the incidents with Vida and then connected her with assistance. Differing frameworks for receiving and interpreting Vida's behavior seemed to make a significant difference in how these teachers ultimately responded to her. While Ms. Gutierrez disengaged from Vida, deeming her behavior out of her teaching range, Mr. Chavez responded to the same student's needs based on his clear sense of how to go about the work of supporting students.

Role Boundaries

The contrasting stories about Vida also evoke role boundaries—what teachers decided the advisor role included and excluded. Teachers with developed advisor role schemas described role boundaries that related to their overarching purpose for advising and for providing social-emotional support to students. Role boundaries were not necessarily broad or narrow for advisors with more developed role schemas; I found evidence of both. Rather, the boundaries that this group of advisors set on their roles had a rationale that connected their personal vision for their role, to the needs of their students, and to their own professional needs.

Mr. Nagel expressed this notion as he described his view of what students needed and how he felt teachers ought to meet these needs:

> I think that students at this school need really clear, high expectations and limits. What they don't need is another parent. And anybody who starts to think they're in a parent role is going to go out of their mind and needs to stop immediately.

Other teachers described setting boundaries on their work with advisees as related to the kind of relationship they wanted to have with them. Ms. Powers voiced concern about grading student advisees simultaneously with knowing about and intervening with personal issues, so she kept conversations about personal issues brief and connected advisees to others for help. Teachers also described skill limitations, opting to refer students to other providers when they did not know how to help their advisees. These kinds of boundaries maintained teacher-advisee connection and additionally reflected teachers' vision for how they wanted to advise.

Teachers with less developed role schemas often involved set boundaries on the advisor roles for purposes of self-protection: guarding their time, avoiding areas of perceived incompetence, or limiting experiences that could be emotionally overwhelming. Mr. Orff told intentionally avoided information about social or emotional matters in students' lives:

> I try to focus mainly on academics and Socratic discussions, developing critical thinking, not investigating students' lives... It helps me to not be overwhelmed by my own emotional responses to the students' lives.

Mr. Orff's boundaries were clear, and in fact represented a strong schema with regard to boundaries. Still, they had little to do with either student needs or his vision for advisory. His boundaries cut students off without reconnecting them in other ways to their advisors or to others who might be of support.

In chapter 6 of this book, I further elaborate upon the boundaries that teachers drew around their work as advisors. At this point, however, teachers' boundaries upon their work as advisors stand to remind us how teachers' actions reflect differing ideas and principles that guide the work of advising.

Teacher-Level Resources Related to the Advisor Role

Aside from guiding principles and ideas about advising, teachers also drew upon their own knowledge, skills, experience, and support as they navigated the work of advising. When teachers serving as advisors described that which helped them know how to advise, they almost exclusively named what Sewell (1992, 2005) calls "human resources." While the number of years spent teaching is an obvious and notable factor, other resources (another career prior to teaching, experience working with children in nonclassroom settings as well as with low-income youth of color, having parented or cared for a dependent adult, support at and outside of the workplace, and constructive life experiences with adversity such as poverty, addiction, and loss) also contributed to participants' overall "package" of relevant resources (see table 5.2). I found that these resources informed advisors' base skills and perspective as they responded to their students'

Table 5.2 Teacher-level advisor role resources (N=45)

Individual Resources	Score Range	Composite Score Mean (S.D.)
1. Years of teaching experience	1–3	14.91 (4.19)
2. Work experience outside of current position, including non-teaching work	1–3	α = 0.7
3. Experience working with children (not classroom instruction)	0–3	
4. Experience working with low-income youth of color	1–3	
5. Experience parenting or caring for an dependent child or adult	0–3	
6. Constructive experiences with adversity	0–3	
7. Support for teaching practice at workplace (colleagues, administrators, workplace mentor)	1–3	
8. Support for teaching practice outside of workplace (e.g., family, friends, non-workplace mentor)	1–3	
9. Formal education (coursework, professional learning experiences)	0–3	
Possible range of total points	5–27	

Note: Scores assigned range from none (0, where applicable) to limited (1) to substantial (3).

circumstances, whether they were academic difficulties, routine tasks of adolescent development, or more acute situations such as exposure to family or community violence. I describe how I applied these criteria to teachers and produced a role resource score for each teacher in appendix B.

Experience beyond Age

Colleagues, friends, and participants alike guessed that a teacher's age would determine her capacity to advise well, but age did not emerge as a significant resource for advising in qualitative analysis. Instead, various experiences—some, but not all of which, accumulated with age—served as substantial advisor role resources. Older teachers were slightly more likely to possess a larger number of the personal resources listed in table 5.2. Five teachers under the age of 25 mentioned age in a more negative manner, referring to limited life experience and difficulties sharing parents' perspectives. Advising was often not a rookie performance for older teachers, many of whom had raised children into adulthood, and had seen adolescent development and school issues up close.

At the same time, several participants in their twenties reported significant personal resources that informed the work of advising. Ms. Janus, a 25-year-old teacher in her fourth year of teaching, reports a combination of role resources, including previous and current work as a team sport coach, a family member who is a secondary educator and provided significant mentoring, familiarity with youth of color from her own experience growing up in a socioeconomically diverse community, youth worker and supervisory experience gained at a local parks and recreation department, and her experience with a prolonged workplace conflict over concerns that she had been hired due to a family connection. These role resources, which did not necessarily correspond with teacher age, seemed to contribute to teachers' comfort with having conversations with students (including advisees and nonadvisees) in which they learned about their students' lives, identified behavior patterns, and connected students with support.

Interestingly, life experience involving adversity informed advisors' work in a number of ways. Difficult experiences such as poverty, the loss of a parent, addiction, and learning difficulties helped teachers to both understand their advisees' personal and family experiences and to come across to their students as capable of understanding them. The experience of failure—both on the job and in school—helped give them the perspective they needed as they attempted the work of advising, with multiple instances of failure, rejection by students, and uncertainty. "Failure was not as hard on me because I was more used to it," Mr. Nagel explained to me about the hidden benefits of his academic difficulties in high school and college. "I struggled academically, and I struggled here. I continue to struggle here."

In contrast, lower-resource teachers tended to have a shortage of advisory-relevant experience upon which to draw. They described feeling inadequately prepared to talk with students or parents about situations such as depression or complicated family circumstances, due to a lack of familiarity with these issues, with the experience of parenting, and with their students' cultural practices and norms. Ms. Saenz, age 25, told me, "I stay away from home issues. I don't feel like I have the right judgment as to when to intervene, when it's not appropriate to intervene. I'm uncomfortable with that, partially because I'm so young." With less life experience under their belts, this group of teachers had little to inform them when they found they had to improvise a response to an advisee's needs.

Prior Professional Experience

A particularly salient dimension of human resources relevant to advising was a professional career prior to teaching. Among the 45 teachers who informed this chapter, I identified 11 who came to teaching from fields such as engineering, graphic design, law, public health, sales, advertising, scientific research, entertainment, and publishing. This group of teachers told me that in previous careers they had developed different skills—such as problem-solving, negotiation, persuasion, and the ability to cope with workplace politics and short-term frustrations—that helped them to do the work of advising and providing support to students. "As a scientist, you know okay, it's not going to work. Try next hypothesis, try the next experiment," Ms. Baca explained of her efforts to persist with advisees where nothing seemed to work. Ms. Bruce, age 27, had come to teaching after another brief career working with youth. "A lot of people came here really, really overwhelmed by the advisor role and I was definitely overwhelmed but felt a little bit more prepared than others," she told me, citing her experience working with parents, helping 8th-grade students apply to high schools, and managing a heavy workload that could easily exceed her scheduled hours. While Ms. Bruce had the chance to learn these moving parts of her job over time *before* taking a position at Los Robles, some lower-resource teachers had never had a job prior to teaching, and found themselves figuring out all of the moving parts—including the advisor role—at once.

Educational Preparation for the Advisory Role

Teachers mentioned formal training, such as undergraduate studies, teacher credential programs, or professional learning experiences, surprisingly infrequently when they described that which informed their work as advisors. Forty-five percent of this study's teachers reported some educational experience that was relevant to their work as advisors. Still, these responses averaged quite low (0.77 out of a possible 3 points), with only three teachers—one with a bachelor's degree in social work and a master's degree in education (Ms. Renato), another with a master's degree in out-of-school education (Ms. Bruce), and a third with a law degree and a master's degree in education (Ms. Carbonell)—reporting a high level of educational preparation for the advisor role. One additional participant (Ms. Reinhardt), who participated in an urban school district's teacher residency program, reported significant training that prepared her to address issues such as child abuse, community violence, and gang involvement. It is noteworthy that among these exceptional participants, the two who followed traditional teacher education pathways did so as part of a second career.

A strong majority of advisors in this sample (91%) said that they had either limited or no training that supported their role of recognizing and responding to social and emotional matters among their students. Some teachers laughed or rolled their eyes when I asked them about their educational preparation for the work of advising; they then told me that their credential programs scarcely, if at all, prepared them for the advisor role. Others, such as Ms. Sosa, described by peers and students as a strong advisor, reported more informal learning experiences:

> In my credential program, we did a practicum course and I think we had a class or two on what to do in these situations, but mostly what I have learned has been sort of talking to other teachers and then having intense experiences with kids.

While the work of knowing, seeing, and intervening with students was framed as important, particularly at Western and Los Robles, teacher education and professional development experiences appeared to be a weak resource for most of the teachers whom I interviewed.

Support

Ms. Sosa's comment above highlights the importance of support that teachers accessed as they negotiated the work of advising. Some teachers turned to trusted colleagues or administrators, such as Mr. Carmichael did: "If I am in a situation that is really difficult, I would turn to a close colleague and I have a lot of faith in their judgment, Ms. Carbonell, Ms. Moré, Mr. Perrales." Others made use of school-based mental health professionals, both for support with individual students and support with their own struggles as they encountered student difficulties and demanding workloads. As discussed in chapter 3, teachers on particularly strong work teams at Western (house teams B and C), enjoyed not only supportive colleagues who knew their advisees well, but also time scheduled into their work days to meet with one another, exchange information about students, strategize, and plan advisory class meetings.

For others, this support came from outside of the school building. Ms. Willis, in a sense, grew up with support, in a family of caregiving professionals where family discussions often turned to one parent's research on human behavior, including work that used the Myers-Briggs test. Others grew up watching their own parents teach, and some still spoke with family members who were current or retired educators for support and guidance. Ms. Williams, to whom advisees and students alike turned frequently for advice and support, consulted frequently with a friend who worked as a therapist about challenging situations—particularly student mental health situations—for which she felt unprepared. "I would call her up and say this is what's happening, what do you think I should do and she would give me strategies and how to listen really well and how to get them to talk about feelings." While Ms. Williams used out-of-school support to compensate for what she did not have at work, others went without. Ms. Reynaldo lacked support as a new hire at Los Robles. She worked largely in isolation, partly due to the nascent state of her relationships with colleagues and partly due to Los Robles' organization of teacher time, which did not allot time for advisors to access each other or their advisees' content-area teachers. Given teachers' limited professional preparation and, at times, a lack of other advisor role resources, support often went a long way when available.

Race, Ethnicity, and Gender

Interestingly, neither race nor ethnicity represented salient advisor role resources, and gender factored in in a minor way. Quantitative analysis of survey results, using a variable to represent individuals with low levels of advisor role resources, showed that this variable had no statistically significant relationship with teachers' reported race or ethnicity. Qualitative analysis revealed that teachers identified multiple points of both similarity to and difference from their advisees, or "all these different differences," as Mr. DeLucia described them. "There is a distance," he explained,

> because by nature teachers (at Los Robles) have master's degrees and they are middle class already, and the students we are teaching mostly are lower,

maybe middle class, mostly lower class. So there is a class difference which sets a power dynamic... and then there is often times an educational difference between community and the teacher.

In addition to these differences, all three schools enrolled students of multiple ethnicities (particularly among diverse Latino and Pacific Islander groups) and races, as well as mixed-ethnicity and mixed-race students. The same applied to the schools' faculties, which had a slight white majority (55%), in addition to 18 percent Latino, 16 percent mixed race, 9 percent Asian-American, and 2 percent African-American teachers (see chapter 1 for additional information on schools' student and faculty demographics). The potential for a true racial, ethnic and socioeconomic match bewteen teachers and students was extremely rare (Warikoo, 2004, reports similar findings). Teachers' connection with advisees from the same racial or ethnic group on a basis of similarity came up very rarely in interviews, and could not generalize to an entire group of advisees because of the advisory classes' diversity. Teachers of color did raise concerns about their colleagues tolerating misbehavior and academic underperformance because of ethnic, racial, and socioeconomic differences. Ms. Reynaldo, a Latina teacher who grew up in poverty, voiced this concern: "Poor work habits, which we can teach them (students), are excused because of socioeconomic background, or upbringing." White teacher participants who had higher levels of other advisor role resources, such as work with lower-income youth of color, caregiving experience, and constructive experience with adversity, however, expressed the same concerns. A teacher's race and ethnicity did not give her a particular leg up on advisor role resources.

Teachers' gender, however, emerged as a somewhat more salient factor. Male teachers were disproportionately represented among teachers with lower levels of advisor role resources. Male teachers with lower levels of resources (n=7) were both younger (average age of 27.6 years) and less experienced (4.1 years of teaching experience) than the larger group of teacher participants (34.4 years and 6.4 years, respectively). But overall, I found no statistically significant differences between males and females with regard to what informed their work as advisors. Some teachers reported difficulty connecting across gender lines with their advisees, particularly when it came to sensitive personal issues such as sexuality or illegal activity. Ms. Janus and her student, Miguel, both told me that Miguel had a stronger connection with one of the school's male paraprofessionals in charge of school discipline and safety, for example. However, I also observed and was told (by teachers and students) about strong cross-gender advising relationships. Further, advisors with more developed social networks engaged colleagues for advice or as quasi coadvisors or when they felt there were differences that might trace to gender. It is fair to note, however, that I saw students recruit informal advisors of both the same and different genders.

Relational Skills

I spent a multimonth period conducting more extended interviews with a subgroup of the 45 teachers who informed this chapter (see appendix B for a description of this subgroup). In these extended interviews, I found that relational skills—interpersonal communication skills used to develop and sustain relationships with others—represented another critical advisor role resource. Since this information emerged from the extended interviews, I could not systematically assess the presence or degree of these resources among all 45 teachers. For this reason, I did not include these findings when I calculated the level of teachers' advisor role resources. However, I found some evidence of relational skills as a resource in the larger group of advisors, and include that information where relevant.

Grossman et al. (2007) describe the "complex relational work" (p. 110) of teaching, and my findings support this characterization. I coded advisor interview text for relational practices and identified 112 instances where teachers described relational practices. Grouping these responses by type, I found two primary types of relational practices reported by advisor participants: communication skills and assertiveness.

Most relational practices employed by subgroup teachers (73 instances) involved general communication skills—how the advisors communicated and what they conveyed with their words. They spoke of listening to students and staying attuned to them without interrupting, judging, or giving suggestions. Responding to students in a positive, calm, respectful, constructive manner also appeared to advisors to help build relationships with their students.

Mr. Chavez described a situation where he turned around a potential conflict with Jaelle, a transfer student new to his advisory class. He saw Jaelle using her phone during advisory class and asked her to put it away:

> She said, "Why? We're not doing anything." So I sat with her and I said, "Have you had this problem in other classes?" and she said yeah. I said, "Well, what happens when you use your phone?" She said "Well, they try to take it or get me in trouble or send me to the office." I said to her, "How is that helping you pass your classes, how is that helping you graduate?" She admitted very freely that it was not. So then I went kind of further and said, "Do you think this is affecting your grades?" She said yeah. "Well...what is it going to take for you to pass?" She said, "I don't get what I'm doing." *That's* when the conversation happened about her classes. She said that she didn't get what was going on in her classes.

This interaction could have escalated into a conflict or a disciplinary situation (and did between Jaelle and other staff members during my time at King). Instead, Mr. Chavez sought more information from Jaelle and used different strategies to diffuse and redirect the conversation, away from Jaelle's phone use and toward a discussion about her adjustment to her new school and her academic struggles.

Other communication skills seemed specifically tailored to adolescent students. I noted nine instances of advisors giving young people power in their shared interactions, consistent with youth development research (e.g., Mitra, 2004) that stresses the importance of student voice, particularly in institutional settings. Teachers gave their advisees the choice of whether, where, and how much they wished to discuss sensitive and/or personal matters. Even though Ms. Renato had skills and knowledge—from her training as a social worker—to intervene when Essie showed signs of depression, she heard consistently from Essie that she did not want to discuss emotional or family issues. Ms. Renato continued her efforts to engage Essie in conversation and held Essie responsible for academic work as well as broken school rules, but did not cross over into territory that Essie had designated as off-limits.

Other responses involved teachers using assertiveness, which Back and Back (2005, p. 1) define as "expressing your needs, wants, opinions, feelings and beliefs in direct, honest and appropriate ways." I saw evidence of assertive communication in participants' direct conversations with students, colleagues, and parents where information was shared and where advisors shared opinions with, and made specific requests of, their partners in conversation. Teachers reported telling their advisees directly about unacceptable behavior, being at risk for failure, and concerns regarding advisees' personal well-being. Other situations called for assertiveness between colleagues. "You're checking each other, did you do this, did you do that," Ms. Dolby explained of her relationship to other teachers at Los Robles. Ms. Powers advocated with a colleague for Javier, an advisee interested in automotive school rather than four-year college:

> When the automotive school came (to Los Robles), she said Javier couldn't leave her class. I said, "There is a recruiter, he really wants to do this," so finally the teacher relented, but the fact that the teacher wouldn't... I said, "If it was Harvard would it be different?" She said that the automotive school is not a real college, and I said that I don't think I get to make that choice for him.

Teachers' relational skills, then, made it more possible to develop not only relationships with advisees, but other relationships that would help them support their advisees.

Role Enactment: Evidence of Intertwined Advisor Role Resources and Schemas

Teachers put their advisor role schemas and resources together in a variety of different ways, consistent with Sewell's (1992/2005) claim that resources and schemas can influence one another in an infinite number of possible combinations. In order to gain perspective on what leads to differences in how teachers advise, I distinguish between different combinations that I observed. A four-quadrant, typological framework (represented in table 5.3) represents how advisor role schemas and resources intersect with one another, and clusters individuals for the purpose of explaining shared characteristics among, as well as differences between, groups of teachers along these lines (Bidwell, Frank, & Quiroz, 1997; Weiss, 1994).

Teachers' resource and schema total scores serve as the basis for distinguishing the four quadrants. I established a threshold for each score, with schema scores below 12 out of 18 considered "low schema," (a more concise way of saying "less-developed schema") and scores 12 and above considered "high schema" (synonymous with "more-developed schema"). Likewise, individuals with a score of 14 or less points out of a total 27 were considered "low resource," while those scoring 15 or above were considered "high resource." Teachers' schema and resource totals determined the quadrant to which I assigned them. I include in table 5.3 quadrant means for these scores, as well as for teacher age and years of teaching experience, in order to show differences and similarities across the four quadrants. Averages highlight similarities in rows and columns, even among teachers whom we might consider different from one another. Schema scores are more similar, for example, between quadrants A and C, and between quadrants B and D. Average age is similar among lower-resource teachers in quadrants A and B, but schema scores are not. This framework suggests that years of teaching experience do not necessarily imply well-developed ideas about how to advise. Quadrant C teachers, who have the highest average years of teaching experience, have the lowest mean schema score.

The distribution of advisors across quadrants, aside from the differences noted above, was fairly even. T-test analyses revealed no statistically significant difference in mean age or years of experience between low- and high-schema participants. In other words, neither age nor years of experience predicted the presence of well-developed schemas for advising. Further, the quadrants did not differ significantly (according to analysis of variance) with regard to race and ethnicity or gender composition. Teachers from each of the sample's three schools were distributed across all four quadrants. Western had the only notably uneven distribution of teachers across quadrants, with only one in quadrant B. Combinations of resources

Table 5.3 Mean scores and standard deviations for individual teacher characteristics, sorted by teacher quadrant (n=45)

	Low Advisor Role Schema	High Advisor Role Schema
Low Advisor Role Resource	**Quadrant A** 13 Teachers Mean Resource Score: 10.38 (2.63) Mean Schema Score: 9 (1.23) Mean Age: 27.31 (3.07) Mean Years Teaching Experience: 4.15 (2.79)	**Quadrant B** 7 Teachers Mean Resource Score: 13 (1.41) Mean Schema Score: 15 (1.73) Mean Age: 26.29 (1.38) Mean Years Teaching Experience: 2.86 (.69)
High Advisor Role Resource	**Quadrant C** 11 Teachers Mean Resource Score: 16.09 (1.22) Mean Schema Score: 8.9 (1.58) Mean Age: 35.81 (11.18) Mean Years Teaching Experience: 9.64 (8.78)	**Quadrant D** 14 Teachers Mean Resource Score: 19.14 (2.83) Mean Schema Score: 16.07 (1.44) Mean Age: 39.64 (10.65) Mean Years Teaching Experience: 6.71 (5.46)

and schemas are unique for each teacher, yet there are particular characteristics that distinguish teachers in each quadrant. Below, I describe the quadrants, using case examples to illustrate each.

Quadrant A: Low Resource/Low Schema

Novice teachers often lacked both advisor role resources and schemas that might have helped them to do the work of advising. They tended to describe both advisory class and the advisor role as stressful and overwhelming. With a limited stock of knowledge, experience, skills, support, or ideas upon which to draw, they often seemed at a loss for how to handle the inevitable challenges of advising young people. Mr. Westerberg, a 24-year-old, first-year teacher who described himself as "a young teacher still figuring things out," represents this group of teachers well.

The first time Mr. Westerberg mentioned Dahlia, a 10th-grade advisee whom he described as "unengaged," "nondefiant," and one of his smartest students, was after she told him that she had quit smoking marijuana. "I'm a little bit baffled about how to get involved with those things, I must say," he said of his response to her disclosure. "Besides providing positive reinforcement and a set of ears to listen, I don't feel like I necessarily have the tools that I need to help in more concrete ways."

Mr. Westerberg suspected, and Dahlia confirmed, that she had limited confidence in his advisory skills. "I'm not sure if Mr. Westerberg has been an advisor before," she commented. "Not that he's not a good advisor, just that there's things that he can improve on." Dahlia described him as a bit hard to approach, struggling with classroom management issues, and as having an awkward relationship with the advisory curriculum. Mr. Westerberg would not have disagreed with any of these statements. Completely new to the advisor role, he felt unsure about how to carry it out. He had some ideas about how to advise, and had developed some early rapport with Dahlia. Still, like other quadrant A teachers, he found it difficult to bring his ideas about advising to fruition. Mr. Westerberg came across to me and to his advisees as personable. But having a more productive rapport with advisees was a struggle for him. He said he would like more structure and guidance related the advisor role, on topics such as interacting with parents, addressing student crises, activities and discussion topics for advisory class, and his duties as an advisor. "I have no clue what to do in advisory," Mr. Westerberg said at the end of the year, even after recognizing his growth over the school year. "I'm just going to do what I can to fill up the space." In general, quadrant A teachers struggled the most with schools' limited structuring of the advisor role. Their schools gave them little to work with as they figured out how to advise.

Midyear, Dahlia told Mr. Westerberg that she would be leaving the following day for El Salvador due to an imminent death in her extended family there, and wanted help keeping up with her school work while she was gone. While concerned, Mr. Westerberg also felt pleased that Dahlia had developed enough of a relationship with him to warrant the conversation. He felt overwhelmed by the responsibility that their conversations generated, both that day and in the emails she sent from El Salvador. As a bright student nonetheless short on academic credits, and getting further behind as her absence lasted for weeks, Dahlia had a lot of questions about what would happen to her schooling upon her return. Mr. Westerberg named a number of individuals who might be able to help him help Dahila, but said that these important matters felt out of his hands. Quadrant A teachers often said that they understood the critical nature of the advisor role, and yet felt limited in their capacity to fulfill it. Mr. Westerberg had weak connections to resources in the school (e.g., the school counselor, his teaching team members) that could have helped him to support his students, however. Accessible resources and schemas at the organizational level were a great help to quadrant A teachers, and they felt the absence of advisory-related organizational structures just as strongly.

Mr. Westerberg cared deeply about students' well-being and progress, but felt consistently doubtful that he could help students move in the right direction. While quadrant A teachers often expended a great amount of effort to help individual advisees, they felt uncertain about whether their actions fit their role responsibilities. Quadrant A teachers at all three schools often described themselves as underperforming their job due to actions they had not taken, yet they often did not know what *was* expected of them. This uncertainty, in turn, had potential to contribute to limited or negative perceptions of their own efficacy, role overload, and burnout.

Mr. Westerberg left Western at the end of the year for another teaching position, but was highly certain that he would not continue long-term in education. "I am being put in a framework of responsibility that is more than I want to take on," he explained, speaking of his responsibilities teaching and advising. Six of the thirteen quadrant A advisors whom I interviewed remained in their positions the year following our interviews. This nearly 50 percent attrition rate raises questions about how well the open-ended advisor role fits the novice teacher.

Quadrant B: Low Resource/High Schema

Quadrant B teachers looked, in many ways, like dream hires. With little experience under their belts, they performed well as both teachers and as advisors. Students sought them out for conversation and advice. In marked contrast to quadrant A teachers, this group demonstrated a clear, guiding view of the advisory program, whether or not it matched the school's stated purpose for advisory. Ms. Bruce, a 26-year-old, 3rd-year teacher, exemplified quadrant B teachers' drive to innovate in the advisor role as well as the strain they felt while doing it.

While short on life and work experience (as suggested by an average of 2.9 years teaching and an average age of 26.3 years), quadrant B teachers capitalized on whatever they had at their disposal. Ms. Bruce frequently tapped into the knowledge and skills that she gained working with youth and their parents in an after-school academic support program. She did not possess a gapless web of ideas and ready-made responses to her advisees, but rather a set of core ideas and a growing toolbox of strategies from which she drew discriminately.

The relationship between Ms. Bruce and her advisee Manuel illustrates quadrant B teachers' principled, thorough responsiveness to their advisees. Manuel's track record did not necessarily inspire teacher optimism and commitment. He frequently missed school and had failed two classes the previous school year. Manuel had also had a series of serious scrapes with school rules leading to police involvement and serious disciplinary action by administrators. Yet Ms. Bruce approached these issues as opportunities. Ms. Bruce described her actions after an incident where he seemed high during a scheduled presentation of his work:

> I said "Manuel, you've broken my heart...you worked your tail off for this." He said, "I understand what you mean by breaking your heart." I called his mother, I told her he failed. I did not tell her he was high. She knows he smokes pot. I said (to a colleague) "Maybe you could help me with this situation, it's clear to me that Manuel was high, what do I do?" He was like, "How do I know what to do?" I did not go to my principal...I told a number of my colleagues. I don't know that our principal would have given me the advice that I was looking for. I worked with Manuel to improve his Power Point. He sat in on other's people's presentations so that he could answer the questions better when it was his turn. He went again and he passed. It was very clear that he was sober. It was a hundred times better than the first time and it was a real victory...It got him a step closer to graduation.

Ms. Bruce's actions reflect the following advisor role schemas: a clear vision (advisory is to help students graduate) that guided her decisions of how to proceed with Manuel after this incident, a high sense of responsibility for Manuel's academic progress, and a sense that she should customize and at times sidestep school norms and procedures. While Ms. Bruce's response to Manuel seemed deliberate, she did not immediately respond with a clear idea of what she would say or do in face of this unfamiliar experience. Yet, her principled approach to advising helped her to quickly move from dismay and surprise to a decisive set of actions.

Ms. Bruce creatively enlisted others in order to support Manuel, including his girlfriend (another of her advisees), Manuel's parents, and a male student-teacher who was of the same ethnic group as and also closer in age to Manuel. Like other quadrant B advisors, Ms. Bruce readily, but selectively, engaged colleagues and other individuals to obtain advice and accommodations for her advisees in her work with them.

Ms. Bruce and Manuel both experienced strain amidst her constant press for him to grow academically and personally. "She be getting on my case, like when I'm doing something dumb," Manuel explained, but he generally described Ms. Bruce in positive terms: "She's cool, she knows mostly everything about my life." Ms. Bruce found her work with Manuel exhausting when it went poorly, and highly satisfying as his attendance and academic performance improved over the course of the school year: "from total burnout to total joy." This time- and emotion-intensive work, however, came at a price. Ms. Bruce dedicated evening and weekend time to her entire teaching job, including advising, and said that this commitment had put substantial strain on her personal life.

Quadrant B teachers often felt overwhelmed by a range of student-related and organizational responsibilities, many of which they took on themselves or were assigned due to others' perceptions of their competence. Ms. Bruce, for example, began coaching an athletic team that had dissolved under previous leadership. The strain from her expanded responsibilities extended to the advisor role. Ms. Bruce wondered aloud whether she should limit her work with Manuel, in terms of hours and commitment. When Manuel faced possible expulsion after a major rule infraction, Ms. Bruce seriously considered whether it would be better for them both for Manuel to leave Los Robles. Manuel would not receive endless chances to redeem himself (one of Ms. Bruce's gripes with Los Robles' administration and teachers), and she would have a lighter pragmatic and emotional workload. "Ultimately," Ms. Bruce said, "I want him to stay and I want him to graduate." Her role schema (advisory is to help students graduate) guided even her approach to this problem.

Quadrant B teachers' driven work wore on them, even as it clearly benefited their advisees. Their well-developed ideas and guidelines about advising led to intense, demanding involvement with advisees, but interestingly, their role resources were not always sufficient to support this ambitious vision for advising. Quadrant B advisors seemed to have an imbalance, with more schemas than resources, or more blueprints than bricks, as they enacted the advisor role. This imbalance did not bode well. Five of seven indicated their intention of moving on to different jobs within the next two to five years. One resigned midyear to take a nonteaching position, and two others left at the end of the school year. Three initiated discussions with me about their interest in doctoral programs, compared to one teacher in the rest of the larger group of 45 teachers. The effort to make their roles work, often without sufficient organizational support or enough of their own advisor role resources, appeared taxing to this group of teachers.

Quadrant C: High Resource/Low Schema

Teachers with high advisor role resources and low advisor role schemas for advising made up the most diverse group in terms of age (from 25 to 62 years) and years of teaching experience (3 to 30 years). One might anticipate that a richness of life and work experience would enhance the advisor role for this group, but it did not. Instead, most quadrant C teachers questioned the rationale for advisory, acknowledged investing minimal energy in advisory, and found the experience frustrating. This group of teachers had less developed schemas for doing the work of advising. While quadrant B teachers had more blueprints than bricks, teachers in quadrant

C had plenty of bricks but lacked the blueprints that could have guided their work.

Ms. Baca, a 37-year-old, 5th-year teacher, illustrates this group well. Her rich advisor role resources include a previous career, stepparenting, her own experience as an adolescent with an undiagnosed learning disability, living in the same community as many of her students, and the close knowledge of family members and friends who struggled with and resolved personal and academic challenges. Her classroom walls, decorated with photos of students and student artwork, and interactions with students, showed her strong relational skills. During an interview, an alumnus visited her room and bantered amicably with Ms. Baca. As he left, she called after him, "Thanks for visiting. I love you."

Despite her rich advisor role resources, though, the advisor role frustrated Ms. Baca. "I wouldn't miss advisory if we did away with it. It's a clusterfuck, a nightmare," she exclaimed. She identified shortcomings of her schools' advisory curriculum, but did not feel she had the ability or time to improve upon it. I saw little evidence among quadrant C teachers of a guiding vision that helped them plot and execute their next steps. Ms. Baca halfheartedly implemented the curriculum, sometimes opting out of it without substituting anything substantive. This passive approach toward the advisor role's problems was common among quadrant C advisors.

Ms. Baca's work with Josué, a 10th-grade advisee, illustrates the combination of limited advisor role schemas and abundant resources that characterized quadrant C teachers. Josué's attendance was poor, he ranked below nearly every other student in King's sophomore class, and Ms. Baca had seen him on local street corners with other gang-identified students. While she worried about Josué, Ms. Baca did not place herself in the center of the school's responsibility to support him. When asked what she thought Josué needed from her as an advisor, Ms. Baca replied,

> I don't know, a slap in the head? I'm just kidding. But honestly, I'm not sure. He needs something. He needs to get out of this school and go somewhere that, I mean, I think he might need me as an advocate perhaps to help him find a new situation.

As happened with other quadrant C teachers, though, her ideas did not come very far forward in her day-to-day work. Ms. Baca likened herself to a border collie with Josué. "All I can do is keep barking and hope that maybe it will make sense or that something will come back to him," she said of her attempts to talk with him about his academic progress or his future. Compared to what her colleagues with richer advisor role schemas did, Ms. Baca's approach was passive.

Josué agreed with Ms. Baca's idea that he should attend a different school, but he got no help from her with this matter. He told me of a meeting between his teachers, mother, and the school guidance counselor in which he asked for transfer to a continuation school (where he hoped he could make up missing course credits), but was told he would have to stay at his current school. "I got so frustrated that I even cried, tears coming out of my eyes," he told me. "They didn't want to listen to me. I just walked out." Ms. Baca never mentioned this meeting. When I asked her about it, she replied that she never knew that the meeting happened. "I've never been included in on a conversation about where a child should go," she explained. Had she participated in this meeting, she said, "I would have advocated to send him where he could succeed." Nevertheless, Ms. Baca did not situate herself where she could activate these ideas.

Ms. Baca's work advising her students left her feeling badly about her work, but she did not make significant changes to it. She felt unsure about whether she had taught her advisees anything, and described having limited impact on Josué. She managed these experiences of doubt by what she called "flushing" them. "I would go insane if I didn't try to let things go," she explained. Ms. Baca drew boundaries but did not shore those boundaries up with any sort of referral to others who might do for her advisees what she felt she could not. Her connections with colleagues, as was the case with other quadrant C advisors, were strong but not she did not use them to leverage support for her students. Josué left King before the end of the year, and Ms. Baca was neither informed nor had she inquired about where he had gone.

Interestingly, on Western's teacher team B (described in chapter 3), three quadrant C teachers received substantial support—in the form of team-level norms, expectations, procedures, and support for the advisor role—that made the experience much more constructive for advisors and advisees alike. Team members relied upon each other, as well as upon colleagues with more developed schemas for advising, and were therefore able to capitalize on the advisor role resources they possessed. Ms. Reinhardt, for example, told me that Western provided a big picture view of advisory, but did not give specific guidance. Her teacher team, whom she described as providing "really great examples of how to support kids mentally and academically," gave her concrete models and guidance about how to advise. Her team compensated for the school's insufficient structuring of the advisor role as well as for its teachers' limited schemas for advising. This situation, however, was rare among all teachers, and highlighted the importance of advisor role schemas for even richly experienced teachers.

Ms. Baca's combination of ample advisor role resources, limited ideas about how to carry out the role, and frustration with and mild disengagement from the role exemplify the quadrant C teacher. Teachers in this group experienced a misalignment of resources and schemas, with resources outweighing schemas and having no figurative place to "go" in these educators' work.

Quadrant D: High Resource/High Schema

Teachers belonging to this group showed an integration of their advisor role schemas and resources that largely seemed to benefit them and their students. Sewell (2005) suggests that "schemas are the effects of resources, just as resources are the effects of schemas," (p. 136), and it is easy to see how quadrant D teachers' skills, experiences, knowledge, support, and ideas reinforced one another. Whether or not their schools structured and supported the advisor role, quadrant D teachers skillfully and confidently conducted their classes and relationships with advisees. Autonomy with the advisor role did not rattle quadrant D teachers, but rather gave them space that they used to enact their vision for the role.

Ms. Powers, a 41-year-old, 5th-year teacher, brought substantial advisor role resources *and* schemas to her work. After a career in sales, she was familiar with workplace dynamics, persuasive rhetoric, and workplace expectations of high school graduates, and activated these resources as an advisor. Her mother was an educator, and Ms. Powers learned about teaching special needs students through frequent visits to her mother's classrooms. She also cared for this parent as she died in later years, and had lost her father during her adolescence. These experiences helped her connect with the grief and family disruption experienced by some of her students. Before joining Los Robles' staff, Ms. Powers had taught in other urban schools with less support for students and teachers, and had learned strategies for coping with the stresses of urban teaching.

Ms. Powers was aware of and used her schemas for the work of advising. She described herself as a "life skills sherpa" to her advisees, and joked that she had a "master plan" for them. This master plan—to help her advisees identify a post-high school plan and take the necessary steps to prepare for it—guided Ms. Powers's work. It is also where Ms. Powers incorporated her previous career, as well as her familiarity with a range of issues, schools, and students, into advising. She activated her background knowledge of various careers and experience as a salesperson as she attempted to help students define and pursue post-high school goals. Dissatisfied with Los Robles' protocol for handling students sent out of class and to their advisors due to misbehavior, Ms. Powers revised the form that students were required to complete and discuss with their advisors. Ms. Powers, like other quadrant D teachers, used school procedures when they supported her vision, and either adapted or ignored those that did not.

Ms. Powers's work with Candace, a 17-year-old advisee, confirms her deliberate, informed approach to advising. Candace had attended three schools in less than two years, missed at least one day of school per week, and barely had enough credits to qualify her as a 10th-grade student. Los Robles evaluated her for special education, at which time she was diagnosed with Attention-Deficit Hyperactivity Disorder and other learning disabilities. Candace had experienced a number of family disruptions and was in the custody of an elderly relative.

Like other quadrant D teachers, Ms. Powers approached advising with intention and focus. Ms. Powers claimed the difficult situations Candace frequently encountered as opportunities, using them to enact her vision for advising Candace and her other students. When Candace threatened to have her brother beat up her math teacher, Ms. Powers did not know how to respond but felt that she needed to. She brought this information to a school administrator, who felt equally stumped. Ms. Powers raised the possibility of involving the police in order to communicate to Candace the gravity of Candace's acts. In quadrant D fashion, Ms. Powers made use of the school's intervention to push the point she wanted to make with her advisee. Ms. Powers recounted her conversation with Candace following the police interview:

> She said to me, "Ms. Powers, I can't believe that happened," and she was angry at the assistant principal. So I said to her, "It was me." She was speechless. She was like, "How could you do that to me?" I said, "No, Candace, how could you do that to *me*? You threatened my colleague, I know you are a better person and you went to a place that nobody can accept. If I care for you, what am I supposed to do?"

Candace's continued engagement with Ms. Powers reflects Ms. Powers's use of this intervention to teach rather than simply to punish. After this incident, Candace described Ms. Powers as "doing any and everything to help me." This incident shows how this quadrant D teacher stepped into an initially puzzling situation and intervened in a way that moved her advisee forward and also built a relationship with her.

Highly resourceful and principled in their interventions with students, quadrant D teachers still acknowledged the limitations of their knowledge and skills, particularly about student social-emotional issues. Like other quadrant D teachers, though, Ms. Powers did not see her lack of situation-specific knowledge or of success with individual advisees as a sign of her own incompetence. Instead, she viewed her work through the lenses of her *life skills sherpa* role schema and her own life experience. "It's like she's out there and I keep throwing a lifeline and she can't catch it," Ms. Powers said of Candace, whose personal and school lives had deteriorated over the course of the school year. This understanding of her limitations did not keep her from continuing and adjusting her efforts with Candace, but did limit how much she let it reflect on her own potential contributions. "As long as I feel that I did what I could, I'm pretty okay with it. I hate to see a kid drift, but whatever the situation is, it's not for me to fix," she explained. This approach reflects a unique and important combination of boundaries and persistent effort that characterizes most quadrant D teachers. In contrast to the disengagement I noted with many quadrant C teachers (and some quadrant B teachers who found themselves overextended and unsupported), most quadrant D teachers drew boundaries in ways that reflected consideration of their potential impact on advisees (I take up this topic again in chapter 6). Not surprisingly, only 2 of the 13 quadrant D teachers left their positions at the end of the study, both for teaching positions elsewhere. This group of teachers made creative use of their own assets to make the advisor role work for themselves and their students.

Conclusion and Implications

On a surface level, this chapter's case examples tell a story about how individual characteristics informed teachers' work. These examples explain that teachers not only interpreted the advisor role in different ways, but that they drew from their own independent toolboxes—whose contents varied substantially from teacher to teacher—as they advised their students. These toolboxes' contents, which I have described as advisor role resources and schemas, were particularly powerful (or particularly missed, if absent) when schools did not fully support teachers' work as advisors. As a result of differences in teachers' advisor role toolboxes, students had a range of experiences with their teachers who advised them—from Manuel's experience of impactful, persistent, attuned advising with Ms. Bruce to Josué's lack of connection to Ms. Baca. Variation in advisor role resources and schemas—teachers having a different assortment of tools—was also associated with differences in teachers' adjustment to the advisor role, as suggested by teachers' engagement in the work of advising, satisfaction with the advisor role, and turnover rates. The content of teachers' toolboxes, and the teacher-to-teacher variation in these contents, mattered to teachers and the students whom they advised.

In addition to this surface story, this chapter also tells us about the importance of individual teachers' match with expanded teacher roles. I touch upon three aspects of this theme: teacher learning related to expanded roles, organizational structuring of expanded roles, and the staffing of expanded roles.

The teachers at King, Los Robles, and Western had experienced almost no formal preparation for the advisor role, but some of them possessed tools that helped them do the work. It is easy to say preservice teacher education programs must prepare teacher candidates for the jobs awaiting them, and educators have made calls for just such actions (National Council for Accreditation of Teacher Education [NCATE], 2010b). Yet much of teachers' tools for their work—their vision for advising, their perspective on their work with students, the skills they used—emerged from practical experience in and out of schools. Those invested in educational preparation for expanded roles might learn from these findings. They could identify core competencies needed to effectively carry out the roles, and then consider how to provide practice-based learning experiences related to expanded roles. These experiences—which could target preservice or practicing teachers—could build these competencies through a combination of instruction, direct experience, and guided reflection (with reflections framed by designated competencies) intended to expose learners to opportunities to gain, and to then bring out, particular competencies. With the case of the advisor role, this chapter's findings suggest that teachers' core competencies involve relational skills (with students and colleagues), advisory class planning (both individual class meetings and the class' overall trajectory), response to emergent student social-emotional issues, problem-solving, boundary setting, and persistence in the face of difficulties advising students. Other expanded roles would involve other competencies.

I must note, however, that individual teachers' tools mattered the most in the absence of schools' structuring of the advisor role. This finding suggests an inverse relationship between role structure and the need for individual teachers' independent readiness for expanded roles—the more structure, the lower the need. Teachers, particularly those with limited resources and schemas, expressed a desire to clearly understand what their administrators and colleagues expected them to do with and for their advisees. Teachers not only wanted to understand the school's purpose for advisory, but also wanted to know specifics of the role—what to do in class, when to intervene, where their responsibilities left off. Some readers might have felt dismay at Ms. Bruce's independent decision to not inform her principal when Manuel came to school high, but it is important to remember that she made this decision largely on her own due to a lack of guidance about her advisor role responsibilities. She did what made the most sense to her. For teachers who do not yet have a solid grasp of the work of advising, explicit guidelines would help guide day-to-day actions. Such firm guidelines, however, might put off more confident, experienced advisors as represented by quadrant D teachers, who thrived on autonomy. Schools could also make the advisor role more manageable (and more accessible to novice teachers) by building in support, a key resource for all teachers I interviewed. Quadrant C teachers, long on experience but short on guiding ideas about advisory, floundered less in the role when they encountered support within formally organized teaching teams. If schools could build in the support that teachers found in teacher teams and scavenged from colleagues, friends, and family members, less grounded advisors might not struggle so much with their role.

Finally, the idea of different teachers benefiting from or struggling in particular school arrangements suggests the importance of staffing expanded roles with teachers who are best suited for them, particularly in schools with fledgling structures to support those roles. My extension and application of structuration theory (Giddens, 1984; Sewell, 1992, 2005) suggests that neither ideas and principles that guide teachers' work (role schemas), nor the knowledge, skills, experience, or support that inform teachers' work (role resources), are alone sufficient for an effective enactment of expanded teacher roles. Teachers seemed to need both. Ideally, then, every expanded role occupant possesses a balanced combination of role schemas and resources. With every advisor a Ms. Renato, a school's advisory program would likely flourish, structured or not. However, no school found itself staffed by a squad of master advisors. In particular, 29 percent—nearly one-third—of the teachers I interviewed fell into quadrant A, the quadrant with the lowest amounts of advisor role resources and schemas. Teachers with such limited preparation for the advisor role, set in a school that does not structure the role for teachers, had less chances of success, with potentially negative implications for their advisees. These findings suggest that school administrators who include expanded roles in teachers' formal responsibilities would do well to consider which teachers will fit these roles, as well as how the school's support of the role influences this fit. They might hire teachers already suited to expanded roles, or give teachers support and learning experiences to suit them to the roles, but doing neither seems likely to result in frustration for administrators, teachers, and students alike.

Questions emerge from these findings: How do teachers cope with performing a role for which many are unsupported and unprepared, particularly a role that includes demands to provide social and emotional support to students? Does greater readiness for the expanded role buffer teachers against any negative experiences of the expanded role? Chapter 6 takes up these questions, focusing on how teachers respond to, and cope with, strains associated with the advisor role.

CHAPTER SIX

OCCUPATIONAL HAZARDS AND
INNOVATION: TEACHERS' RESPONSES
TO THE ADVISOR ROLE

When teachers take on roles that expand their formal responsibilities beyond conventional parameters, strain seems expectable. Today, for example, many "mainstream" teachers work in "inclusion" classrooms that blend special education students—with learning challenges including autism, learning disabilities, communication disorders, cognitive disabilities, and behavior disorders—together with other non-special education students for the majority of their school day. Research on this particular expanded teacher role finds teachers who feel underprepared for, and at times experiencing increased job stress due to, their responsibilities on top of the demands of "just" teaching (Forlin, 2001; Idol, 2006).

An additional, unique strain comes along with expanded teacher roles that ask teachers to engage in the social and emotional aspects of their students' lives. When required to know their students well and address problems that threaten their academic progress, teachers end up learning about the difficult life and family circumstances, mental health issues, and dangers that some of their students face. When teachers respond—by intervening themselves, finding others who can offer students support and assistance, or simply by continuing the conversation—they find themselves working with their students' emotions as well as their own. Scholars (e.g., Brennan, 2006; Brown, 2011; Oplatka, 2011; Tsang, 2011; Winograd, 2003; Zembylas, 2002) contend that all teachers encounter demands to perform a degree of *emotional labor*, in which they meet their employers' and professions' expectations to display and suppress different emotions in order to produce particular emotional states in their students, students' parents, and colleagues. "Confronted on a daily basis with a variety of emotions," Zembylas (2002, p. 201) elaborates, "Teachers must control emotions of anger, anxiety and vulnerability, and express empathy, calmness, and kindness." Teachers encounter implicit and explicit *emotional display rules* (EDRs), which specify which emotions they should and should not convey to others, although scholars continue to raise questions about the degree to which these rules are enforced, regulated, and institutionalized (e.g., Oplatka, 2007). These rules take on a more pronounced form with the advisor role, which requires teachers to go beyond expressing empathy, calmness, and kindness and to take the position of caring for and supporting their student advisees on behalf of their school, and to create a sense among students that their schools care for them.

Teachers who served as advisors at King, Los Robles, and Western encountered both pragmatic and emotional demands as a result of their role expansion. The latter were particularly prominent at Los Robles and Western, schools that explicitly required teachers to provide social-emotional support to their advisees. Teachers did not respond to these demands in one uniform way, however. They reported satisfaction and dissatisfaction, commitment and intention to leave their positions, invigoration and burnout, involvement with students and detachment from them. The variation I found in teacher responses traced both to their schools and to individual teachers themselves. Schools that required teachers to provide social-emotional support to their advisees, which also had weak structural support of the advisor role including vaguely defined EDRs, tended to have teachers reporting more negative outcomes such as role overload and job dissatisfaction. Teachers' responses also seemed grounded in their own advisor-role-related ideas, knowledge, skills, experience, and support. Those with less of these assets—particularly novice teachers—struggled the most with the role and reported higher rates of role overload, burnout, and intention to leave their positions. By contrast, teachers who found ways to engage with and manage the advisor role's pragmatic and emotional demands responded more positively.

Ms. Renato and Ms. Li demonstrate the range of responses to persistently demanding advisor roles. "I don't humanly understand how we can do what we're being asked to do," Ms. Renato told me midway through the school year. As a second-year teacher, she carried an advisory class and also held a school leadership role, taught all of her classes to mixed-age and -ability groups, and developed curriculum and benchmark assessments in her subject area. Similarly, Ms. Li taught a full courseload (including 3 different courses, each of which required separate lesson plans, texts, and exams), carried an advisory class, and supervised King's after-school tutoring program. The advisor role added to each teacher's already heavy load.

Besides the pragmatic demands of a multitude of assigned tasks, Ms. Li and Ms. Renato also grappled with the emotional demands of advising students—many of whom struggled academically and socially, while also living in communities affected by poverty, violence, and inadequate public services. These demands took their toll. Both teachers described themselves using the word "callous." Ms. Li told me that she no longer felt renewed by collaborating with colleagues or attending professional development sessions, and said she had to be "selectively" callous—which she defined as not letting her students' shortcomings or problems bother her too much—in order to continue with her work. She responded to her advisee Randy's slow but steady process of dropping out of school by viewing him as a student where "you just have to let go." Ms. Renato described herself as callous as she explained her loss of affection for Omar, an advisee who struggled academically throughout the school year and had a left a trail of behavioral outbursts and broken agreements with teachers in his wake. She elaborated that even though "I still want the best for him and I believe he's a sweet and earnest young man who deserves to have the life that he wants…he also helps me recognize that I'm not going to be able to change the lives of every single student that I encounter." In order to continue with their work, both teachers had to emotionally distance themselves from it, but neither viewed that distance in a positive light. Citing workload and the physical and emotional fatigue that came along with their work, Ms. Li and Ms. Renato both expressed doubt about their ability to effectively support their students, as well as about their long-term futures in teaching.

Differences in how Ms. Renato and Ms. Li responded to the strain of advising, however, illustrate the range of teacher responses to the advisor role's demands. As Ms. Li described her emotional disengagement from parts of her job, she also described herself in critical terms such as "in a rut," and said of her difficulties advising, "I need to kick myself." She thought she could find herself more satisfied with her job if she could do it "better," in her words, but acknowledged that she engaged minimally with her advisees. Ms. Li identified a difference between "that big picture in my head" of how she wanted to advise and her day-to-day practice with her advisees and described her practice as insufficient.

In contrast, Ms. Renato did not blame herself or her abilities for her difficulties on the job. She instead saw her efforts as part of the work of teaching and advising well, adding, "Even when I'm failing, that's when I'm doing my job." In addition to accepting her shortcomings and returning persistently to the tasks of advising, often with great skill and ultimate success, Ms. Renato also questioned whether teachers should credit (or blame) themselves for their advisees' academic performance and well-being. At a faculty meeting where Western's teachers analyzed student performance and attendance data by advisory class, she heard people say,

"'Oh, I'm just the worst advisor,' or, 'Man, I thought I was a much worse advisor than that!' People would just immediately equate it (student outcomes) with their (own) ability to be an advisor." While she held herself to high standards, Ms. Renato did not so directly connect her efforts to her students' results. She also considered the impact of schoolwide systems, available supports, and student and family factors when evaluating her students' progress and her own performance as an advisor. While Ms. Li stood back from her advisees and then criticized her own performance, Ms. Renato dove decisively into advising, accepting failure as part of the job but not letting those failures slow her or her work as an advisor down.

This chapter considers much more than a teacher kindly going out of her way one time to talk with one student who needs a sympathetic ear or help connecting to a community agency. Rather, I explore the formalized expansion of teachers' professional role, which required teachers to engage in the support of students in multiple, cascading ways every day with any of the student advisees assigned to them. This expansion adds to the existing teacher role, which is well-known for including a diverse array of tasks and responsibilities in the first place, while teachers' work has also "increased, intensified, and expanded in response to federal, state, and local policies aimed at raising student achievement" (Valli & Buese, 2007, p. 520). When teachers respond to the demands of the advisor role, they respond to the bundle of all of these conditions.

I frame this chapter with a question, which makes it possible to sort through and make sense of teachers' different reactions to the advisor role. I ask: *How do teachers respond to the advisor role's pragmatic and emotional demands?* With this question, I delve into how teachers handled formally expanded roles by considering outcomes—role load perception, efficacy, job satisfaction, turnover, and burnout—that indicate how teachers are managing and coping with the advisor role's demands. I also focus on teachers' responses to the aspects of their jobs that involve emotional labor, in which they assume responsibility for caring for and supporting students. In so doing, I get at the advisor role's uniqueness among formally expanded teacher roles, as a role that requires teachers to step into students' personal lives and into matters of student wellness and strive to create a feeling in the students that their schools care for them.

This chapter continues with a brief introduction to the survey data that, along with this study's qualitative data, informs my discussion. I then discuss school-to-school variation in teacher responses to the advisor role, with special attention paid to the role played by schools' EDRs for advisors. Finally, I consider between-teacher variation. I use the four-quadrant model (related to teachers' advisor-role-related ideas, knowledge, skills, experience, and support) that I introduced in chapter 5 to parse out differences among teachers in how they responded to the advisor role. I also discuss my findings from the perspective of emotional labor research, and identify a positive relationship between teachers' engagement in the emotional labor of advising and their willingness to set boundaries upon this aspect of their work. I conclude this chapter by discussing my findings' implications for expanded teacher roles in general, teachers' work providing social-emotional support to students, and emotional labor research.

Gauging Teachers' Responses to the Advisor Role

Expanded roles, such as the advisor role, require teachers to assume additional responsibilities in areas for which they have not always received training. How does this work out for teachers? I interviewed and surveyed teachers regarding a range of responses to their responsibilities as advisors. My questions gauged teachers' sense of their role's feasibility and difficulty (role load perception, see Byrne, 1994), their sense of their own efficacy at and satisfaction with their jobs, and the extent to which they experienced burnout (as indicated by emotional exhaustion, a reduced sense of accomplishment, and depersonalization) (Maslach, Jackson, & Schwab, 1996). As another way to gauge teachers' sense of their jobs' manageability and their satisfaction with their work, I asked teachers whether they intended to remain at or leave their positions before the beginning of the next school year.[1] I gathered only qualitative information on teachers' responses to implied and explicit demands that they perform emotional labor, since this dimension of teachers' responses was not part of my original study design but rather emerged as a theme in teachers' comments. This assortment of teacher responses helped me to get a broad sense of teachers' pragmatic and emotional responses to the advisor role.

Between-School Variation in Teacher Responses

Comparing survey results across King, Los Robles, and Western (see table 6.1), I identified two patterns. First, about half of the teachers in all three schools reported high levels of efficacy in the advisor role. Second, schools that explicitly included social-emotional support as an advisor responsibility had higher concentrations of teachers experiencing role overload and teacher turnover. At these same schools, fewer teachers reported job satisfaction.

Table 6.1 Teacher responses to the advisor role, sorted by school

Teacher Response	Response Subcategory	King	Los Robles	Western	Statistically significant differences between schools
Role Overload		21%	75%	39%	Yes
Efficacy		50%	43%	58%	No
Job Satisfaction		60%	33%	46%	No
Intention to stay in position the following academic year	Intend to stay	86%	37.5%	54%	Yes
	Intend to leave	7%	25%	31%	Yes
	Unsure	7%	37.5%	15%	Yes
Burnout	Reduced Accomplishment	0%	0%	0%	No
	Emotional Exhaustion	27%	27%	23%	No
	Depersonalization	20%	31%	15%	No

Note: N=43 for school data.

Teacher Efficacy Hovered Near 50 Percent

Since the advisor role at King, Los Robles, and Western lacked substantial detail about what constituted success as an advisor, I was curious about how teachers at these schools determined their own efficacy as well as the extent to which they felt efficacious in their work. Tschannen-Moran, Woolfolk Hoy, and Hoy (1998) describe teacher efficacy as "the teacher's belief in his or her capability to organize and execute courses of action required to successfully accomplish a specific teaching task in a particular context" (p. 233). This definition relates teachers' judgments of their own efficacy to their performance of specific tasks and situations that they encounter on the job. The figurative glass of teacher efficacy was half-full *and* half-empty at these three schools. About half of the participants overall reported a sense of efficacy, and differences between mean school scores were present but not statistically significant. It is encouraging to know that half of the schools' teachers experienced efficacy in the advisor role, but of concern that the other half did not.

Most teachers described advisor-role-related efficacy as coming from their relationships with, and impact upon, advisees, such as seeing advisees improve their academic performance or attendance following their (teachers') efforts to support them. Across schools, negative efficacy experiences concerned a sense of not performing the advisor role well, difficulties conducting advisory class, and knowing about student needs yet feeling unable to respond effectively to them. For example, teachers experiencing low efficacy spoke of feeling unsure of how to "use" advisory class minutes, inundated by expectations they could not meet, wondered whether they were helping their advisees at all, and felt unable to connect with their advisees. Ms. Saenz, a quadrant A teacher at Los Robles, had substantial negative efficacy experiences as she advised 12th-grade students:

> I think graduation sucks, college entrance sucks, because I have no idea what I'm doing. FAFSA[2], what? And you feel shitty. Whenever we have advisory time I feel shitty about what I'm not doing and what I don't really want to do...I do enjoy the majority of it (advisory), but when there is something lacking in the school and it hasn't been thought out well...when these things are out of our control, on our shoulders, and we don't have time to do it, it's just very frustrating because again, you feel guilty and like you're going to have to break your back to do it.

Ms. Saenz's comments illustrate a strong sense that she could not positively impact her advisees, even though she liked advising them. Facing a combination of limited knowledge and skills, a high workload that seemed to hinder the completion of advisory-related tasks, and a lack of support for her work, Ms. Saenz responded with a negative assessment of her own performance.

Teachers' responsibilities to provide social-emotional support to advisees led to differing efficacy outcomes depending on whether teachers could count on support for their own work in this area. When schools made social-emotional support services available to students, teachers spoke of their efficacy in connecting students to providers who could help them. Without the option to connect students to needed services, though, advisors sometimes found themselves "holding the ball," stuck with information about a student situation that they themselves could not address effectively, if at all. Ms. Greggs had nowhere to turn for help for one advisee, but felt unable to help this advisee on her own before Western hired a mental health counselor:

> Some tag lines I heard a lot last year are: "Advisory is a cornerstone of our school. You really need to cultivate these relationships with your advisees. That's a big step in helping students to succeed." But when it came down to it, here's a kid who is really struggling and suffering and I feel like I've reached my limit. After checking in with different staff members or with our principal, nobody was able to offer me a direction to pursue.

Ms. Greggs saw her self as stuck and incapable. Her experience illustrates how schools can scaffold (or fail to scaffold) teachers' efficacy in expanded roles by connecting their responsibilities to necessary supports.

Different Response Patterns Existed at Schools That Required Teachers to Provide Social-Emotional Support

Teacher responses differed along the lines of schools' requirement that teachers provide social-emotional support as part of the advisor role. At King, which did not require social-emotional support as part of the advisor role, teachers reported slightly higher rates of job satisfaction, a greater proportion of teachers intending to remain at their jobs (positive responses to the advisor role), and lower rates of role overload compared to Los Robles and Western. Teacher comments suggest that the mere assignment (or nonassignment) of these responsibilities did not create such different teacher responses; rather, the combination of responsibilities and limited support did.

Teachers at all three schools perceived substantial role loads. Advisor role responsibilities—including parent outreach, monitoring advisees' grades and attendance, assisting with college applications, planning and overseeing the advisory class period, and intervening with academically struggling, misbehaving, truant, or distressed students—added to existing responsibilities carried by teachers in these small schools. Teachers also sat on school committees, wrote curriculum, supervised bus loading and yard areas, judged student project presentations after school, led extracurricular activities (which Western required of all teachers), and even drove students to sporting events at Los Robles. "Here it's not one of those things like, 'Oh, it's not my job,'" explained Ms. Mahali at King. Further, teachers at all three schools said that they did not have adequate time during the school day to plan and prepare materials for advisory class (along with their other courses they planned and taught, of which some teachers had three or more), and were on their own to contact advisees' other teachers or mental health professionals if they wished to collaborate with them.

Still, King's administrators limited their expectations of teachers who served as advisors. King explicitly expected teachers to *not* engage in substantial social-emotional support of students, and the school supported this expectation with a guidance counselor and a school health center (which employed a number of mental health providers) who did this work. Even though Los Robles and Western also employed school-based mental health professionals, these schools still assigned substantial social-emotional support tasks to teachers via the advisor role. These responsibilities further increased teachers' role load. As I discussed in chapter 3, none of the schools specified nor fully supported the advisor role (with the exception of two teacher teams at Western). When these conditions applied to social-emotional support tasks, for which few teachers are prepared, teachers found themselves all the more loaded down with highly demanding, unfamiliar responsibilities. Teacher comments such as, "Teaching here is not sustainable," "Taking on that role will create problems," and "Advisory is what makes me feel overcommitted" illustrate how a number of teachers at Los Robles and Western encountered expectations in excess of their perceptions of their own perceived capabilities and time.

Differences across schools in teacher responses to the advisor role reflect these different constructions of the role. Los Robles' rate of teacher-reported role overload (75%) exceeded King's (21%) by more than a factor of three, while it nearly doubled Western's role overload rates (39%). Similarly, Los Robles' rate of teacher-reported job satisfaction (33%) was half that of King's (60%), with Western closer to Los Robles (46%). Finally, King's rate of teachers intending to remain in their positions the following year (86%) distinctly exceeded rates at Los Robles (37.5%) and Western (54%). "They are not realistic," Ms. Coltrane, who left her position at Los Robles at the end of the school year, told me of the expectations she encountered as an advisor. "There are so many things that an advisor has to do when you just really don't have enough time in a day to do it." As undersupported expectations associated with the advisor role mushroomed, so did negative responses to it.

Between-Teacher Variation in Responses to the Advisor Role

While school-to-school differences in teacher responses highlight differences and reasons underpinning those differences, they do not reveal variation across teachers. Even at schools that failed to balance expectations of teachers serving as advisors against support for their work, some teachers appeared to thrive in the advisor role. Other groups of teachers—particularly novice teachers—languished across all three schools, with their survey numbers reflecting even more negative responses trends than school averages did.

To explore differences among teachers, I grouped them according to advisor-role-relevant ideas, knowledge, skills, experience, and support. As I did in chapter 5 (where I discussed differences in teachers' enactment of the advisor role), I compare results across four quadrants of teachers that represent different combinations of teachers' (1) advisor-role-related ideas (which I call *teacher schemas for the advisor role*), such as a vision for advising students, and (2) knowledge, skills, experience, and support (which I call *teacher advisor role resources*), such as experience working with children aside from classroom instruction (see figure 6.1). Quadrant A contains teachers with limited role schemas and role resources, quadrant B contains teachers with more developed role schemas and limited role resources, quadrant C contains teachers with less developed role schemas and more extensive role resources, and quadrant D contains teachers with more developed role schemas and greater role resources. Survey analysis results, grouped by teacher quadrant, follow in table 6.2.

	Limited Advisor Role Schema	Developed Advisor Role Schema
Limited Advisor Role Resources	**Quadrant A** 13 Teachers	**Quadrant B** 7 Teachers
Extensive Advisor Role Resources	**Quadrant C** 11 Teachers	**Quadrant D** 14 Teachers

Figure 6.1 Teacher quadrants used for analysis of between-teacher variation in teacher responses to advisor role.

Table 6.2 Teacher responses to the advisor role, sorted by teacher quadrant

Teacher Response	Response Subcategory	Quadrant A	Quadrant B	Quadrant C	Quadrant D
Role Overload		60%	100%	14%	27%
Efficacy		40%	80%	33%	70%
Job Satisfaction		30%	80%	57%	70%
Intention to stay in position the following school year	Intend to stay	40%	60%	100%	70%
	Intend to leave	20%	20%	0%	0%
	Unsure	40%	20%	0%	30%
Burnout	Reduced Accomplishment	0%	0%	0%	0%
	Emotional Exhaustion	20%	40%	0%	33%
	Depersonalization	40%	20%	0%	9%

Note: N=31.

Novice Teachers Struggled the Most with the Advisor Role

Teachers with lower levels of advisor-role-relevant resources (knowledge, skills, experience, and support) reported markedly higher levels of role overload and burnout, suggesting that novice teachers had a more difficult time with the advisor role. The majority of quadrant A and B teachers—predominantly in the first years of their teaching careers and under 30 years of age—reported role overload on their survey responses, and did so at a rate approximately four times that of their respective higher-resource colleagues. Even more strikingly, quadrant B teachers—those who often performed so well as advisors in spite of their limited professional and personal experiences—showed a 100 percent rate of reported role overload. They all spoke of multiple points of engagement with their students, colleagues, and advisees, and also spoke of being overextended. Ms. Bruce characterized her workload at Los Robles as "unbelievably difficult," while Mr. Chavez, at King, describing his role mentoring students (advisees and nonadvisees), said that "taking it (formal and informal advising) too far in this environment is to be spread too thin." Even though quadrant B teachers possessed more developed schemas for their work as advisors, they resembled their quadrant A colleagues in their struggle to manage daunting extended role workloads.

Novice teachers also reported elevated levels of burnout. While no teachers reported high levels of a reduced sense of personal accomplishment (one of the dimensions of burnout established by Maslach et al, 1996) on their survey responses, I encountered teachers who expressed a sense of guilt about their inability to help their advisees with their needs or to advise the way they envisioned their job. Other advisors said that they did not see what they could effect in their position, given the enormity and complexity of their students' needs and problems. I also found evidence of emotional exhaustion—which teachers expressed as feeling "drained," "run down," "tired," and often "exhausted"—among novice teachers (and also, interestingly, quadrant D teachers, who as a group had very few negative responses to the advisor role). They described feelings such as physical and psychological fatigue and frustration with their colleagues, administrators, and students. Teachers' exhaustion seemed to come in response to both the general strain of working in the small school environment and the demands of student-teacher relationships that came with the advisor role. The closeness of these relationships, while appealing to so many, also took its toll. Ms. Curran, a quadrant A advisor at Los Robles, cried as she told me of a pregnant, undocumented advisee who planned to attend a competitive state university that had admitted her. This student would not receive any federal financial aid, had little family support, and would deliver her baby during November of her first year of college. Ms. Curran described the difficulty of "living through their (advisees') traumas" along with them. Other teachers told me of speaking with advisees about experiences such as sexual abuse, abandonment by their parents, and community violence that they found distressing to take in and process, in addition to their often limited sense of how to best support students in such circumstances.

Depersonalization, burnout's third subdomain, seemed strongly connected to teachers' experience of the advisor role as pragmatically and emotionally overwhelming. Maslach and colleagues (1996, p. 4) define this phenomenon as "an unfeeling and impersonal response toward recipients of one's service, care, treatment or instruction." Forty percent of quadrant A teachers and 20 percent of quadrant B teachers reported depersonalization, compared to 0 percent of quadrant C teachers and 9 percent of quadrant D teachers. These teachers reported and showed detachment that manifest as a lack of demonstrated concern about students' progress or difficulties, and stepping back from or refusing responsibility for advisee support that their schools had assigned to them. Referring back to Ms. Curran, she said that she found herself leaving school before she finished her advisor-role-related work but not completing it when she got home:

> Something happens to my brain. I leave at 4. I need to leave at 4. I have a half hour home. Somewhere in between when I leave here and when I get home, I shut off. I don't remember to do anything. I just shut off. I might complain about something at school, but I don't remember to make phone calls, or do any work at home. I just shut down and I can't handle it any more.

As a result, a number of Ms. Curran's advisor-role-related tasks went incomplete, which she acknowledged but did nothing to change, such as reporting her time crunch to her principal, or delegating or declining expected tasks. Mr. Chavez, a quadrant B advisor who had a reputation at King for mentoring his advisees and students, also found himself increasingly detached:

> I've got students that cut (class) a lot. I might have a conversation with them like, "What is going on?" But I don't pursue it and really hammer it because I think I'm going to be wasting my breath. So I have a few students where last year I tried more with them and I see that nothing is really happening.

The association between lower levels of advisor role resources and depersonalization suggests teachers' distancing from relationships and situations where they lacked the capacity to help their advisees. Different rates of reported role overload and burnout across advisor quadrants tell us that the advisor role itself does not directly produce these outcomes among all teachers. However, advisory responsibilities seemed to create an elevated, difficult-to-manage extended role load for novice teachers. Contending productively with this role load proved too great of a challenge for a number of quadrant A and B teachers, particularly when their schools lacked sufficient structures to support the advisor role and teachers lacked the capacity to compensate for their schools' shortcomings.

Guiding Ideas about How to Advise Mattered

While novice (and sometimes nonnovice) teachers struggled with the advisor role, teachers of all levels of experience who had more developed ideas about how to advise (or advisor role schemas) reported higher levels of job satisfaction and efficacy than did their colleagues with less developed role schemas. Exploring this information further, I found that role schemas did not simply account for differing levels of job satisfaction and efficacy. Instead, schemas were associated with different ways of experiencing these phenomena in the first place.

Mean job satisfaction scores differed across teacher quadrants. Quadrant A teachers, those with both limited advisor role schemas and resources, show a strikingly lower level of job satisfaction (30%) than advisors in other quadrants. Teachers with more developed advisor role schemas (quadrants B and D) had higher levels of job satisfaction and generally found student and professional growth satisfying. In comparison, teachers with less developed advisor role schemas (quadrants A and C) focused on the quality of the student-teacher relationships themselves—whether students seemed to like and respect them, whether they as advisors could engage their advisees. I found this interesting as lower-schema teachers, particularly those in quadrant A, also often struggled to establish relationships with advisees. That which provided them job satisfaction also proved quite difficult to achieve, which may explain lower rates of job satisfaction among this group. Further, those who had less developed role schemas tended to experience advisees' difficulties (e.g., academic failure, behavior perceived as disrespectful, unplanned pregnancy) as sources of job *dis*satisfaction, while those with more developed schemas did not to such a strong degree. Stronger role schemas appeared to buffer teachers' job satisfaction from the effects of day-to-day experiences with students; the more developed the schemas, the less these experiences inflated (or deflated) teachers' sense of satisfaction.

Similarly, most teachers described their advisor-role-related efficacy as coming from their relationships with, and impact upon, advisees, but advisors with more developed role schemas judged their own efficacy based on a broader range of experiences. In their interviews, teachers with more developed role schemas said they experienced efficacy not only from direct interactions with advisees and from those advisees' responses to those interactions (as was the case among teachers with less developed schemas), but also from more complex experiences. These experiences included seeing advisees treat one another well, advisees meeting their own goals, succeeding at their (teachers') self-defined roles, seeing the effect of the broader school community upon an advisee, mentoring less experienced teachers, experiencing professional growth from advising experiences, and successfully connecting students to other needed supports. This finding suggests a relationship between advisor efficacy and a broader, more complex range of efficacy "inputs" as described above. A wider range of such inputs may explain why teachers with more developed advisor role schemas had approximately double the rate of efficacy as their colleagues with less developed schemas did.

"High" schema teachers' own ideas about how to advise also seemed to help them independently judge their own efficacy. When teachers had a vision for advising—such as stewarding students to college, serving as their *life skills Sherpa* or ensuring that they were the person at their school who knew each student well—they could use that vision as a lens to interpret their experiences as evidence of their efficacy (or lack thereof). Without that vision, teachers had to rely on their schools to confirm their efficacy, and, as I discuss in chapter 3, neither King, Los Robles, nor Western provided substantial guidance about or feedback on teachers' performance as advisors. Teachers whose own role schemas could make up for schools' lack of guidance could determine their own efficacy; those who lacked these schemas had less that could guide their judgments. Advisor role schemas seemed to provide guideposts to teachers that helped them understand how they were doing at their jobs and how well their jobs suited them.

Boundaries on the Emotional Labor of Advising Supported Positive Teacher Responses to the Advisor Role

Some teachers in the advisor role contended with role overload and burnout while their colleagues instead found job satisfaction and efficacy. I now turn to how teachers assigned to this role avoided the former and experienced the latter. To do so, they responded to their role's demands—particularly the demands to perform emotional labor by demonstrating care and creating a sense among their advisees of being cared *for*—with a combination of authentic engagement in the work and firm boundaries upon that work. In order to illustrate this finding, I begin by briefly grounding my findings in the existing knowledge about emotional labor: how organizations express expectations for employees' emotional labor, and how employees tend to respond to those expectations.

Expectations for Advisors' Work: Emotional Display Rules

Organizations that require emotional labor of their employees convey expectations of what emotions those employees will show, withhold, and produce in their customers, also known as *emotional display rules* (Ashforth & Humphrey, 1993; Brotheridge & Grandey, 2002; Diefendorff & Richard, 2003). At Los Robles and Western, and to a somewhat lesser extent at King (the school that explicitly did not require teachers to provide social-emotional support to students via the advisor role), teachers encountered emotional display rules (EDRs) that guided their work advising students.

Emotional labor literature characterizes EDRs as often vague and having multiple origins, and I found this to be the case at King, Los Robles, and Western. Teachers encounter EDRs from professional bodies, the public, and school administrators (Brennan, 2006; Winograd, 2003), such as the expectation that teachers should love their work. Yet, Diefendorff, Richard, and Croyle (2006) found that organizations often enact vague, nonexplicit EDRs, which employees then have a hard time grasping. So while teachers encounter EDRs from multiple sources, they do not necessarily get clear messages about what to do. I found just this in chapter 2: literature about teachers and teaching practice often conceptualizes social-emotional support as part of teachers' work but does not describe what teachers do (or ought to do) in detail. The same thing occurred at King, Los Robles, and Western.

At these three schools, I regularly encountered evidence of EDRs related to the advisor role. Teachers and administrators characterized their schools as caring places where adults knew students well. The advisor's role, particularly at Los Robles and Western, is what Ms. Sosa described as the "cheap way to get the school personalized," by designating one teacher to be the school's agent of caring for each student. Similarly, Western explicitly used advisory as its vehicle for promoting strong student-teacher relationships, one of its charter management organization's core goals for their students' learning experience. Teachers at these two schools described their role with advisees in terms including "support system," "counselor," "parent," "go-to person," and "advocate," implying an emotionally close, supportive relationship. "It's pretty much the advisor's job to make sure that every individual gets what they need," summarized Ms. Coltrane. King's teachers, by contrast, described their role as having a relationship with their advisees, but uniformly did not use such strong terms. The EDRs at Los Robles and Western required teachers in the role of advisor to express and demonstrate the following:

- A caring attitude toward advisees
- Concern about advisees' academic and personal well-being
- Commitment to their advisees
- A desire to help advisees with any problems that interfered with their academic progress or personal well-being.

I saw evidence of the first EDR at King as well, but did not see evidence of the other EDRs, which go beyond a general sense of teacher caring, there.

These EDRs, though, were rarely made explicit to teachers. When I asked teachers at Los Robles and Western how they learned about these EDRs, they told me of colleagues requesting that they support specific advisees (for example, with behavioral issues or missing assignments), of seeing colleagues model these EDRs through their own work with advisees, and of realizing that no one else would do the work that was needed in order to support their advisees. "You know when you take this job it's a pretty unspoken rule that you plan on staying through your advisory (class) graduating," Ms. Dolby explained of expectations at Los Robles that teachers demonstrate commitment to their advisees by not leaving before they graduate as a cohort. Teachers also heard school leaders express expectations that they support and care for advisees, but at Western these expectations were presented as brief "bullet points," per Ms. Greggs's description, rather than as detailed expectations of what advisors would do. Ms. Mitchell said that she understood she was to report suspected child abuse and neglect, but that beyond those legal requirements, she found that expectations of her responsibilities to support her advisees were a "vast gray area." Teachers serving as advisors had a sense of what feelings they were to convey and produce, but these expectations came across indirectly and implicitly.

Responding to Emotional Display Rules with Surface Acting and Deep Acting

One of the central tenets of emotional labor research is that that workers respond to EDRs by engaging in surface acting or deep acting. I saw limited evidence of these responses at Los Robles and Western. Hochschild (1983/2003) describes surface acting as a response in which employees display emotions that they do not actually feel (such as feigning interest, happiness, or impassivity, depending on the job's emotional demands). Deep acting, in contrast, she describes as employees trying "to feel what we sense we ought to feel or want to feel" (Hochschild, 1983/2003, p. 43) in order to more authentically convey emotions in line with their work requirements. In both situations, employees feign emotions in order to meet workplace demands for emotional labor.

As an example of surface acting in response to EDRs for the advisor role, Ms. Dolby demonstrated superficial, minimal compliance with EDRs for advisors in her work with Cleo, an advisee who had reported suicidal ideation to a counselor earlier in the year, had lost her father, and lived far away from the rest of her immediate family. She told me that she did not always ask Cleo how things were going for her "because I didn't really want to know, because I wasn't sure I couldn't handle it. Like she would tell me something and I wouldn't know how to deal with it." While she did not want to express caring for Cleo by learning more about her life or helping her with difficult situations, though, she did comply with her school's EDRs by making referrals to others who could help her. When Ms. Dolby learned of problematic student situations such as Cleo's, she informed the school's administrators or support professionals, but said she did this mostly to protect herself. "I think that's a cover-your-ass thing," she explained. "If something awful were to happen, at least I did something. I may not have done as much as I should have, but I told more people." She demonstrated concern, but in a limited way and out of self-interest. I saw fewer examples of deep acting, but what I saw involved teachers who felt unable to meet their schools' EDRs for the advisor role even though they understood and often believed in the EDRs. Ms. Saenz and Ms. Curran, two quadrant A teachers who showed multiple signs of burnout, spoke of having to put themselves in a frame of mind in which they could appear empathetic, caring, and responsive with their advisees. When pressed to fulfill EDRs that stretched them far beyond their capacity or their preferred range of teaching activities, teachers acted in ways that complied, sometimes minimally, and provided a limited amount of social-emotional support to students.

Authentic Responses to Emotional Display Rules and the Importance of Boundaries

Frequently, teachers did not "act" in order to comply with EDRs, but instead responded authentically to these expectations—displaying emotions with advisees, which often, but not always, matched EDRs' specifications. This finding is consistent with a recent development in emotional labor research in which workers responded to EDRs not with surface or deep acting, but rather with more spontaneous, authentic emotions (Diefendorff, Croyle, & Gosserand, 2005; Martinez-Iñigo, Totterdell, Alcover, & Holman, 2007; Mesmer-Magnus, DeChurch, & Wax, 2012; Naring, Briet, & Brouwers, 2006), exercising more autonomy over how they engaged in emotional labor. For teachers in this study, their efforts to draw boundaries on the advisor role's EDRs—upon the extent to which they demonstrated care for, concern about, or commitment to advisees, or showed a willingness to do whatever it took to support struggling advisees—at times contributed to their engagement with their advisees. I first discuss these boundaries and how they worked, and then share examples of boundaries on the advisor role that contributed to teachers' authentic emotional engagement with their advisees.

Teachers serving as advisors drew boundaries upon their work for three reasons: their own needs, their students' perceived needs, and skill limitations. Some teachers set boundaries related to their own needs to promote or defend their own physical and psychological well-being ("I'm not going to kill myself"), honor family responsibilities ("If I am devoting all this time to my work my family is getting dissed"), or avoid uncomfortable topics or situations (e.g., discussing students' illegal activity or reproductive health issues). Teachers also set boundaries upon their work due to perceived student needs. They expressed concerns about the potential to enable students too much while mentoring and supporting them ("Sometimes when you try to help them too much, you cripple them."). Teachers also voiced a desire to model healthy interpersonal boundaries, to acknowledge students' sources of support ("You have to have a lot more respect for the students' families and the students' own networks."), and to honor what they perceived as a developmentally appropriate adolescent preference for self-determination ("I don't really push kids to talk; they'll talk when they want to talk.").

Skill limitations also led teachers to draw boundaries on their emotional labor with advisees. "It's not that social-emotional support is not my job," Ms. Aron told me. "It's like asking me to pole vault. You could put out the mat and give me the pole and I could run, but I just don't know that I could make it over the bar." When it came to issues such as helping students with matters related to family conflict, community violence, unplanned pregnancy, and immigration, advisors often told me that they didn't do what they didn't know how to do. Mr. Perrales, a teacher sought out frequently by students at King for informal mentoring, did not attempt to help students who had become involved with local gangs. "I'm not going to tell them 'You're going to get out of this (gang) and I'm going make sure you do,' because I don't know how to get them out of it." No teachers expressed guilt about not having more sophisticated social-emotional intervention skills. Teachers, including those who *did* involve themselves in their students' social-emotional issues, felt that it was best for other, more specialized professionals to take the lead when acute student needs called for intervention.

From the teachers most confident about advising to those more rattled by it, all tended to draw boundaries for similar reasons. Yet sometimes the boundaries promoted connection with students in a way that seemed to reinvigorate teachers, while at other times they created more distance that led teachers to feel less effective in the advisor role. Mr. Orff, a novice teacher who left classroom teaching at the end of the school year, set boundaries on the advisor role that seemed to cut him off from his students. "When expectations (about student-teacher relationships) have been communicated to me, what's been communicated is really too much for me to do," he explained, going on to describe how he "quickly detached" himself from intense engagement from his advisees and other students. He said he worried that he should be "more knowledgeable about the different aspects of their lives, and on the other hand, I'd like to have some distance." In my visits to his advisory class, I saw this distance as he interacted minimally with his advisees, joking or playing card games with them or speaking to them in order to reinforce classroom rules or check on homework completion. He set boundaries on his work where it felt unmanageable, but those boundaries created distance between him and his advisees and did not seem to improve his experience of teaching, as suggested by his decision to leave the profession.

Other teachers drew boundaries that seemed to preserve and even promote their engagement with advisees, as the EDRs for the advisor role required. "I had to figure out how to feel intimate with students without being drawn into their personal dilemmas," Ms. Aron explained. This group of teachers intentionally engaged with advisees in close, long-term relationships, and often took on issues related to social-emotional stresses present in their advisees' lives, but did not allow these efforts to dominate their work or their appraisal of their own work. Ms. Moreno, for example, said she loved her job and felt fulfilled in it. She was no stranger to her job's EDRs ("There's no written (document), but it's there," she said of the expectations she encountered), and she engaged in the emotional labor of her work heartily. She regularly visited the residential shelters where two of her advisees lived, had confronted advisees who used abusive language toward their teachers, and described a desperate phone call she received from a student whose boyfriend told her he planned to commit suicide. While deeply engaged in the emotional labor of her work, though, Ms. Moreno also set limits upon what she did as an advisor. She regularly attended funerals in her students' families, but always declined their invitations to birthday parties and mother's day celebrations (unlike some of her colleagues, who she said felt compelled to accept such invitations). Although she worked closely with many of her advisees' parents, she had ceased communication with a parent when their conversations became too acrimonious ("Too bad for her child, but I couldn't play that game. It was affecting the kid."). Ms. Moreno limited how much she helped her advisees in order to avoid creating dependence, and acknowledged when her their difficulties were beyond her powers to solve ("There's only so much I can change."). But she did so while continuing her efforts to reach and support her students, stepping into their lives often at complicated and distressing times.

Teachers who involved themselves in students' social-emotional issues found themselves drawing boundaries on this work as well. Ms. Pozo spoke of boundaries she drew around how she would respond the pressing demands that advisees often presented. She often did not respond immediately, dropping her other tasks and responsibilities, to a situation that seemed urgent to a student. "You're pregnant," she said, painting a hypothetical picture: "That's not an emergency. You'll still be pregnant for 9 months! No need to drop everything I'm doing to figure that out." Similarly, Ms. Pozo set boundaries but stayed engaged when she offered to continue talking with Georgia, an advisee with a history of suicidality, but encouraged her to communicate with her (Georgia's) psychiatrist. "When Georgia started talking about what was bothering her, I would say, you know, if you really need to talk right now, I'm here, but I really think it's better for you to talk to your psychiatrist." Ms. Pozo described her rationale:

> I'm helping her get to a person who can really help her, that's actually a bigger source of caring. I wasn't ignoring it, I wasn't listening and not knowing what to do with it. *That's* not being caring or thoughtful.

By finding Georgia someone who could help her, yet staying connected, Ms. Pozo created boundaries that made the advisor role productive for herself and remained responsive to her advisees.

Teachers also set boundaries about what their work with students, and the results of that work, meant about their own job performance or abilities. Ms. Powers told me of how she bounded the meaning of her advisees' day-to-day successes and struggles. When her students did well, she told me,

> I don't think that's like, "Whoo, yeah, I'm so successful!" And when it doesn't happen, I have to start rethinking what I'm doing and try something else. It's a process more than, oh, look at my advisees, they are doing so well!

Ms. Powers used student progress (or problems) to guide her subsequent work with them, but she never interpreted her students' performance or well-being as a reflection of her efforts, efficacy, qualifications, or skills. "I don't wrap my success in that," she explained. "My heart is still heavy and I still worry about the student, but it is not going to make me say 'I suck, it's my fault.'"

While remaining involved and concerned, Ms. Powers did not succumb to some of the negative thoughts about herself as an advisor that I saw among other teachers. This stance seemed to buffer her from the impact of the inevitable strains and abrasions involved in advising. Supported and perhaps protected from negative reactions to the advisor role by the boundaries she drew, Ms. Powers engaged willingly and persistently with her advisees.

Interestingly, of the 11 teachers who drew boundaries on their work while also responding authentically to the advisor role's EDRs, 9 had well-developed schemas for the work of advising. Eight of the eleven had higher levels of personal resources that informed their work as advisors. These findings suggest that advisors who bring higher levels of personal schemas and resources to the work are the most likely to set deliberate boundaries that keep them engaged with and responsive to students. Teachers' boundaries on the emotional labor of advising did not always immunize them against negative outcomes—two of these eleven advisors showed moderate levels of burnout, and two left teaching for other careers. Still, most teachers who set boundaries upon the emotional labor they performed managed to sustainably meet their schools' expectations to engage in supportive, caring, committed relationships with their advisees.

Conclusion and Implications

This chapter's framing question—*How do teachers respond to the advisor role's pragmatic and emotional demands?*—led toward many answers rather than just one. Teacher outcomes such as role load perception, efficacy, job satisfaction, turnover, and burnout varied, with more negative responses to the advisor role concentrating among teachers with less knowledge, skills, experience, support, and ideas that could inform their enactment of the role. Los Robles, the school that combined high, complex expectations of teachers with limited specification of and support for the advisor role, also had more pronounced levels of negative teacher outcomes. Looking more closely at the social-emotional support and emotional labor demands that came along with the advisor role, I again found varying responses, ranging from innovation to marked disengagement from advisees, an ironic and unfortunate outcome given advisory programs' goals of promoting stronger connections between students and their schools and teachers. Among this range of responses, some teachers engaged productively in formally expanded roles, even roles that involved a substantial degree of social-emotional support. It is important to remember that these teachers' impressive work related to their own specific assets as well as to their deliberate efforts to limit the advisor role's demands—all characteristics that the school might have inspired, but did not build into the advisor role (except at King) or help teachers to develop. These findings carry implications for expanded teacher roles, for teachers' involvement in the social-emotional support of students, and for continued research on emotional labor.

Implications for Expanded Teacher Roles

Teachers such as Ms. Moreno and Ms. Renato demonstrate that some teachers will work skillfully and innovatively with expanded roles, even in the absence of professional or organizational support. On one hand, this finding offers a sense of promise: teachers *can* fulfill formally expanded roles. A warning must accompany this promise, however: not all teachers will have this optimism-inspiring experience, particularly when their schools expand their positions but abandon them with a combination of high pressure, vaguely expressed expectations, and minimal support. Substantial rates of undesirable teacher responses to the role, such as role overload, burnout, and turnover, suggest that expanded roles have the potential to negatively impact teachers.

Consistently higher levels of negative outcomes among the least experienced teachers (from quadrants A and B) raise serious concerns, given that novice teachers have been, and remain, a substantial part of America's teacher workforce. Teachers with less than five years of experience represent one-quarter of America's teachers (Ingersoll & Merrill, 2012), and 47 percent of the teachers at King, Los Robles, and Western. Among that group of teachers, those who came up short on advisor-role-relevant knowledge, skills, experience, support, and ideas (quadrant A teachers) showed troubling trends: a 60 percent experiencing role overload, 40 percent intending to continue in their positions the following school year, 40 percent seeing themselves as effective in their jobs, and a 30 percent reporting job satisfaction. Teachers who ran equally short on experience, but who brought ideas about advising (role schemas), found their jobs more satisfying, experienced more efficacy on the job, and were more likely to remain in their positions. They also, however, experienced a 100 percent rate of role overload and a 40 percent rate of emotional exhaustion. Handling teachers—particularly those in schools that strive to individually engage historically underserved youth—in such a way bodes poorly for teachers, the schools that employ them, and their students. Schools such as King, Los Robles, and Western attempt to do better with their students than conventional high schools do, yet if they wear out or lose their teachers in the process, their chances of meeting this goal diminish. My findings strongly suggest that expanded teacher roles, particularly those that intensify and require social-emotional support responsibilities, run a serious risk of adversely impacting the work of novice teachers expected to implement those roles.

This study's findings suggest that, at a minimum, teachers that are assigned an expanded role would benefit from guidance about how they go about fulfilling that role and about how it fits into the school's—and students'—big picture. Quadrant B teachers, who averaged less than four years of teaching, formulated their own guidelines and expectations, or schemas, about how the role was to work for them when schools did not provide these things. And aside from higher role overload levels than their novice colleagues who did not have such a strong sense of how to go about advising (quadrant A teachers), this subgroup of novice teachers generally had more positive responses to the advisor role. Quadrant A teachers—who lacked role schemas *and* had limited knowledge, skills, experience, and support related to their expanded role—had the most negative responses to their roles of all of the teacher groups analyzed in this chapter. School administrators who do not support novice teachers in expanded roles by helping them to develop needed role resources and schemas via professional learning experiences and support built into the organization should anticipate novice teachers' negative reactions to expanded roles, including turnover, a particularly costly consequence (Barnes, Crowe, & Schaefer, 2007), role overload, and burnout, which will ultimately limit the impact of expanded teacher roles upon students, their intended beneficiaries.

Implications for Teacher Involvement in the Social-Emotional Support of Students

The advisor role provides a rich opportunity to explore what happens when a diverse group of teachers provides social-emotional support to their students. This exploration builds upon the work of others concerned with teachers' mental health competencies (Burke & Paternite, 2007; Weston et al., 2008) by adding qualitative and quantitative teacher data to the conversation. And, like the above discussion of teachers' responses to role expansion, the data tell a mixed story: some, but not all, teachers *can* competently do the work of providing social-emotional support to their students. Teachers such as Ms. Pozo and Ms. Powers dealt in sophisticated ways with students' social-emotional difficulties, their own emotional reactions to their students' situations, and the need to connect with students while still maintaining boundaries. Teachers at King, Los Robles, and Western at times faced frightening, overwhelming situations that impacted their students: students who harmed themselves or planned to do so, who dealt with long-term mental health difficulties, who lived in highly conflictual families, who willingly affiliated with street gangs, who struggled to understand their own gender identity and contend with a world that did not always accept it, and who grieved the loss of parents and siblings. That some teachers knew how to handle crises, build relationships with students who did not always trust them, and collaborate effectively with colleagues and social service professionals is impressive. This group of teachers demonstrated that teachers can competently address students' social-emotional issues without feeling pressed to mimic psychologists or social workers, or forced to take on work that they cannot handle pragmatically or emotionally.

Teachers can and do make their own unique, critical contributions to students' lives. They can play a role in the identification of student social-emotional support needs, and in schools' day-to-day responses to those needs, that mental health professionals simply cannot play from their more formalized, treatment-oriented vantage point. But all teachers do not stand ready to step confidently and competently into such a role, as teachers' range of responses to the advisor role show. That some teachers stepped away from the advisor role, drawing boundaries that shut their advisees out, makes sense given the limited skills so many said they had, and the limited support they received. Many of the participating teachers lacked intervention skills (suited to addressing students' crises or ongoing difficulties) related to their students' needs, not to mention the professional skills that other mental health professionals learn related to how to establish relationships, how to compassionately and professionally set boundaries, and how to cope with the emotional strains that social-emotional support work creates for the professionals themselves. Such shortcomings come as no surprise, given that the vast majority of teachers did not have any preservice or inservice learning experiences related to these topics. With teachers pressed to engage in ongoing, caring relationships with their advisees, address their issues, connect them with needed services, and carry on their other teaching responsibilities, these skills—oriented to teachers, not mental health professionals—seem essential.

Teachers' learning needs are related to student-teacher relationships and the social-emotional support of students and call upon both teacher educators and school-based mental health professionals to assess how they could more thoroughly and effectively support teachers' unique social-emotional support role. These needs also call upon schools and teacher educators to reflect more thoroughly on the EDRs of teaching. Do we want all teachers to develop engaged, caring relationships with their students? Do we want the same of teachers serving as advisors? If the answers to either of these questions are yes, schools and teacher educators will need to convey clearer expectations of teachers and will also need to back up those experiences with tangible support and preparation. I make specific recommendations to these ends in chapter 7.

Implications for Emotional Labor Research

My analysis of teachers' responses to the EDRs of advising also extends the knowledge available about teachers' emotional labor, particularly the ways in which teachers experience and exercise autonomy when faced with explicit requirements to perform emotional labor on the job. While Oplatka (2007) describes the emotional aspects of teachers' work as "discretionary, nonobligatory role elements" (p. 1394), the advisor role differs because of its requirement that teachers engage in emotional relationships with students and produce emotional states in them. Still, teachers at King, Los Robles, and Western exercised autonomy in how they responded to these requirements. Whether they avoided the emotional labor of advising, engaged in it superficially, or took it on affirmatively, they all exercised significant agency related to the EDRs that they encountered on the job. This finding contradicts Hochschild's (1983/2003) portrayal of flight attendants' expression of emotion as controlled by their employers via training, required procedures, and rules ("The worker is restricted to implementing standard procedures," p. 120), and lends support to assertions that workers in positions that require emotional labor also exercise autonomy and discretion over their emotional expression on the job, even when they cannot necessarily control their circumstances or assigned tasks (Bolton & Boyd, 2003; Hargreaves, 2000 & 2001). These previous assertions hint at, but do not fully explore, the possibility of workers setting boundaries on emotional labor demands while also striving to meet them. Evidence that teachers in this study did just that—such as Ms. Moreno engaging deeply, willingly, and consistently with her advisees while still knowing and communicating her own limits about how far she would go to support and care for her students—suggests that workers may end up complying with EDRs as long as they can determine how they will do so.

However, employers and scholars must remember that the *kind* of discretion, or autonomy, that workers have over their engagement in emotional labor matters. On one hand, teachers had limited amounts of what Brotheridge and Grandey (2002, p. 32) call *emotional autonomy*. Teachers knew that they, as advisors, were supposed to ensure that students felt cared for by their school, and had to convey emotions accordingly. While some teachers chose to avoid emotional labor associated with advising, the expectation stood and seemed to contribute to some teachers' sense of role overload and reduced efficacy (because they perceived that they could not advise the way they thought they were supposed to). But even as schools limited advisors' emotional autonomy, they provided much more *practice autonomy*. Unlike the extensive training and supervision that emotional labor scholars describe workers getting from some employers such as Mary Kay Cosmetics (Rafaeli & Sutton, 1987) and Disney World (Reyers & Matusitz, 2012), teachers found themselves largely on their own to determine the nature, extent, and content of their work with advisees. *That* teachers cared for advisees was not optional; *how* they cared was up to them. Some teachers welcomed practice autonomy, as Hochschild might anticipate they would, others found it overwhelming and expressed a preference for explicit guidance, and still others exercised their practice autonomy by essentially cutting out as much emotional labor from their jobs as possible. When school administrators or scholars reflect on how teachers might benefit from autonomy with regard to how they respond to EDRs, it is important that they remember that practice autonomy is not equally welcome among all teachers.

My findings also add to emotional labor literature the understanding of additional individual characteristics that underpin different ways of performing emotional labor. Existing emotional labor research considers how teachers' personality characteristics, such as conscientiousness or extraversion (Brotheridge & Grandey, 2002; Brotheridge & Lee, 2002; Diefendorff et al., 2005; Kim, 2008; Judge, Woolf, & Hurst, 2009), influence different forms of emotional expression at work. Evidence from King, Los Robles, and Western suggests that teachers' knowledge, skills, experience, support, and ideas can also influence teachers' choices of how to respond to EDRs. Ms. Dolby's distance from Cleo traces to her feeling unprepared for and unable to manage the advisor role, just as Ms. Pozo's steady, purposeful yet bounded engagement with Georgia connects to her clear vision for her work as an advisor and collegial support for her role. It will remain important for emotional labor scholars to consider a range of worker characteristics—including their skills and support related to emotional labor demands—when drawing conclusions about why workers respond to EDRs in particular ways.

The variety of teachers' responses to emotional labor demands and forms of autonomy stands as a reminder that the advisor role is neither a bad one nor a good one for teachers. Instead, this chapter reveals the advisor role as one that contributes to a range of teacher responses and outcomes depending on school and teacher characteristics (and how those characteristics combine with one another). I turn in this book's final chapter to synthesizing my findings across all six chapters so that those interested in expanded teacher roles, and the advisor role in particular, can bring these findings into K-12 schools.

Chapter Seven

Tying It All Together: Lessons about Formally Expanded Teacher Roles, Teachers Advising Students, and Teachers Providing Social-Emotional Support

King, Los Robles, and Western are, like all schools, constantly evolving. In this book, I offer a snapshot of each school and its teachers at a particular point in time, understanding that each school's advisory program has likely changed since my final interviews. The "snapshots" in this book's preceding chapters show what can happen when schools formally assign teachers expanded roles and how support from the teaching profession and from K-12 schools frames these roles' feasibility.

From the early chapters' focus on the advisor role's professional and organizational contexts to the middle chapters' examination of individual teachers' experiences with this role, this book pulls together different factors that are critical to consider when designing, evaluating, or otherwise studying expanded teacher roles. I saw from these vantage points that, with a few exceptions, neither the profession of teaching nor the schools substantially helped teachers at King, Los Robles, and Western fulfill their obligations as advisors. Under these circumstances, teachers had varied experiences within this role, ranging from satisfaction and effectiveness to burnout and avoidance of the work of advising. Some of these experiences, such as teachers pulling away from students in crisis, are cause for caution when assigning expanded roles to teachers. Other teacher experiences, such as innovation in spite of limited school support, offer suggestions for how to scaffold and develop expanded teacher roles so that they might more fully benefit students and their schools. In the rest of this chapter, I summarize and discuss those suggestions in detail.

When anyone takes steps to expand the teacher's role, I recommend that they take a broad, anticipatory view first, given, how stable the teacher's traditional role has been over time. How does an expansion of the teacher role depart from business as usual for teachers? Are the differences minor or major, limited or comprehensive? What, if any, school, professional, teacher education, or community resources might support this expansion? What might emerge as obstacles to teachers effectively taking up the expanded role? My research also strongly suggests considering how the school (or school district) sets up and supports the expanded role and the qualities of teachers who will occupy it. What do teachers bring, or need to bring, in terms of relevant preparation or experience?

Key to expanded roles' prospects for success is the fit between the school's structuring of the role—how it assembles necessary resources, formalized procedures, and informal norms and expectations that pertain to the expanded role—and individual teachers' toolboxes that inform their work within the role. This perspective does not credit (or blame) teachers or schools for what happens with expanded teacher roles, but rather focuses on the fit between the two. The achievement of such a fit would require fine-tuning, as the school adds or changes supports such as guidance, time, or materials that teachers need to perform the role, and adapts the role (or lets teachers adapt the role) to fit how teachers can best fulfill it given their background and school context. Ideally, the role and the teachers who occupy it will fit one another without overburdening teachers to the extent that they burn out, refuse to do the work associated with the expanded role, or cannot perform the role adequately in spite of their best efforts.

In the rest of this chapter, I develop these ideas with an eye toward how they can become part of the larger school and classroom teaching practices in three related, but distinct, areas: expanded teacher roles, teachers' work advising students, and teachers' provision of social-emotional support to students. I also explore conditions of teaching that may facilitate or stand in the way of such ideas coming to fruition.

Lessons about Expanded Teacher Roles

A central lesson from this study of the advisor role is the imperative nature of the fit between how schools structured the expanded teacher role and teacher responses to it. If readers began this book at its fourth chapter, looking just at teachers' enactments of the advisor role, they would miss out on how schools' support of the expanded teacher role has much to do with what teachers are able to then do with that role. They might see innovative, distressed, or checked-out teachers doing vastly different things with the advisor role and think that individual teachers' skill, background knowledge, vision, or effort determines teacher-to-teacher differences. The experiences of teachers at King, Los Robles, and Western, however, caution us against jumping to such premature conclusions.

Schools need to provide adequate, balanced structure for expanded teacher roles. In chapter 3, I explore how schools set up the advisor role, and argue that schools' internal and external alignment of the expanded role is critical to how that role will work. When an expanded teacher role's resources (such as dedicated time during the school day), formalized procedures (such as written performance evaluation criteria), and cultural dimensions (such as informal norms) are sufficient and balanced with one another, the role has enough scaffolding that teachers know what they are supposed to do (and not do), have places to turn with uncertainty, and have sufficient time and information with which to carry out the role. I describe this state as the expanded teacher role's internal alignment, in which the role's different elements align with one another.

External alignment of expanded teacher roles, in which those roles work in tandem with other school structures for teaching and learning (such as the school schedule or academic departments), also support teachers' work in expanded roles by reinforcing, rather than competing for, time, resources, energy, and priority. When Western's house team structure assembled teachers of the same one hundred students together for departmental meetings, for example, it also gave them an opportunity to discuss and troubleshoot their work advising students. These findings strongly suggest that those who design, oversee, and evaluate expanded teacher roles should ensure that expanded teacher roles have a well-developed, balanced structure that aligns with, rather than competes against, other school structures.

The importance of clear expectations. One critical element in expanding teacher roles is the presence of clear expectations. Looking at this book's second chapter, one can see that teachers have long encountered *some* expectations for providing social-emotional support to their students. The nature of those expectations, however, has been far from specific or clear. As a result, teachers carried out that particular expansion of the traditional teacher role in divergent ways. Teacher participants at King, Los Robles, and Western similarly traveled different directions with the advisor role, but this did not occur as a result of teachers' radically different agendas for the work of advising. With very few exceptions, teachers came in with *no* agenda for advising. Rather, they found themselves forced to improvise in the wake of minimal guidance about how to carry out the role. Some teachers, such as Ms. Powers, the self-appointed "life skills Sherpa," had no problem doing just that. Others, though, found themselves marooned, with limited skills, knowledge, support, or ideas in their figurative advisor role toolboxes that could have helped them figure out how to advise. The absence of a fully fleshed out script for the expanded role turned out well for some—particularly those who had fuller repertoires of experiences, knowledge, skills, and support—to move boldly into these expanded roles. But it turned out poorly for just as many others insofar as job satisfaction, turnover, role overload, and burnout rates indicate in chapter 6. Novice teachers, in particular, seemed willing to give up some flexibility with their expanded roles in order to have guidance about what to do and how to do it.

These findings make it clear that not all teachers are ready to take the reins of an open-ended expanded role and independently guide it. Role theorists' assertion that the role serves as a resource for action (e.g., Baker & Faulkner, 1991) held true for some, but not all, teachers in this study. Teachers such as Ms. Li, Mr. Westerberg, and Mr. Carver, given maximum flexibility but limited support, did not use the advisor role as a license for work that they wanted to do with their students. Some did what they could and struggled, while others did as little as they had to do. Their experiences tell us that neither role theorists nor educators should view a nonprescriptive expanded role as a universal recipe for success or a trigger for innovation. If architects of expanded teacher roles have a particular goal in mind for the role, my findings strongly suggest that they are better off pointing teachers explicitly toward that goal.

Clear expectations about expanded role performance can also inform the consistency with which teachers carry out that role. In chapter 4, I describe how teachers interpreted the advisor role in diverse ways. While airtight uniformity in expanded role is most likely neither possible nor desirable, highly divergent interpretations of being an advisor are probably not ideal either. Differing interpretations among teachers reveal the lack of clear expectations for performance of the advisor role at King, Los Robles, and Western, and highlight important questions that expanded role architects (such as policymakers and administrators) must ask. How much flexibility do promoters of the role want to allow? Does the possibility of innovation justify the risk (or the actual experience) of inconsistency in implementation? Answering these questions should clarify how much specificity about role performance is needed. My findings suggest that when expanded roles take teachers, particularly novice teachers, into uncharted territory, more clarity in expectations is essential.

Teachers can make or break expanded roles, but do best with school support. When Ms. Li said, "If I could do it (advisory) right, there would be a positive impact," her words implied that her difficulties as an advisor came only from her. Such a perspective denies the critical contributions that schools make to setting up and supporting expanded teacher roles, and leaves teachers vulnerable to blame even when they do their best to succeed with poorly structured roles. Certain teacher characteristics, though, do make a difference with expanded role implementation, particularly when schools fail to adequately set these roles up for success.

In chapter 5, I identify what goes into the advisor role toolbox, which role resources (such as experience working with youth outside of teaching positions) and role schemas (such as a vision for advising students) informed teachers' work as advisors. This approach to understanding what informs teachers' work adds to the set of characteristics used in sociologically oriented research on teachers, such as teachers' gender, race or ethnicity, or teachers' preparation, certification, and performance, as is emphasized in teacher effects research (summarized by Konstantopoulos, 2012). In considering which individual characteristics inform teachers' work within expanded roles, it is important to remember that each unique role has its own nature, and so would not necessarily draw upon the same resources and schemas that the advisor role did at King, Los Robles, and Western. The idea here is to identify which role resources and role schemas would ideally inform teachers' work in a particular expanded role. Beyond contemporary arguments about the merits of traditional or alternative forms of teacher certification, what specific learning experiences prepare teachers for the jobs that await them? With such information in hand, principals would stand in a better position to hire teachers ready to assume expanded roles. Teacher educators would similarly have a better sense of how to prepare generalist teacher candidates for expanded roles such as special education inclusion or ELL instruction in mainstream classrooms.

My findings strongly suggest that individual teacher characteristics—those that make for an especially well-stocked toolbox for use on the job—also compensate for schools' inadequate structuring of expanded teacher roles. Teachers at King, Los Robles, and Western who had well-developed advisor role resources and role schemas, particularly those who had both, often transcended flimsy expectations, insufficient support, and underwhelming curricula and created dynamic, impactful advisory class experiences for their advisees. However, I did find that teachers who had well-developed schemas for the advisor role but lacked substantial knowledge, skills, and support that might inform their work (whom I describe in chapters 5 and 6 as quadrant B teachers) had just enough rope with which to hang themselves. Their rich ideas and aspirations for their expanded role helped them to connect with their advisees and fueled their persistent efforts to help their advisees make it through often-difficult straits. However, this group of teachers also found themselves often fatigued as evidenced by their 100 percent rate of reported role overload. Their ideas alone could not make the expanded role work for them over time. Even teachers with more role resources and schemas struggled with the strain of a poorly structured advisor role.

These findings carry two implications. First, the right individual teacher characteristics can "float" teachers in expanded roles in schools that have yet to figure out how to structure those roles. A school with a poorly structured advisor role but full of ridiculously overqualified advisors (such as a faculty loaded with Ms. Renatos, Ms. Powerses, and Ms. Morenos), would look like it had a strong advisory program due to those teachers' individual qualifications and efforts. However, my findings also imply that a school's overreliance on teachers' individual toolboxes can potentially wear teachers out and therefore undermine the expanded role's long-term benefits for schools and students.

I suggest that schools, districts, or other educators interested in developing effective, sustainable expanded teacher roles (or fixing ineffective, unsustainable ones) engage in the tandem task of developing a balanced structure for those roles while also identifying ideal teacher qualities that will contribute to strong implementation. Schools lucky enough to have toolbox-rich teachers while they develop expanded roles would do well to capture these teachers' experiences figuring out the role and finding ways to use their experiences and ideas to forge more permanent structures for newcomers or less experienced faculty members. Beyond the key steps of developing structures to frame the expanded role and giving teachers the support they needed to carry out the role, educators' next step would be to connect expectations to teacher learning opportunities and school-based support that would enable strong performance of the role.

Teachers' lack of prior experiences with expanded roles. While schools' and teachers' contributions to expanded teacher roles' viability are essential, it would be a mistake to ignore the world outside of schools, particularly preservice experiences and professional development. Very few teachers at King, Los Robles, and Western had learning experiences in their preservice programs or ongoing professional development that prepared them for the work of advising students. Rather than reacting to this finding by saying, "This proves that teachers need to learn more about supporting and mentoring students" (which they may or may not need to do, depending on the results expected), we must examine why teachers do *not* have those learning experiences in the first place and what that means for the prospects for the advisor role's success.

Historic and contemporary factors that create and reinforce narrow teacher roles. Chapters 1 and 2 of this book together tell a story: the teacher's role has narrowed over time. Teachers have encountered vague but persistent appeals to step beyond this role and engage in their students' personal and social-emotional lives (one form of role expansion), and atop this all, many teachers now encounter formal requirements to provide social-emotional support to their students. This example of the expansion of teachers' roles shows how it happened without full support from teachers' workplaces or learning experiences. Schools, and particularly secondary schools, remain set up for teachers to concentrate on traditional content-based instruction. Stable, long-term patterns of school organization differentiate teachers by grade level and specialization (Tyack & Cuban, 1995), reinforcing teachers' grade level- and discipline-specific organizational identity and their exchange of information with others who have similar instructional responsibilities rather than with those who have a range responsibilities for shared students. Schools also differentiate mainstream instruction from "special" instruction and support, which is often provided to students perceived not to fit into the generalist teacher's classroom (Deschenes, Cuban, & Tyack, 2001), reinforcing the notion that that generalist teachers' responsibilities center on the instruction of adequately progressing students (Haberman, 2005).

Teacher education programs likewise tend to emphasize a narrow teacher role, in spite of many educators' and programs' independent efforts to promote teachers' broad understanding of their students and their learning needs. Ongoing debates over whether teacher education ought to focus on teachers' content expertise (e.g., in mathematics or foreign language) or build their pedagogical expertise (Herbst, 1989; Sedlak, 2008) have nonetheless maintained a focus on how teachers learn to connect students with curriculum. Some teacher educators committed to further articulating a curriculum of teaching practice (e.g., Ball and Forzani, 2009; Grossman et al., 2007) call for teacher learning that prepares teachers for the broader range of demands they will encounter in the classroom. Meanwhile, however, scholars of education have found generalist teachers typically ill-prepared for work beyond curriculum-based instruction such as teacher leadership (York-Barr et al., 2008), student mental health issues (Koller & Bertel, 2006; Roeser & Midgley, 1997), general child development (NCATE, 2010a), and effective student-teacher relationships (Grossman et al., 2007; Hamre et al., 2012). Similarly, scholars find that many teachers lack sufficient preparation to work with students with more particular learning needs such as ELL (Villegas & Lucas, 2011) and special education students (Cook, 2004; Swain, Nordness, & Leader-Janssen, 2012).

At the same time, teachers continue to encounter calls for additional work beyond the subject matter and skills their schools traditionally require them to teach. Many encounter this call every day, as the steady policy drumbeat of standards-based accountability has raised the stakes for standardized student testing and has ratcheted up demands on teachers to spend instructional time covering tested subjects and conducting test preparation activities (Darling-Hammond, 2010). Beyond these demands, the trend of expanding teacher work responsibilities is particularly evident in contemporary demands upon teachers to provide social-emotional support. This under-the-table expansion of teachers' responsibilities became pronounced during the 2012 Chicago teachers' strike. The Chicago Teachers Union (CTU) leadership called consistently for increased counseling and social work services, citing an absence of sufficient services (illustrated by the district's employing one social worker for approximately every 1,000 students) and the pervasive poverty and violence that impacts Chicago's student population (Chicago Teachers Union, 2012; Ellis, 2012). CTU president Karen Lewis described the connection between inadequate support services and demands upon teachers:

> With the huge uptick in the amount of murders in the city, we feel that our kids need help. We have been told by parents that if it is not an immediate family member (who was murdered), they (students) are not entitled to (school district-sponsored) services... With the mental health clinics closing, with the regular public health clinics closing... our kids are getting hit on both sides. So we (teachers) have to make up the slack for some of the things that don't actually happen and we are feeling extraordinarily overworked, extraordinarily underprepared. (Gill, 2012)

This example, extreme as it may appear, illustrates how, even as district administrators, schools, and teacher educators reinforce narrow academic instructional roles for teachers, classroom teachers find themselves pressed to do more work for which they have received neither preparation nor support. In many situations, then, teachers have to work beyond their bounded role. When they do this, though, they have not changed their working conditions but rather do their work in spite of these conditions. When policymakers formally and unilaterally broaden the teacher role, they exacerbate an already untenable situation.

Contending with obstacles to the expanded teacher role. When educational leaders and policymakers graft expanded roles onto what teachers already do, they will most likely find themselves working against a current of narrow roles. Schools are organized that way. Teachers have been trained that way. What can be done? My analysis suggests that certain types of expanded roles may fare better, and that the time is ripe to scaffold expanded teacher roles.

Since school organization and teacher education have largely supported teachers' instructional role, role expansions that concern instruction stand to receive more adequate support. The increasing availability of ELL-related coursework for teacher candidates, for example (Villegas & Lucas, 2011; Walker & Stone, 2011), suggests that a framework is growing to support generalist teachers required to teach ELLs. Teacher educators, under such circumstances, expand upon what they have already been doing—teaching teachers how to instruct students.

Role expansions that stray farther from teachers' instructional role, however, seem much less likely to garner support, as these matters have not been a widespread part of teacher education, nor of teachers' "official" work in schools. The increasing presence of master's degree programs in teacher leadership, for example, suggests an awareness of the need (or at least entrepreneurial opportunities for higher education) to prepare teachers in this area. But stand-alone degree programs are divorced from what individuals seeking certification as teachers must learn. Tyack and Cuban (1995) suggest that reforms that strive to change peripheral aspects of schools will take hold more readily than reforms that take aim at schools' core functions. Adding to the curriculum that teachers (or teacher educators) already teach is far less paradigm-shifting than reorganizing schools and teacher education programs around additional foci for teachers' work. Teacher professional development for practicing teachers, perhaps more nimble and less mired in stable patterns of organization than university-based teacher education programs, may offer other avenues by which teachers' learning opportunities could adapt to prepare teachers for expanded roles.

Meanwhile, teacher education and certification programs in the United States find themselves the focus of reevaluation, concerned with what teachers need to learn in order to serve their students well. This reevaluation holds at least some promise for larger shifts in what teachers learn to do. Calls come from multiple directions to overhaul what teachers learn and how they learn. Among the nearly endless demands placed upon teacher education programs come calls to fit school-based, clinical education to teacher candidates' learning needs and university-based coursework experiences (Zeichner, 2010; Darling-Hammond, 2010), to demonstrate teacher education programs' effectiveness by measuring graduates' job placement rates and subsequent K-12 students' test scores (US Department of Education, 2011), and to ready teacher candidates to educate diverse learners for success in our information-driven, global economy (Council on Foreign Relations Task Force, 2012; Levine, 2006). While different parties disagree about what needs to change or how, all agree that many certified teachers begin their careers without adequate preparation for the demands they will face, and that teacher education must change to remedy this situation. These exhortations suggest that the door is open to looking at what teachers need to know in order to effectively teach the students in front of them. In such a climate, teacher educators have an opportunity to consider what their current candidates and graduates face in K-12 classrooms and to reengineer teacher learning experiences accordingly. This opportunity, however, is not a promise of change that would prepare teachers for formally expanded teacher roles, but only a chance at it. Those concerned about teachers' ability to perform formally expanded roles would need to insert themselves in relevant conversations about the shape of teacher education and highlight what specific learning experiences teacher candidates and practicing teachers lack.

Those who pursue such goals, though, will likely find themselves facing the question: How important is it for generalist educators (as opposed to only specialists who work in K-12 schools) to perform an expanded teacher role such as the advisor role, or special education inclusion, and to perform it consistently well? Then, if it is important enough, what changes have to be made by those who educate and certify teachers in teacher education programs, and by those who organize teachers' day-to-day work in schools?

I'll answer those questions with another question: What if we don't? What if we continue to assign expanded roles to teachers without giving teachers different learning opportunities to prepare them and without changing the schools in which they work? The schools and teachers described in this book give reason to expect that, under such conditions, expanded teacher roles will at times work out well by fortunate coincidence and will lead to mediocre or poor results otherwise. Such a situation promises costs to schools and students via squandered resources such as student instructional time, teachers' personal time devoted to unfinished work (above and beyond the extra-hours work already expected of teachers), and the human and financial costs of replacing teachers who burn out under the weight of unmanageable expectations.

Feasible, sustainable expanded teacher roles require not only strong teachers, but also teachers with strengths that particularly suit them for those roles, schools that structure and support these roles, and broader professional support. Whether by adapting monolithic systems and practices or working with programs, groups, and organizational forms that promise more nimble responsiveness to expanded roles' demands, those invested in assigning expanded teacher roles must include teachers but also look beyond them in order to make these roles work in today's schools.

Lessons about Teachers and Advisory

While this book considers the advisor role as an example of expanded teacher roles, it also provides a detailed view into the advisor role and advisory programs in action. That view tells us that advisory programs run a very real risk of overrelying on teachers who may or may not be ready for the task. I found this particularly true regarding teachers' responsibility to provide social-emotional support as part of their advising duties. These findings underscore the importance of (1) schools' structuring support for the advisor role and (2) specifying teacher competencies for it. Below, I provide suggestions in both areas.

Advisory programs must rely on teachers, but require sufficient structure and support in order to work. It is impossible to think about advisory programs—designed to create stronger connections among students and teachers—working without teachers. King's, Los Robles', and Western's advisory programs relied heavily on teachers. When an overarching vision for the advisory program was missing, incompletely defined, or contested, teachers found themselves on their own to define it for their advisees and themselves. When advisory programs did not suggest or provide activities for advisory class, teachers figured out how to spend that class time. Many teachers dug into their own reserves and made advisory work, but most did so in spite of their schools' advisory program rather than because of its support.

Literature on advisories consistently tells schools to structure their advisory programs before launching them. Long before I wrote, or researched, this book, the many manuals dedicated to supporting advisory programs told schools and educators interested in advisory what to do, and they uniformly counseled schools to structure their advisory programs before implementing them. "Are you ready?" Poliner and Lieber (2004, p. 15) ask in *The Advisory Guide*. They ask readers to answer a series of questions, including the following:

> Can your advisors finish the following sentences with ease and confidence?
> The goals of our school's advisory program are...
> My goals for my advisory group are...
>
> Does the school schedule have time assigned for advisory groups to be held and for advisors to do preparation?
>
> Will anybody know if advisors are fulfilling their roles effectively?
>
> Has the relationship between advisory and other school structures been articulated? For example, in what ways are advisors to be involved in disciplinary matters? (p. 15)

Without these structures and supports, teachers assigned to lead advisory classes must work out the details themselves. King, Los Robles, and Western consulted different resources on advisory, and Los Robles and Western even sent faculty to observe other advisory programs in action. Still, teachers' reports from these schools reflect that their advisory programs fell far short of fully implementing recommendations for these programs' structure. Teachers made up for this shortfall everyday.

Echoing advisory guidebook authors and my own recommendations, I contend that schools must structure their advisory programs and the advisor role as much as possible *before* asking teachers to advise students.

Such work involves determining and specifying broad goals for advisory programs (e.g., ensuring that all students get necessary academic support, building student community, or helping students develop and carry out college and career plans) as well as graspable year-by-year, quarter-by-quarter, or even week-by-week goals. I saw examples of the latter kind of goals in King's focus on college readiness and application support in upper grades, as well as Western's use of advisory to help students with graduation portfolios, required internships, and college admissions. Schools can also adjust and add to advisory programs in response to teacher and student feedback on programs once they are in action.

Recommendations for structures that support advisory and teachers who advise. It is essential that schools structure their advisory programs in keeping with their goals for those programs. I suggest particular structures with the understanding that they must fit schools' goals for advisory programs, or will otherwise come across as confusing and wasteful. In chapter 3, I describe three structural elements—resources, formalized procedures, and cultural dimensions—that I found to underpin the advisor role structure. Thinking about advisory and the advisor role, I recommend that schools with advisory programs create the following structural elements:

- *Develop, communicate, and periodically revise an overarching vision for school advisory programs.* Knowing what an advisory program and teachers who carry it out are trying to accomplish will help schools determine what is needed for the program in terms of personnel, time, curriculum, professional learning opportunities, support, materials, meeting time, and formalized procedures. This vision will require revision as the program and the school evolve.
- *Designate and support leadership for the advisory program.* Teachers will have questions about their schools' advisory programs and their roles in it, and, while they will ask each other, their family members, or friends if they have to, they should ideally receive guidance from someone whom their school has designated to support the advisory program. Based on feedback from some teachers that such work was draining, individuals in such roles need sufficient expertise and time within the school day in order to develop and support school advisory programs.
- *Provide clear expectations about the advisor role and advisory class meetings.* The school's goals for its advisory program can and should determine the scope and limitations of teachers' responsibilities as advisors. Should advisors engage in social-emotional support, college planning, behavioral guidance, parent contact? What is the difference between an advisor and an administrator, a school-based

mental health practitioner, and a guidance counselor, with regard to their responsibility toward advisees? Specification along these lines would help teachers know when they are doing well at their jobs and should hopefully prevent at least some role overload by letting teachers know what lies beyond their role requirements. Similarly, clear expectations can guide how advisory class time is spent, particularly in schools with many novice teachers. Schools that want teachers to customize their advisory classes would need to specify any base requirements that teachers also need to meet, and need to remember that some teachers will prefer that schools guide their practice. The communication of such expectations, both verbal and written, informal and formal, will need repetition over time, so that new teachers will learn what is expected of them.

- *Schedule time for advisory-related activities that cannot take place during advisory class.* Advisory class needs time designated in a school schedule, but advisory programs and teachers who serve as advisors also use other kinds of time outside of class. Teachers in this study used nonclass time to plan, collaborate with other advisors and advisees' other teachers and school-based specialists, meet privately with students, and contact parents. Schools with advisory programs need to factor in diverse time demands such as these when initiating programs and scheduling teachers' time.

- *Support teachers with professional development.* Few teachers in this study felt prepared for their work as advisors, suggesting that teachers who become advisors may find themselves in the same situation. Organizations such as the Wildwood School and Educators for Social Responsibility provide advisory-specific professional development, but other learning opportunities exist for teachers as well, related to needed competencies in areas such as child and adolescent development, crisis management, and college and career planning. Members of schools' internal or local communities may be able to provide professional development opportunities that build teachers' advisory-relevant knowledge and skills.

- *Align advisory programs and advisor roles with other school structures.* If advisory stands apart from the rest of the school, it will compete against other programs and goals for time, priority, and other resources. Likewise, teachers may find themselves forced to choose between fulfilling their advisor role responsibilities and their myriad other responsibilities. In chapter 3, I discuss how Western's teacher teams—which took on a variety of curricular, administrative tasks—also incorporated advisory curriculum and mental health consultation and allowed advisors and content-area teachers together to consult about advisees. These teams' alignment with Western's advisory program used existing resources in ways that supported the advisory program and teachers' work within it, and connected advisors' knowledge of advisees to those students' content-area teachers and mental health providers. When advisory structures align with other school structures, advisory programs can support and receive support from their schools.

Advisor role competencies for teachers. As I call for schools to sufficiently structure their advisory programs so that teachers can work effectively and sustainably within them, I also recognize that advisory programs need teachers with particular competencies. In chapter 4, I detail what teachers did in the advisor role, revealing that they took on tasks, including academic guidance, social-emotional support, life skills development, and discipline, which varied across teachers and schools. In chapter 5, I discuss the different knowledge, skills, experiences, support, and ideas that teachers drew upon in order to do their jobs as advisors. Together, these chunks of information suggest that there is an array of tasks that most advisors perform and that certain capacities made it possible for teachers to do these tasks well. With this understanding, I propose competencies that teachers need for their work as advisors, again with the understanding that individual schools' advisory programs will largely determine which competencies teachers need. Schools with advisory programs might seek to hire teachers with these competencies, or might seek to build these competencies among their teaching faculty.

Competencies for the advisor role involve the many tasks that advisors do beyond the classroom. Within advisory class, teachers need basic *advisory class facilitation skills.* Since advisory class does not tend to rely on an academic discipline or curriculum, teachers may find themselves facing new challenges as to how to structure class time, sustain group conversation, or help their students connect to curriculum. In schools that require teachers to conduct individual consultation with advisees during advisory class time, I learned that many teachers found it difficult to focus on one advisee while ensuring that other advisees were engaged in other activities. *Advisory content-area expertise* may be necessary depending on an advisory program's focus, such as college readiness, career education, life skills, or community-building. Teachers' knowledge in these areas should not be assumed, even though some teachers may bring rich experience to their work.

Relational skills, which I discuss in chapter 5, represent another competency related to teachers' advisor role, and are critical to the individual relationships that advisory programs ask teachers to develop with their advisees. Given teachers' and students' generational, sociocultural, and within-school power differences, teachers' relational skills, such as the ability to listen, to build rapport with students, and to communicate with assertiveness, are often critical to student-teacher relationships (I discuss student perspectives on teachers' relational practices in Phillippo, 2012). These skills are particularly important when advisory programs include student-teacher relationships that touch upon students' academic progress, personal issues, and life plans. Finally, teachers who work as advisors should have a strong command of *relevant school policies* that impact their advisees, such as graduation requirements or discipline policies. This information should help teachers to not only inform their advisees, but also to understand what, if any, role advisors have in addressing emergent student needs.

Teachers in this study also found themselves involved in multiple out-of-class activities on behalf of their advisees. As a result, advisor role competencies must extend beyond the classroom as well. To describe these competencies, I borrow language from school-based mental health professions, but stress that teachers occupy a different role than social workers or school psychologists. The competencies I discuss below are not intended to transform teachers into school-based mental health professionals, but rather adapt those professionals' knowledge and skills for teachers' use. When teachers serve as advisors, they find themselves collaborating with a range of professionals—such as other teachers, school mental health professionals, foster care workers, probation officers, and college admissions programs—about their advisees. For this reason, one advisor role competency involves *consultation*, in which teachers understand when and how to consult with others on behalf of their students, and use these consultations to make service referrals and to provide and receive relevant information about their advisees. Effective consultation can benefit not only advisees, but also teachers who take in needed information and support pertaining to their advisees and share the work of supporting them. Collaboration also requires *advocacy* skills, used by Ms. Renato, for example, when she inserted herself into school meetings (whether invited or not) that pertained to her advisees, challenged administrative decisions about advisees based on her deeper knowledge of them, and commanded support from colleagues who had expertise that promised to help her work with advisees. As teachers strive to help advisees navigate school requirements and systems, they need the ability to effectively advocate with their colleagues for students while still respecting student choice and self-determination.

As teachers work closely with advisees over time, my results suggest that they will likely encounter student social-emotional issues such as depression, peer harassment, family disruption, and exposure to violence. For this reason, teachers who serve as advisors would get many opportunities to exercise *teacher-specific social-emotional support* competencies. I discuss such competencies in detail in this chapter's next section, but briefly define them here as teachers' ability to recognize and respond to student social-emotional issues that present themselves in the classroom or at school. Such issues are likely to come to an advisor's attention in schools that designate advisors as the teachers in charge of overseeing and supporting an assigned group of advisees.

While one of teachers' most important social-emotional support skills is the ability to successfully refer students to the appropriate mental health provider, teachers in this study often found themselves noticing or learning about student issues before specialists did. Social-emotional support competencies would support teachers in just those moments. When Ms. Moreno's student contacted her about another student's intention to commit suicide, Ms. Moreno did not "treat" the student herself but instead gathered information and contacted the appropriate authorities to arrange for help. Such actions came easily to Ms. Moreno, who had parented, worked in other human services jobs, and taught for ten years, but seemed to escape other teachers with less advisory-relevant backgrounds. It is important to remember that many teachers at Western and Los Robles did not take up the social-emotional support aspects of the advisor role as their schools designed it, and did not see social-emotional support as part of their job, even when it was. Teachers didn't do what they didn't know how to do. Increased competency in this area would improve teachers' responsiveness to their advisees, and therefore, advisees' experiences.

Lessons about Teachers and Social-Emotional Support

Teachers at King, Los Robles, and Western showed a clear need for additional knowledge, skills, and support in the area of providing social-emotional support to their advisees. The lessons learned from their experiences, though, pertain to the broader population of K-12 teachers, many of whom will encounter students contending with social-emotional challenges in their lives. These lessons pertain both to what teachers already do and what they have the potential to do to help support their students.

There are plenty of reasons why teachers might not want to involve themselves in the social-emotional support of their students. As I demonstrate in chapter 2, the conditions of teaching—such as large-group instruction and expectations for impartial treatment of students—stand as obstacles to student-teacher relationships in general and teachers providing social-emotional support in particular. Further, I found that not everyone in the field of education supports the idea of teachers providing social-emotional support to their students—some have vehemently opposed this idea. Even proponents of teachers providing social-emotional support tend to fail to specify what teachers should actually *do*. Not surprisingly, then, teachers at King, Los Robles, and Western had a number of compelling reasons to avoid, underperform, or misunderstand expectations that they address their students' social-emotional needs.

Nevertheless, I found that teachers consistently encounter expectations to provide social-emotional support to their students. Although some educational leaders have *discouraged* teachers from involving themselves in the social-emotional support of students, I also report in chapter 2 that other literature for and about teachers *encourages* this very work by providing compelling examples of it and by directly exhorting teachers to do it. The fact that we have made these implicit and explicit requests of teachers for over a century suggests that teachers' social-emotional support responsibilities remain on K-12 education's collective mind. What teachers ought to do, though, is not yet clear. My findings from King, Los Robles, and Western suggest a way forward.

In spite of mixed and often vague messages about teachers providing social-emotional support, and a work environment that does not favor such work, some teachers in this study demonstrated a vision for and sense of comfort with it. They talked with their students about issues such as personal safety, struggles with gender identity, grief, and drug use. No teacher strived to move in on school-based mental health professionals' turf by taking on a therapist-type role (and none wanted to). Instead, teachers listened to students' concerns and pointed out their own, asked students to reflect on how their issues impacted their school lives, and connected students to school- and community-based services. These teachers also knew how to give to their students without overextending themselves by promising support they did not know how to provide or by emotionally overcommitting themselves. However, just like the "virtuoso" teachers (such as Leonard Covello or KIPP Schools founder Dave Levin) whom I discussed in chapter 2, who skillfully provided social-emotional support with no apparent help from their schools, teachers in these three schools often did this work in spite of their professional preparation and school structures. If they spoke with their schools' mental health providers about their students at all, they often did so before or after school, or while running in between classes. After referring their students to these providers for support services, many teachers did not hear back about whether their students were receiving services, and did not have opportunities to exchange information about their students' progress or needs. Most teachers had had no formal professional learning experiences that addressed student social-emotional wellness issues. Teachers provided social-emotional support to their students, but did so within an infrastructural vacuum.

Furthermore, not all teachers stepped into the social-emotional support role, even when their schools foisted it upon them. At Los Robles and Western, teachers knew that their schools wanted them to address social-emotional issues that came up with their advisees. Still, most did not see social-emotional support as their primary responsibility: only 25 percent of Western's participating teachers did, and none of Los Robles' teachers did. Most teachers did not gravitate toward social-emotional support responsibilities.

If schools, or the broader fields of teacher education and K-12 education, want to encourage teachers to use their unique relationships with students to provide them with certain kinds of social-emotional support, they will do better to support teachers in this area than to hope that they figure out how to do this work on their own. Certainly, some teachers at King, Los Robles, and Western had background experiences—such as undergraduate majors in psychology or social work, experience as participants and mentors in substance abuse recovery programs, or previous work as hotline counselors—that helped. Some teachers relied on family members or friends with professional mental health backgrounds to help them sort out how to respond to their students' situations. But such assets helped only those who already possessed them.

Social-emotional support competencies for teachers. Karen Weston and her colleagues (Weston et al., 2008) have done foundational work in which they identify specific areas of teacher mental health competence, and my findings lend empirical support to their efforts. I note, though, that my data and recommendations extend beyond matters related to student mental health. Young people encounter other distressing situations—such as homelessness, immigration difficulties, struggles related to sexual orientation and gender identity, pregnancy, peer harassment, and family challenges such as a family member's death, incarceration, substance abuse, or unemployment—that may cause mental health problems to develop. These situations, however, are not themselves diagnosable student mental health conditions. For this reason, I consider social-emotional support to be something that includes but extends beyond mental health counseling, an array of supports and services that assist students in dealing with the broad range of issues that cause them trouble in their personal and academic lives.

Weston and her colleagues identify six domains of teacher competence that apply to student mental health as well as a wider range of social-emotional issues. These domains are as follows: (1) Policies and laws related to learning support in schools, such as regulations related to teachers' responsibilities to report child abuse and neglect; (2) The provision of learning supports, for example, teachers' use of strategies identified in student behavior plans; (3) Data collection and use, in which, for example, teachers identify and record signs of student distress or improvement; (4) Communication and relationship-building, such as teachers' development of caring and respectful relationships with their students; (5) Multiple system engagement, in which teachers navigate and refer students to school and community resources when needed; and (6) Personal and professional development and well-being, such as teachers' use of coping and self-care strategies in face of workplace stress. My recommendations for developing teachers' social-emotional support competencies connect directly to Weston and her colleagues' domains, as I illustrate in figure 7.1. I recommend three areas of emphasis for developing teachers' social-emotional support

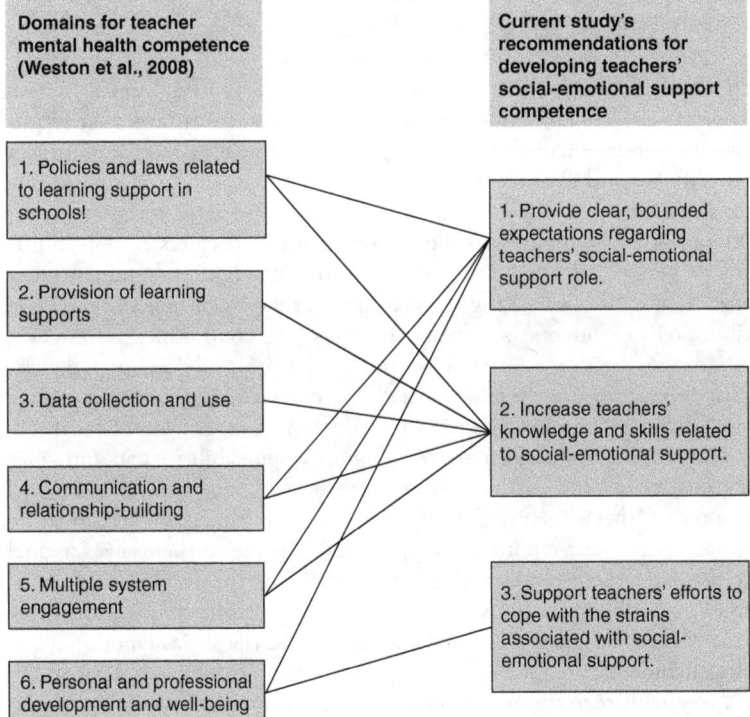

Figure 7.1 Recommendations for developing teachers' social-emotional support competence.

competencies: (1) Providing clear, bounded expectations, (2) increasing teachers' knowledge and skills, and (3) supporting teachers' own coping efforts.

Provide clear, bounded expectations regarding teachers' social-emotional support role. Teachers need to know what their schools and profession expect of them in the area of social-emotional support. I found that teachers stand in a unique position as "first responders" to student social-emotional difficulties and have the potential to support students by connecting students to needed services as well as through ongoing classroom interactions once service referrals have been made. A shift toward more specific expectations would require broader discussions involving a diverse range of stakeholders, including teachers, students, parents, school administrators, teacher educators, and school- and community-based support providers. These discussions would need to clarify what different stakeholders want to ask of teachers (and what teachers want to, and feel they are able to, offer) so that, ideally, consensus could be reached and could lead to clearer communication of expectations to teachers.

Clear expectations would specify not only what local stakeholders, schools, and the teaching profession want teachers to do, but also those expectations' limits. When laws and policies—such as laws that require teachers to report child abuse or neglect, school policies requiring teachers to notify the authorities when students are suicidal, and informal expectations that teachers will refer students to needed social-emotional support services—require teachers to take action, where do teachers' responsibilities end? When we ask teachers to step into students' personal and emotional lives, how far are we asking them to go? Teachers can make critical contributions to students' well-being by engaging community resources or providing a regularly available sounding board for advisees experiencing difficulties. However, teachers usually do not stand in a position to independently and indefinitely support a student in distress. The specification of when teachers' social-emotional support responsibilities end and where administrators' and other support professionals' responsibilities begin is essential. Otherwise, my findings suggest that teachers may under- or overperform social-emotional support tasks, perceive themselves as ineffective, find themselves overloaded, or distance themselves from social-emotional support responsibilities all together. None of these outcomes bode well for teachers' sustained engagement in the social-emotional support of students.

Increase teachers' knowledge and skills related to social-emotional support. Specific social-emotional support expectations of teachers would need to be accompanied by knowledge and skills that would help teachers meet those expectations. I found a number of areas in which teachers would benefit from being more able to recognize, find out more about, and take steps to address students' social-emotional issues and needs. Teachers encountered a range of student social-emotional issues such as family conflict, pregnancy, and peer harassment. They did not always recognize these issues until a crisis occurred, though, and did not always know what to do or say when they became aware of student problems. These findings suggest that teachers would benefit from having more information that would help them recognize and then respond—as teachers, not as school-based mental health professionals—to commonly experienced student social-emotional issues for the age groups and communities that they serve. As student issues vary across individuals and communities, and available information that could support teachers' efforts likely changes over time, teachers might do best if they gain general, adaptable knowledge, and skills (on topics such as crisis management) in combination with training specific to particular issues (such as depression, eating disorders, or gangs) that are relevant to their school's student population.

Teachers would also benefit from knowing how to address different social-emotional issues that arise in the classroom. If a student, for example, has posttraumatic stress disorder (PTSD) following community, intimate, or family violence, a teacher would not be the primary person to treat this condition but could find herself in the position of being the first person at school to notice, adapting instruction or providing classroom-based support for that student. Likewise, teacher involvement in carrying out student intervention plans or behavior plans (such as those developed by schools' Positive Behavior Interventions and Supports (PBIS) or Response-to-Intervention (RtI) programs) requires teacher knowledge and skill about student needs and how to meet them, which teachers may not have, given the limited learning opportunities I have described elsewhere in this book. Guidance and information about student social-emotional issues and support needs—in the form of preservice training, induction program-sponsored teacher coaching, school-based professional development, or more informal support from school-based mental health professionals—could boost teachers' work that occurs in conjunction with the work of others who serve their students.

In addition, teachers' connections with students were strengthened by their relational skills, or their abilities to productively engage with their students and build relationships with them. Teachers' possession of these skills, however, was very scattered—some had a solid grip of how to develop relationships with their students while others felt at a loss. While other helping professions take steps to support workers' connection with their clients or consumers of their services, teachers do not receive substantial preparation in this area (Grossman et al., 2007) and could put learning experiences in this area to work. Finally, teachers in this study simply needed more information about available school- and community-based resources that could support their students. They recognized their own support skill and time limitations, and wanted to make sure students got the supports they needed. Available information, however, went out of date as agencies changed their service offerings or closed, and teachers did not always know how or where to find information about services for their students. If teachers are to engage with school and community systems, as Weston et al. (2008) rightly suggest, they need accessible, up-to-date information on how to access different services. They would also benefit from clear, teacher-friendly protocols for making referrals to and receiving follow-up information from frequently used support providers in and out of school. Teachers complained to me about filling out lengthy referral forms and then not receiving information about what happened with the information they provided. They responded more affirmatively to simpler protocols such as directly emailing or speaking to a particular staff member, having regularly scheduled access to mental health professionals through school-based team meetings, and phone numbers (such as national programs' toll-free numbers and city- or countywide referral numbers) that were easy to remember and connected callers to a variety of service options. More usable information about students and supports for them would make it easier for teachers to provide social-emotional support.

Support teachers' efforts to cope with the strains associated with social-emotional support. Weston and colleagues' (2008) sixth competence domain—personal and professional development and well-being—connects directly to my findings that teachers often struggled with the work of providing social-emotional support to students. When teachers learned about students' challenges and vulnerabilities, and then tried to address them, often with limited skills, they understandably experienced strain. I found that teachers weren't waiting for ideas about how to address this strain but were addressing it in ways that ranged from productive to troubling. In chapter 6, I discuss how teachers drew different kinds of boundaries on their work advising students. Some of these boundaries were thought-out and aimed at supporting students' and teachers' well-being, while other boundaries were drawn reactively and defensively in response to overwhelming student needs, with little regard for impact upon students. Both cases show teachers' attempts to cope with potentially draining and upsetting work demands, such as helping a student who disclosed that she had been raped or working with a student who was involved in a gang and faced danger in and out of school because of it. I recommend that schools and teacher educators build in experiences that help teachers anticipate and constructively cope with the strains of providing social-emotional support, rather than merely hoping that teachers will cope in ways that are good for themselves and their students. These experiences could focus on topics such as how to set boundaries on their work with students, stress management, and self-care, and would complement the efforts I describe above, which specify, delimit, and inform teachers' provision of social-emotional support.

School-based mental health: Obstacle or key to teachers developing social-emotional support competence? I have already suggested that, when making recommendations for changed practice, one must consider why these recommendations have not already come to fruition. Earlier in this chapter, I review characteristics of K-12 schools and teacher education programs that reinforce narrow roles. Those characteristics likewise work against teachers acquiring social-emotional support competencies. In addition, school-based mental health professionals (SBMHPs) have not historically promoted the development of these competencies. Changes in the relationship between these professionals' work and teachers' work, however, could alter this pattern and make substantial contributions to teachers' readiness to provide social-emotional support.

SBMHPs and teachers have long served the same students, but these groups of professionals have tended to work separately from one another. Waxman, Weist, and Benson (1999) note the differing perspectives and goals that each group of professionals has, with teachers focusing on academic growth for more-or-less normally developing groups of students, and SBMHPs addressing individual students' needs and issues and anticipating students' departure from developmental norms. In this way, SBMHPs' and teachers' work has always differed from each other's. School-based mental health professions gained and have maintained their foothold in K-12 education *because of* these differences, by providing services that teachers do not perform, particularly clinical, therapeutic services (Sedlak, 1997). Furthermore, school-based mental health professions have created stability for themselves largely by staying *out* of K-12 education's core activities of teaching and learning. By focusing on office-based clinical services for students (Brener, Weist, Adelman, Taylor, & Vernon-Smiley, 2007; Frey & Dupper, 2005; Kelly, Berzin, Frey, Alvarez, Shaffer, & O'Brien, 2010), these professions have become what Tyack and Cuban (1995) describe as structural add-on reforms, which take place in schools but do not challenge schools' basic structures or practices. School-based mental health refrains from reaching too far into the classroom or into teachers' practice, and so asks minimally for schools or teachers to change their practice. In this way, school-based mental health professions maintain stability via their peripheral status (Phillippo & Stone, 2011; Sedlak, 1997). To ask SBMHPs to reach further into teachers' practice might amount to asking them to destabilize their own status in schools. In addition, SBMHP training reinforces the separation of SBMHPs from educators by providing minimal exposure to school-related issues while prioritizing trainees' clinical knowledge (e.g., Berzin & O'Connor, 2010). SBMHPs have had little reason to engage with teachers. In my research with SBMHPs at King, Los Robles, and Western (Phillippo & Kelly, 2011), I learned that teachers and SBMHPs worked largely in isolation from one another unless one sought the other out. Even though they worked in the same building as one another, SBMHPs, often to their own disappointment, had little to do with teachers' work advising students, which represented a missed opportunity for SBMHPs to reinforce and expand teachers' social-emotional support capacity.

Yet, school mental health scholars have begun to call for SBMHPs to collaborate with teachers in ways that could promote teachers' social-emotional support competencies. Paternite and Johnston (2005) criticize SBMHPs' hierarchical, "expert-consultee" approach to working with teachers, and challenge SBMHPs to instead view teachers as possessing equal standing with them with regard to their knowledge of, and ability to support, shared students. Further, Burke and Paternite (2007) question the "exclusivity" of office-based individual therapy among SBMHPs' different options for serving students and their schools. They call for SBMHPs to immerse themselves in their schools and provide a range of services including prevention, wellness promotion, and problem-focused intervention that respond to schools' concerns and needs. Part of such work, Burke and Paternite assert, involves SBMHPs providing professional learning opportunities that respond to teacher-identified needs. Assuming that teachers, such as the teachers at King, Los Robles, and Western, would identify a need to better understand and respond their students' social-emotional issues and difficulties, I contend that such SBMHP-led professional development could take powerful steps to empower teachers to promote student wellness and help identify student issues before they mushroom into full-blown problems.

Changes in SBMHPs' work with teachers would require parallel changes in the organizations that prepare and employ them. Such changes would represent a departure from business as usual for many SBMHPs, and would press their own professional preparation programs to position them as potential educators and leaders in the K-12 school setting. It would also require schools to change the ways in which they work with SBMHPs, such as aligning their services with other school structures such as those for faculty meetings and professional development. A shift toward greater SBMHP-teacher collaboration would also require schools to exercise flexibility with how they used SBMHPs' time—no practitioner could conduct a full week's schedule of individual counseling sessions and also engage meaningfully in educative, prevention, and promotion activities. However, Kelly and Lueck (2011) find that SBMHPs in schools that ask them to engage in a wider range of services still drift toward a focus on individual and small group intervention, which suggests that this shift is only in its very earliest stages. Finally, SBMHPs' enhancement of teachers' social-emotional support competence would need to be accompanied by schools' enhancement of support for teachers. If teachers acquire more social-emotional support skills, they would likely end up learning more about their students' social-emotional lives and would need to be able to turn to colleagues to refer students for services and obtain professional support for their own ongoing work with distressed students. SBMHPs and administrators would need to be ready for this additional layer of work. Are SBMHP training programs and K-12 schools ready for such changes? The teachers at King, Los Robles, and Western suggest that they ought to get ready, and quickly, for the sake of having strong teachers who can truly support their students.

Final Thoughts

The teachers of King, Los Robles, and Western have shown how expanded teacher roles work, how advisory programs turn out for teachers, and what teachers need to know and do in order to provide social-emotional support to their students. Together, these three clusters of findings and their implications stand as a reminder that as people tinker with and contemplate teachers' responsibilities they are really saying what teachers should and should not do, what should and should not matter to teachers, and what teachers should and should not be able to do in order to optimally educate their students. As expanded roles become increasingly formalized, teachers may reach a tipping point beyond which they simply cannot add more tasks to their job and do them well enough. It is incumbent upon the organizations that employ and prepare teachers to understand this situation so that that they can enrich and support teachers' potential to serve their students rather than squander that potential by unthinkingly heaping more upon teachers with little regard for teachers' capacity to do the work or for the role that school structures play in supporting or defeating that important work. My hope is that this book advances the quest to gain a fuller understanding of what we ask of teachers, and pushes policymakers, teacher educators, school districts, and school administrators to fairly and fully set teachers up to meet these expectations.

Appendix A
Teacher Interview Participants, Sorted by School

These lists include all teachers (by pseudonym) who participated in the interviews that informed this book. One asterisk denotes teachers who also participated in more extensive mini-case study interviews, as described in appendix B. Two asterisks denote teachers participated in part, but not all, of the teacher interview process.

King High School

1. Ms. Baca*
2. Ms. Brice
3. Ms. Byrd
4. Ms. Carbonell*
5. Mr. Carmichael
6. Mr. Chavez*
7. Mr. Colvin
8. Ms. Gutierrez
9. Ms. Hamilton
10. Ms. Li*
11. Ms. Mahali
12. Ms. Moré
13. Mr. Perrales
14. Ms. Sobotka**
15. Ms. Williams

Los Robles

1. Ms. Aron
2. Ms. Baker
3. Ms. Bruce*

4. Ms. Colbrane
5. Ms. Curran
6. Mr. DeLucia
7. Ms. Dolby*
8. Ms. Gillespie
9. Ms. Goodman
10. Mr. Hart
11. Ms. Little
12. Ms. Mitchell
13. Ms. Moreno
14. Mr. Nagel
15. Mr. Orff
16. Mr. Palmieri**
17. Ms. Powers*
18. Ms. Pozo
19. Ms. Reynaldo
20. Ms. Saenz*
21. Ms. Sosa

Western

1. Mr. Bell
2. Mr. Carver
3. Mr. Bennett
4. Mr. Freamon
5. Ms. Greggs
6. Ms. Janus*
7. Ms. Reinhardt
8. Ms. Renato*
9. Ms. Sathe
10. Mr. Westerberg*
11. Ms. Willis*

APPENDIX B
OVERVIEW OF RESEARCH METHODS

Study Design and Site Selection

Due to my multifaceted interests in the advisor role—in how it relates to the broader teaching profession and the organizational context of the K-12 school, teachers' preparation and qualifications to perform the role, and teachers' enactment of and responses to it—I selected a comparative case study design for this study. This approach—employing observations, interviews, and surveys—enabled me to take in a wealth of information about the advisor role through the experiences of a range of teachers and students in multiple schools (Yin, 2009). Multiple methods provided for what Eisenhardt (1989) calls a "synergistic relationship between data types" (p. 538), in which quantitative data and qualitative data balance each other and facilitate a nuanced understanding of the phenomena under study.

The comparative case study design led me to select three small high schools as the sites for this study. The schools I chose—King, Los Robles, and Western—all had an advisory program in which classroom teachers served as advisors. Beyond the convenience factor of selecting three schools with advisory programs in the same metropolitan area, I sampled for maximum variation in key school characteristics. I sought schools with differing levels of support and guidance for teachers serving as advisors, which I gauged by the advisory programs' degree of formalization (e.g., a set curriculum or no curriculum), and the amount of school-based mental health services (e.g., counseling, social work) made available to students and their teachers.

I selected schools with at least 40 percent of their students qualifying for free or reduced-price lunch (as a proxy for lower socioeconomic status) and at least 65 percent students of color, which helped me to hold demographic factors relatively constant across schools. Finally, I sought small high schools for this study's sample, given that the small high schools model stresses the importance of teachers knowing students well and often uses advisory as one way to personalize the school (as I describe in chapter 1). I intentionally sought schools that identified as small schools, ascribed to the small schools philosophy, and enrolled less than five hundred students.

This study had three phases. During phase 1, which took place late in the 2006–2007 academic year, I piloted the study at Los Robles by collecting observational and teacher interview data. I expanded the study, with revisions based on pilot study results, to all three school sites during the 2007–2008 academic year, for phase 2. This phase added in a teacher survey as well. For phases 1 and 2, I interviewed all teachers who were willing to participate. In phase 3, which also took place during the 2007–2008 academic year, I conducted a series of 12 minicase studies with a smaller group of teachers, along with a group of their student advisees.

For Phase 3, I selected four teachers from each school (totaling twelve across the three schools) to participate. From each school, I recruited one teacher from each of the four teacher quadrants (the criteria for which I developed using pilot study data) that I describe in chapter 5, with each quadrant representing a different combination of advisor role-relevant resources and schemas (low resource/low schema, low resource/high schema, high resource/low schema, high resource/high schema). I strove to maximize gender, age, and ethnic diversity within this group of 12 teachers. One phase-3 teacher left midyear to accept another position. Since I could not identify anyone else in the same quadrant at his site, I chose another teacher whose scores were the closest to his.

Once teacher participants agreed to be part of phase 3, I asked them to nominate three advisee participants apiece. I wanted to include advisees experiencing social-emotional stressors that might come to their advisors' attention, since teachers' work providing social-emotional support is one of this study's foci. I also wanted a narrow range of the types of stressors that participating students would present, since phase 1 and 2 interviewees described a wide array of such stressors among their students. I asked teachers to nominate advisees who, to their knowledge, met one or more of the following criteria: a history of disruptive behavior in class, known engagement in health or safety risk behavior such as substance use or delinquent behavior, or living in substitute care (not in either parent's custody). These criteria represent issues that pilot study teachers readily identified among their group of advisees. I asked phase 3 teacher participants to introduce me to students who met one or more of these criteria (without specifying which of the criteria they met). When teachers introduced me to the advisees whom they nominated, I explained the study, its goals, and privacy measures. If advisees expressed a willingness to participate, I arranged to obtain parent or guardian consent using contact information that advisees provided.

Data Collection

In phase 1, I piloted the study at Los Robles. I used modified ethnographic methods (e.g., Spindler and Spindler, 1987) in order learn about the school. Over the course of six weeks, I visited all content-area and advisory classrooms, observed unstructured periods of the day (passing periods, dismissal, lunch recess), and attended staff meetings. During this observation period, I also engaged in brief, informal conversations with students and educators. I kept field notes on both observations and conversations. At the end of this observation period, I scheduled interviews with all teachers serving as advisors who were willing to meet with me (19 of 20 teachers, with 1 additional teacher completing only part of the interview and then deciding to discontinue participation). In these interviews, I sought information on teachers' experience at the school (both teaching and advising), any school or personal resources they used while advising, what kind of expectations they encountered about their work advising students, their interpretation of the advisor role and its purpose at the school, and their responses to the advisor role. I made minor adjustments to the interview protocol during this phase and contacted participants as needed to ensure that I asked all phase 1 participants the same questions.

Phase 2 of this study brought King and Western on as sites. I conducted the observation and interview portions of the study, as I did in phase 1, at King and Western. Eleven of 13 Western's eligible teachers participated, and 14 of 16 eligible teachers participated at King (one additional teacher participated in an abbreviated interview only). I interviewed one additional teacher (a new hire) from Los Robles as well, bringing the total of teacher interview participants (including participants who completed partial interviews only) to 47. I also administered teacher surveys midyear at all three sites, which 45 teachers completed (15 at King, 17 at Los Robles, and 13 at Western, a 95.75% overall response rate). The survey instrument consisted of validated items that assessed teachers' views of their responsibilities for student social-emotional support (Roeser & Midgley, 1997), sense of efficacy at performing different advisor-role-related and social-emotional support tasks (adapted from Bandura, 2006), role load perception (Byrne, 1994), job satisfaction (Pettegrew & Wolf, 1982), and burnout (Maslach et al., 1996). I also included original survey items, developed following this study's pilot phase, that measured support for teachers' work (within and beyond the workplace), prior learning experiences that prepared teachers for advising, and teachers' individual interpretations of the advisor role. These items all used a Likert scale, indicating either the degree of agreement with statements (e.g., "I believe I must be both a teacher and a counselor to my students."), confidence about performing role-related tasks (e.g., "Recognize signs of family violence"), or the amount of the phenomenon being measured (e.g., low, moderate, or high levels of peer support). The survey also asked teachers to indicate their intention to continue in their current position for the following school year (yes, no, or unsure), and requested demographic and employment history information of respondents.

Phase 3 consisted of 12 mini-case studies in which I conducted 3 interviews apiece with 12 teachers serving as advisors and 3 interviews with each advisee, over the course of approximately 6 months. I focused teachers' interviews on their work with their three focal advisees by asking the same series of questions about each advisee. I gathered information about each of their advisees' academic performance and any known social or behavioral issues, interactions with this specific advisee (specifically those concerning social, emotional, or behavioral matters), teachers' sense of their own and others' expectations of them regarding this advisee, any individual or school resources that helped them in their work, and teachers' responses to working with each advisee. I also inquired about any collaboration between phase 3 teachers and others (teachers, administrators, school mental health professionals) about their selected advisee. In the final interview, I asked teachers to think back over the year of working with their advisee, to describe who or what had helped them in this work, what complicated it, and what, if any, kinds of additional support they wished they could have had.

In each advisee interview, I asked participants to describe their experiences in advisory class, as well as recent interactions with their advisors and their responses to these interactions. In the final interview, I also asked student participants to identify any adults at their school whom they felt knew them well, and what they would recommend to teachers or advisors who wanted to support their students. I sought 36 advisees (3 per advisor) for these interviews, and 35 participated.

Data Analysis

With the qualitative data from this study's phases 1 and 2, I began with the combined analytic strategies of reviewing field notes, discussing preliminary findings with participants, memo-writing, and exploratory readings of interview transcripts (Taylor and Bogdan 1998). I developed a list of codes for analysis while collecting data, and developed the list further once I had read all interview transcripts. In forming this list, I combined methods characteristic of a "tight, prestructured qualitative design" (Miles and Huberman 1994, p. 17) with a more open-ended stance, allowing for themes to emerge (Charmaz, 2006). I included and applied descriptive codes for key concepts (e.g., school expectations for teachers' performance of the advisor role, teachers' job satisfaction), derived from research that frames this study, along with more inductive codes that identified emergent themes in the data (Merriam, 2009). I applied the full set of codes to transcripts using HyperResearch software. During the early stages of the coding process, I refined and expanded my code list, so I went back and recoded data where necessary in order to ensure that all transcripts had the same set of codes applied to them. After I coded all the data, I used visual case display strategies (Miles and Huberman 1994) to order and focus my interpretation of coded data.

The small number of survey respondents (N=45) limited my options for quantitative analysis, but these responses were enhanced by their connection to teacher interview and observational data. I primarily conducted cross-tabulation to sort and interpret survey data, due to the small cell sizes of subgroups such as teacher quadrant groups (in chapters 5 and 6), although I was able to conduct analysis of variance (ANOVA) of teacher responses between schools. I also constructed a series of composite variables from survey items that measured advisor job satisfaction, efficacy, role load perception, and burnout. I confirmed the internal reliability of each composite variable by obtaining a Cronbach's alpha statistic on each, and removed one survey item from the job satisfaction variable in order to establish reliability via this statistic. To indicate high levels of each variable, as I discuss in chapter 6, I established a cutoff score as close as possible to the top quartile of possible points. Dr. Susan Stone and I conducted exploratory factor analysis of survey indicating how teachers interpreted the advisor role (e.g., "I see advisory as a place where students should focus on academics."). This analysis generated three factors (with Eigenvalues greater than 1), which we interpreted as three underlying dimensions of teachers' advisor role definition, as I discuss in chapter 4.

Notes

1 Advisory: A View into Expanded Teacher Roles

1. School, teacher, and student names (as well as other information that could identify individuals) have been changed to protect participants' privacy.

2 "Very Nice, but Not Very Helpful": The Education Profession's Divergent Representations of Teachers' Social-Emotional Support Responsibilities, 1892–2011

*Beth Wright is a doctoral student in Cultural and Educational Policy Studies at Loyola University Chicago's School of Education. She previously taught high school history in Chicago. Her research interests involve the sociology of education and school choice policies.

1. Our criteria excluded documents that focused solely on single-subject curriculum approaches (e.g., math instruction) or concerned classroom instructional methods alone. Since secondary historical texts did not always address recent trends in American education and teacher education, we also identified major movements and events in American schooling since 1980 (e.g., comprehensive school reform, attempts to redefine teacher quality) and then located documents related to these movements that were widely circulated and discussed in educational and news media. We refined this list following two rounds of expert review apiece with two senior historians of American K-12 and teacher education.
2. We initially applied the criteria to a small set of documents, discussed where our interpretations converged and diverged, and refined our criteria to promote consistent application. Following these steps, we each coded half of the remaining documents, discussing unusual cases that emerged.

3 Advisor Role Structure: How Schools Support or Undermine Expanded Teacher Roles

1. Nonclassroom teacher faculty members, such as special education resource teachers and administrators, also led advisory groups at Western.
2. Students' responses to advisory, described in a separate publication (Phillippo, 2012), strongly suggest that they did not want their advisors to discuss personal information in front of others.

4 Consistency and Variation in Teachers' Implementation of the Advisor Role

1. The factor analysis that influenced this portion of chapter 4 was conducted by Susan Stone as part of collaborative work between Dr. Stone and this book's author from their forthcoming publication (Phillippo & Stone, in press).

6 Occupational Hazards and Innovation: Teachers' Responses to the Advisor Role

1. Appendix B describes the instruments as well as variable construction.
2. FAFSA stands for the Free Application for Federal Student Aid.

REFERENCES*

*Entries preceded by an asterisk were included in the document analysis discussed in chapter 2.

Ackerman, R. H., & Mackenzie, S. V. (Eds.). (2007). *Uncovering teacher leadership: Essays and voices from the field*. Thousand Oaks, CA: Corwin Press.
*AED National Institute for Work and Learning. (2001). *Teachers for a new era*. New York: NY: Carnegie Corporation. Retrieved February 22, 2012, from http://www.teachersoforanewera.org/index.cfm?fuseaction=home.prospectus.
Alexander, W. M., & McEwin, C. K. (1989). *Schools in the middle: Status and progress*. Columbus, OH: National Middle School Association.
Alexander, W. M., Williams, E. L., Compton, M., Hines, V. A., Prescott, D., & Kealy, R. (1968). *The emergent middle school* (Vol. 23). New York, NY: Holt, Rinehart and Winston.
Allen, D., Nichols, P., Tocci, C., Hochman, D., & Gross, K. (2006). *Supporting students' success through distributed counseling*. New York: Institute for Human Achievement.
Allensworth, E., Ponisciak, S., & Mazzeo, C. (2009). *The schools teachers leave: Teacher mobility in Chicago public schools*. Chicago, IL: Consortium on Chicago School Research.
Ancess, J. (2003). *Beating the odds: High schools as communities of commitment*. New York: Teachers College Press.
Antrop-González, R., & De Jesús, A. (2006). Toward a theory of *critical care* in urban small school reform: Examining structures and pedagogies of caring in to Latino community-based schools. *International Journal of Qualitative Studies in Education, 19*(4), 409–433.
*Armstrong, D. G., Henson, K. T., & Savage, T. V. (1993). *Education: An introduction* (4th ed.). New York: Macmillan.
Ashforth, B. E., & Humphrey, R. H. (1993). Emotional labor in service roles: The influence of identity. *Academy of Management Review, 18*(1), 249–280.
Ashforth, B. E., Kreiner, G. E., & Fugate, M. (2000). All in a day's work: Boundaries and micro role transitions. *Academy of Management Review, 25*(3), 472–491.
Ayers, W. (2000). Simple justice: Thinking about teaching and learning, equity, and the fight for small schools. In M. Klonsky, W. Ayers, and G. H. Lyon (Eds.), *A simple justice: The challenge of small schools* (pp. 95–109). New York, NY: Teachers College Press.
Ayers, W., Klonsky, M., & Lyon, G. H. (Eds.). (2000). *A simple justice: The challenge of small schools*. New York, NY: Teachers College Press.

Back, K., & Back, K. (2005). *Assertiveness at work: A practical guide to handling awkward situations* (3rd ed.). Berkshire, England: McGraw-Hill.
Baeder, J. (2011). The "90/90/90" schools myth. *Edweek*. Retrieved from http://blogs.edweek.org/edweek/on_performance/2011/05/909090_schools_revisited.html.
Baker, W. E., & Faulkner, R. R. (1991). Role as resource in the Hollywood film industry. *American Journal of Sociology, 97*(2), 279–309.
Ball, D. L., & Forzani, F. M. (2009). The work of teaching and the challenge for teacher education. *Journal of Teacher Education, 60*(5), 497–511.
*Baltimore City Teaching Residency. (2012). Baltimore city teaching residency. Retrieved January 9, 2012, from http://bcteachingresidency.ttrack.org/.
Banchero, S., & Maher, K. (2012). Strike puts spotlight on teacher evaluation, pay. *Wall Street Journal*. Retrieved from http://online.wsj.com/article/SB10000872396390443921504577643652663814724.html.
Bandura, A. (1997). *Self-efficacy: The exercise of control.* New York: W. H. Freeman.
*Banks, J. A., & Banks, C. A. M. (Eds.). (2010). *Multicultural education: Issues and perspectives* (7th ed.). Hoboken, NJ: John Wiley & Sons, Inc.
Barker, R. G., & Gump, P. V. (1964). *Big school, small school: High school size and student behavior.* Stanford, CA: Stanford University Press.
Barnes, G., Crowe, E., & Schaefer, B. (2007). *The cost of teacher turnover in five school districts: A pilot study.* Washington, DC: National Commission for Teaching and America's Future.
*Barr, A. S., Worcester, D. A., Abell, A., Beecher, C., Jensen, L. E., Peronto, A. L., Rongness, T. A., & Schmid, J. (1961). *Wisconsin studies of the measurement and prediction of teacher effectiveness: A summary of investigations.* Madison, WI: Dembar Publications.
Bartlett, L. (2004). Expanding teacher roles: A resource for retention or a recipe for overwork? *Journal of Education Policy, 19*(5), 565–582.
Bates, F. L., & Harvey, C. C. (1975). *The structure of social systems.* New York, NY: Wiley and Sons.
Beauboeuf-Lafontant, T. (2002). A womanist experience of caring: Understanding the pedagogy of exemplary black women teachers. *The Urban Review, 34*(1), 71–86.
Bechky, B. A. (2006). Gaffers, gofers and grips: Role-based coordination in temporary organizations. *Organization Science, 17*(1), 3.
Berzin, S., & O'Connor, S. (2010). Educating today's school social workers: Are school social work courses responding to the changing context? *Children & Schools, 32*(4), 237–249.
*Bestor, A. E. (1955). *The restoration of learning: A program for redeeming the unfulfilled promise of American education.* New York, NY: Knopf.
Biddle, B. J. (1997). *Recent research on the role of the teacher* International Handbook of Teachers and Teaching (Part 1). Norwell, MA: Kluwer.
Biddle, B. J., & Berliner, D. C. (2002). Small class size and its effects. *Educational Leadership, 59*(5), 12–23.
Bidwell, C. E. (1965). The school as a formal organization. In J. G. March (Ed.), *Handbook of Organizations* (pp. 972–1022). Chicago, IL: Rand McNally.
Bidwell, C. E., Frank, K. A., & Quiroz, P. A. (1997). Teacher types, workplace controls and the organization of schools. *Sociology of Education, 70*(4), 285–307.
*Bill and Melinda Gates Foundation. (2010). Working with teachers to develop fair and reliable measures of effective teaching. Retrieved March 5, 2012, from http://www.metproject.org/downloads/met-framing-paper.pdf.

Bloom, H. S., & Unterman, R. (2012). Sustained positive effects on graduation rates produced by New York City's small public high schools of choice. New York, NY: MDRC.

Bolman, L. G., & Deal, T. E. (2008). *Reframing organizations: Artistry, choice, and leadership* (4th ed.). San Francisco, CA: Jossey-Bass.

Bolton, S. C., & Boyd, C. (2003). Trolley dolly or skilled emotion manager? Moving on from Hochschild's Managed Heart. *Work, Employment and Society, 17*(2), 289–308.

Brener, N. D., Weist, M. D., Adelman, H. S., Taylor, L., & Vernon-Smiley, M. (2007). Mental health and social services: Results from the school health policies and programs study 2006. *Journal of School Health, 77*(8), 486–499.

Brennan, K. (2006). The managed teacher: Emotional labour, education and technology. *Educational Insights, 10*(2). Retrieved from http://www.ccfi.educ.ubc.ca/publication/insights/v10n02/html/brennan/brennan.html.

Bridgeland, J. M., DiIulio, J. J., & Morison, K. B. (2006). *The silent epidemic: Perspectives of high school dropouts.* Washington, DC: Civic Enterprises.

Brotheridge, C. M., & Grandey, A. A. (2002). Emotional labor and burnout: Comparing two perspectives of "people work." *Journal of Vocational Behavior, 60*, 17–39.

Brotheridge, C. M., & Lee, R. T. (2002). Testing a conservation of resources model of the dynamics of emotional labor. *Journal of Occupational Health Psychology, 7*(1), 57–67.

Brown, E. L. (2011). Emotion matters: Exploring the emotional labor of teaching. (Unpublished doctoral dissertation), University of Pittsburgh, Pennsylvania.

Brown, K. M., & Anfara, V. A. (2001). Competing perspectives on advisory programs: Mingling or meddling in middle schools? *Research in middle level education annual, 24*, 1–30.

Bryk, A. S., Sebring, P. B., Allensworth, E., Luppescu, S., & Easton, J. Q. (2010). *Organizing schools for improvement: Lessons from Chicago.* Chicago, IL: University of Chicago Press.

Burke, P. J., & Stets, J. E. (2009). *Identity Theory.* New York, NY: Oxford.

Burke, R. W., & Paternite, C. E. (2007). Teacher engagement in expanded school mental health. *Report on Emotional and Behavioral Disorders in Youth, 7*(1), 3–4, 22–27.

Byrne, B. M. (1994). Burnout: Testing for the validity, replication, and invariance of causal structure across elementary, intermediate, and secondary teachers. *American Educational Research Journal, 31*(3), 645–673.

Cadiero-Kaplan, K., & Rodriguez, J. L. (2008). The preparation of highly qualified teachers for English language learners: Educational responsiveness for unmet needs. *Equity and Excellence in Education, 41*(3), 372–387.

*Carnegie Council on Adolescent Development. (1989). *Turning points: Preparing American youth for the 21st century.* New York, NY: Carnegie Corporation.

*Carnegie Foundation for the Advancement of Teaching. (1988). *Report card on school reform: The teachers speak.* Princeton, NJ: Carnegie Foundation for the Advancement of Teaching.

Cervantes, W. D., & Hernandez, D. J. (2011). Children in immigrant families: Ensuring opportunity for every child in America. First focus and foundation

for child development. Retrieved from http://www.firstfocus.net/sites/default/files/FCDImmigration.pdf.
Charmaz, K. (2006). *Constructing grounded theory: A practical guide through qualitative analysis*. Newbury Park, CA: Sage.
*Charters, W. W., & Waples, D. (1929). *The commonwealth teacher-training study*. Chicago, IL: University of Chicago Press.
Chicago Teachers Union (2012). Press release: CPS fails to negotiate fair contract to prevent first strike in 25 years. Retrieved from http://www.ctunet.com/blog/cps-fails-to-negotiate-fair-contract-to-prevent-first-labor-strike-in-25-years.
Coalition of Essential Schools. (2012). What we do. Retrieved March 15, 2012, from http://www.essentialschools.org/items/2.
Coburn, C. E. (2001). Collective sensemaking about reading: How teachers mediate reading policy in their professional communities. *Educational Evaluation and Policy Analysis, 23*(2), 145–170.
Coburn, C. E. (2005). Shaping teacher sensemaking: School leaders and the enactment of reading policy. *Educational Policy, 19*(3), 476–509.
Coburn, C. E., & Russell, J. L. (2008). District policy and teachers' social networks. *Educational Evaluation and Policy Analysis, 30*(3), 203–235.
Cohen, D. K., Raudenbush, S. W., & Ball, D. L. (2003). Resources, instruction and research. *Educational Evaluation and Policy Analysis, 25*(2), 1–24.
*Comer, J. P. (1995). *School power: Implications of an intervention project*. New York: Free Press.
*Commission on Teacher Education (1946). The improvement of teacher education. In M. L. Borrowman (Ed.), *Teacher education in America: A documentary history* (pp. 224–251). New York, NY: Teachers College Press.
*Committee on Secondary School Studies. (1892). *Report of the committee of ten on secondary school studies*. Washington, DC: National Education Association.
*Conant, J. B. (1958). *The American high school today*. New York, NY: McGraw-Hill.
———. (1963). *The education of American teachers*. New York, NY: McGraw-Hill.
Cook, B. G. (2004). Inclusive teachers' attitudes toward their students with disabilities: a replication and extension. *The Elementary School Journal, 104*(4), 307–320.
Copeland, M. (2005). *Socratic circles: Fostering critical and creative thinking*. Portland, MN: Stenhouse Publishers.
Cotton, K. (1996). *School size, school climate and student performance*. Portland, OR: Northwest Regional Educational Laboratory.
———. (2001). *New small learning communities: Findings from recent literature*. Portland, OR: Northwest Regional Educational Lab.
Council on Foreign Relations Task Force (2012). *u.s. education reform and national security*. Washington, DC: Council on Foreign Relations. Retrieved from http://www.cfr.org/united-states/us-education-reform-national-security/p27618.
*Covello, L. (1958). *The heart is the teacher*. New York, NY: McGraw-Hill.
*Cremin, L. A. (1964). *The transformation of the school: Progressivism in American education, 1876–1957*. New York, NY: Random House, Inc., Vintage Books Edition.
Crosnoe, R., Johnson, M. K., & Elder, G. H. (2004). School size and the interpersonal side of education: An examination of race/ethnicity and organizational context. *Social Science Quarterly, 85*(5), 1259–1274.

Crosnoe, R., Morrison, F., Burchinal, M., Pianta, R., Keating, D., Friedman, S. L., et al. (2010). Instruction, teacher–student relations, and math achievement trajectories in elementary school. *Journal of Educational Psychology, 102*(2), 407–417.

Cuban, L. (2010). *As good as it gets: What school reform brought to Austin.* Cambridge, MA: Harvard University Press.

*Cubberley, E. (1909). *Changing conceptions of education.* Boston, MA: Houghton-Mifflin.

Cushman, K. (1990). Are advisory groups "essential"? What they do, how they work. *Horace, 7*(1). Retrieved from http://www.essentialschools.org/resources/4.

Cusick, P. A. (1992). *The educational system: Its nature and logic.* New York: McGraw-Hill.

*Darling-Hammond, L. (1997). *Doing what matters most: Investing in quality teaching.* New York, NY: National Commission for Teaching and America's Future.

Darling-Hammond, L. (2010). *The flat world and education: How America's commitment to equity will determine our future.* New York, NY: Teachers College Press.

David, J. L. (2008). Small learning communities. *Educational Leadership, 65*(8), 84–85.

Deschenes, S. S., Cuban, L., & Tyack, D. B. (2001). Mismatch: Historical perspectives on schools and students who don't fit them. *Teachers College Record, 103*(4), 525–547.

*Dewey, J. (1916). *Democracy and Education.* New York, NY: Macmillan.

Diefendorff, J. M., Croyle, M., & Gosserand, R. H. (2005). The dimensionality and antecedents of emotional labor strategies. *Journal of Vocational Behavior, 66*(2), 339–357.

Diefendorff, J. M., & Richard, E. M. (2003). Antecedents and consequences of emotional display rule perception. *Journal of Applied Psychology, 88*(2), 284–294.

Diefendorff, J. M., Richard, E. M., & Croyle, M. H. (2006). Are emotional display rules formal job requirements? Examination of employee and supervisor perceptions. *Journal of Occupational Psychology, 79*(2), 273–298.

*Dill, V. S., & Stafford-Johnson, D. (2001). Belief-based screening: How to find uncompromising quality in a time of teacher shortage. In *Why alternative teacher certification programs are uniquely designed to meet the needs of at-risk students.* Houston, TX: The Haberman Educational Foundation. Retrieved February 22, 2012, from http://www.altcert.org/Articles/Default.aspx?id=49.

*Dryfoos, J. G., Quinn, J., & Barkin, C. (Eds.). (2005). *Community schools in action: Lessons from a decade of practice.* New York, NY: Oxford University Press.

*Edson, A. W. (1896). Legitimate work of a state normal school. *Education, 16,* 274–277.

EdSource. (2012). Charter school history and policy. Retrieved March 20, 2012, from http://www.edsource.org/iss_charter_policy.html.

*Educational Policies Commission. (1944). *Education for all American youth.* Washington, DC: National Education Association.

Eisenhardt, K. M. (1989). Building theories from case study research. *Academy of Management Review, 14*(4), 532–550.

Ellis, R. (2012). Chicago strike reveals a broken system. *NBC News.* Retrieved from http://usnews.nbcnews.com/_news/2012/09/20/13991699-chicago-strike-reveals-a-broken-system?lite.

Elmore, R. (2004). *School reform practice from the inside out: Policy, practice and performance.* Cambridge, MA: Harvard Education Press.

*Elsbree, W. (1939). *The American teacher: Evolution of a profession in a democracy.* New York, NY: American Book Company.

*Evenden, E. S. (1933). *National survey of the education of teachers: Summary and interpretation.* Washington DC: Department of the Interior, Office of Education.

Fantuzzo, J. W., LeBoeuf, W. A., Chen, C.-C., Rouse, H. L., & Culhane, D. P. (2012). The unique and combined effects of homelessness and school mobility on the educational outcomes of young children. *Educational Researcher, 41*(9), 393–402.

Fine, M. (1991). *Framing dropouts: Notes on the politics of an urban public high school.* Albany, NY: State University of New York Press.

Firestone, W. A., & Louis, K. S. (1999). Schools as cultures. In J. Murphy & K. S. Louis (Eds.), *Handbook of research on educational administration* (2nd ed., pp. 297–322). San Francisco, CA: Jossey-Bass.

Firestone, W. A., & Rosenblum, S. (1988). Building commitment in urban high schools. *Educational Evaluation and Policy Analysis, 10*(4), 285–299.

*Flexner, A. (1916). The modern school. *American Review of Reviews, 53,* 465–474.

*Ford Foundation. (1972). *A foundation goes to school: The Ford Foundation comprehensive school improvement program.* New York, NY: Ford Foundation.

Forlin, C. (2001). Inclusion: Identifying potential stressors for regular class teachers. *Educational Research, 43*(3), 235–245.

Franklin, C., Kim, J. S., Ryan, T. N., Kelly, M. S., & Montgomery, K. L. (2012). Teacher involvement in school mental health interventions: A systematic review. *Children and Youth Services Review, 34*(5), 973–982.

Fraser, J. W. (2007). *Preparing America's teachers: A history.* New York, NY: Teachers College Press.

Freedberg, L. (2012). Pioneered in California, publishing teacher "effectiveness" rankings draws more criticism. *EdSource.* Retrieved from http://www.edsource.org/today/2012/pioneered-in-california-publishing-teacher-effectiveness-rankings-draws-more-criticism/6732#.UMdURY7Ocvg.

Frey, A. J., & Dupper, D. R. (2005). A broader conceptual approach to clinical practice for the 21st century. *Children and Schools, 27*(1), 33–44.

Fry, R. (2005). *The high schools Hispanics attend: Size and other key characteristics.* Washington, DC: Pew Hispanic Center.

Galassi, J. P., Gulledge, S. A., & Cox, N. D. (1997). Middle school advisories: Retrospect and prospect. *Review of Educational Research, 67*(3), 310–338.

Gallucci, C., Van Lare, M., Yoon, I. H., & Boatright, B. (2010). Instructional coaching: Building theory about the role and organizational support for professional learning. *American Educational Research Journal, 47*(4), 919–963.

Garza, R. (2009). Latino and white high school students' perceptions of caring behaviors. *Urban Education, 44*(3), 297–321.

*Gay, G. (2010). *Culturally responsive teaching* (2nd ed.). New York, NY: Teachers College Press.

Gewertz, C. (2007). An advisory advantage. *Education Week, 26*(26), 22–25.

Giddens, A. (1984). *The constitution of society: Outline of the theory of structuration.* Cambridge, UK: Polity Press.

Gill, A. (Producer) (2012). Afternoon Shift #139, Interview with Chicago Teachers Union president Karen Lewis, August 31, 2012. Chicago, IL: WBEZ. Retrieved from http://www.wbez.org/results?s=Afternoon%20shift%20Karen%20Lewis%20August%2031.

*Goodman, P. (1964). *Compulsory mis-education*. New York, NY: Horizon.

Grant, G. (1988). *The world we created at Hamilton High*. Cambridge, MA: Harvard University Press.

*Greene, M. (1988). *The dialectic of freedom*. New York, NY: Teachers College Press.

Grossman, P., Compton, C., Shahan, E., Ronfeldt, M., Igra, D., & Shaing, J. (2007). Preparing practitioners to respond to resistance: A cross professional view. *Teachers and teaching: Theory and Practice, 13*(2), 109–123.

Haberman, M. (2005). *Star teachers: The ideology and best practice of effective teachers of diverse children and youth in poverty*. Houston, TX: Haberman Educational Foundation.

*Halleck, R. P., Brown, J. S., Brooks, S. D., Nightingale, A. F., & Brown, J. F. (1905). What constitutes the ideal secondary teacher? *The Education and Training of Secondary Teachers, National Society of the Study of Education Yearbook, 4*(1), 27–48.

Hamre, B. K., Pianta, R. C., Burchinal, M., Field, S., LoCasale-Crouch, J., Downer, J. T., et al. (2012). a course on effective teacher-child interactions. *American Educational Research Journal, 49*(1), 88–123.

Hargreaves, A. (2000). Mixed emotions: Teachers' perceptions of their interactions with students. *Teaching and Teacher Education, 16*, 811–826.

———. (2001). Emotional geographies of teaching. *Teachers College Record, 103*(6), 1056–1080.

Harris, D. N. (2006). *Ending the blame game on educational inequity: A study of "high flying" schools and NCLB*. Tempe, AZ: Education Policy Research Unit.

Hemphill, C., & Nauer, K. (2009). *The new marketplace: How small-school reforms and school choice have reshaped New York City's high schools*. New York: Center for New York City Affairs.

Herbst, J. (1989). Teacher preparation in the nineteenth century: Institutions and purposes. In D. Warren (Ed.), *American teachers: Histories of a profession at work* (pp. 213–236). New York, NY: Macmillan.

*Hess, F. M. (2002). *Tear down this wall: The case for a radical overhaul of teacher certification*. H. W. Wilson Company, 169–183. Retrieved February 22, 2012, from http://vnweb.hwwilsonweb.com.flagship.luc.edu/hww/results/external_link_maincontentframe.jhtml?_DARGS=/hww/results/results_common.jhtml.44.

Hochschild, A. R. (1983/2003). *The managed heart: Commercialization of human feeling* (2nd ed.). Berkeley, CA: University of California Press.

Hoffman, M. (1996). *Chasing hellhounds: A teacher learns from his students*. Minneapolis, MN: Milkweed Editions.

*Hollingshead, A. B., & University of Chicago. (1949). *Elmtown's youth: The impact of social classes on adolescents*. New York, NY: J. Wiley.

Holme, J. J., & Rangel, V. S. (2012). Putting school reform in its place. *American Educational Research Journal, 49*(2), 257–283.

*Holmes Group. (1986). *Tomorrow's teachers: A report of the Holmes Group*. East Lansing, MI: Holmes Group, Inc.

*Holmes, M. J. (1905). The present provision for the education and training of secondary teachers in the United States. *The Education and Training of Secondary Teachers, National Society of the Study of Education Yearbook, 4*(1), p. 63–82.

Hurn, C. (1985). Changes in authority relationships in schools: 1960–1980. In A. C. Kerckhoff (Ed.), *Research in Sociology of Education and Socialization* (Vol. 5, pp. 123–169). Greenwich, CT: JAI.

Iatarola, P., Stiefel, L., Schwartz, A. E., & Chellman, C. C. (2008). Small schools, large districts: Small-school reform and New York City's students. *Teachers College Record, 110*(9), 1837–1878.

Idol, L. (2006). Toward inclusion of special education students in general education. *Remedial & Special Education, 27*(2), 77–94.

Ingersoll, R. M. (2001). *Teacher turnover, teacher shortages and the organization of schools*. Seattle, WA: Center for the Study of Teaching and Policy.

———. (2003). *Who controls teachers' work? Power and accountability in America's schools*. Cambridge, MA: Harvard University Press.

Ingersoll, R. M, & Merrill, L. (2012). *Seven trends: The transformation of the teaching force*. Paper presented at the annual meeting of the American Educational Research Association.

Ingersoll, R. M., & Perda, D. (2010). Is the supply of mathematics and science teachers sufficient? *American Educational Research Journal, 47*(3), 563–594.

Jackson, P. W. (1990). *Life in classrooms* (2nd ed.). New York: Teachers College Press.

James, J. H. (2010). Teachers as mothers in the elementary classroom: Negotiating the needs of self and other. *Gender and Education, 22*(5), 521–534.

Jennings, J., & Rentner, D. S. (2006). Ten big effects of the No Child Left Behind Act on public schools. *Phi Delta Kappan, 88*(2), 110–113.

Jennings, J. L. (2010). School choice or school's choice? Managing in an era of accountability. *Sociology of Education, 83*(3), 227–247.

Johnson, S. M., & Kardos, S. M. (2008). The next generation of teachers: Who enters, who stays and why. In M. Cochran-Smith, S. Feinman-Nemser, D. J. McIntyre, & K. Demers (Eds.), *Handbook of research on teacher education: Enduring questions in changing contexts* (pp. 445–467). New York, NY: Routledge.

Johnson, S. M., & Landman, J. (2000). "Sometimes bureaucracy has its charms": The working conditions of teachers in deregulated schools. *Teachers College Record, 102*(1), 85–124.

Johnson, S. M., & the Project on the Next Generation of Teachers. (2004). *Finders and keepers: Helping new teachers survive and thrive in our schools*. San Francisco, CA: Jossey Bass.

Judge, T. A., Woolf, E. F., & Hurst, C. (2009). Is emotional labor more difficult for some than for others? A multilevel, experience-sampling study. *Personnel Psychology, 62*(1), 57–88.

Kafka, Judith. (2008). Thinking big about getting small: An ideological geneaology of small-school reform. *Teachers College Record, 110*(9), 1802–1836.

Kahne, J. E., Sporte, S. E., de La Torre, M., & Easton, J. Q. (2008). Small high schools on a larger scale: The impact of school conversions in Chicago. *Educational Evaluation and Policy Analysis, 30*(3), 281–315.

Katzenmeyer, M., & Moller, G. (2001). *Awakening the sleeping giant: Helping teachers develop as leaders*. Newbury Park, CA: Corwin Press.

Kelly, M. S., Berzin, S., Frey, A., Alvarez, M., Shaffer, G., & O'Brien, K. (2010). The state of school social work: Findings from the National School Social Work Survey. *School Mental Health, 2*(3), 132–141.

Kelly, M. S., & Lueck, C. (2011). Adopting a data-driven public health framework in schools: Results from a multi-disciplinary survey on school-based mental health practice. *Advances in School Mental Health Promotion, 4*(4), 5–11.

*Kidder, T. (1989). *Among schoolchildren*. Boston, MA: Houghton Mifflin Co.

*Kilgore, S. B. (2003). *Guiding principles of the modern red schoolhouse design: Research-based solutions for 21st century schools*. Modern Red SchoolHouse Institute. Retrieved February 22, 2012, from http://mrsh.org/pdf/Guiding%20Principles%204.28.06.pdf.

*Kilpatrick, W. H. (1922). The project method: The use of the purposeful act in the educative process. New York, NY: Teachers College Bulletin.

Kim, H. J. (2008). Hotel service providers' emotional labor: The antecedents and effects on burnout. *International Journal of Hospitality Management, 27*(2), 151–161.

Kirkpatrick, M. G. (1917). *The rural school from within*. Philadelphia, PA: J. B. Lippincott Company.

Klonsky, M. (2000). Remembering Port Huron. In M. Klonsky, W. Ayers, & G. H. Lyon (Eds.), *A simple justice: The challenge of small schools* (pp. 23–32). New York, NY: Teachers College Press.

*Koerner, J. D. (1963). *The miseducation of American teachers*. Boston, MA: Houghton Mifflin.

*Kohl, H. (1967). *36 Children*. New York, NY: Signet.

———. (1984). *Growing minds*. New York, NY: Harper & Row.

*Koller, J. R., & Bertel J. M. (2006). Responding to today's mental health needs of children, families and schools: Revisiting the preservice training and preparation of school-based personnel. *Education and Treatment of Children, 29*(2), 197–217.

Konstantopoulos, S. (2012). Teacher effects: Past, present and future. In S. Kelly (Ed.), *Assessing teacher quality: Understanding teacher effects on instruction and achievement* (pp. 7–32). New York, NY: Teachers College Press.

*Kopp, W. (2001). *One day, all children: The unlikely triumph of Teach for America and what I learned along the way*. New York: PublicAffairs.

Kumashiro, K. K. (2012). *Bad teacher! How blaming teachers distorts the bigger picture*. New York, NY: Teachers College Press

Labaree, D. F. (2008). An uneasy relationship: The history of teacher education in the university. In M. Cochran-Smith, S. Feinman-Nemser, D. J. McIntyre, & K. Demers (Eds.), *Handbook of research on teacher education: Enduring questions in changing contexts* (pp. 290–306). New York, NY: Routledge.

Labaree, D. F. (2010). *Someone has to fail: The zero-sum game of public schooling*. Cambridge, MA: Harvard University Press.

Lawrence, B. K., Abramson, P., Bergsagel, V., Bingler, S., Diamond, B., Greene, T. J., et al. (2006). *Dollars and sense II: Lessons from good, cost-effective small schools*. Cincinnati, OH: KnowledgeWorks Foundation.

*Learned, W. S., & Bagley, W. C. (1919). *The professional preparation of teachers for American public schools*. New York, NY: The Carnegie Foundation for the Advancement of Teaching.

Lee, V. E., Bryk, A. S., & Smith, J. B. (1993). The organization of effective secondary schools. *Review of Research in Education, 19*, 171–267.

Lee, V. E., & Ready, D. D. (2007). *Schools within schools: Possibilities and pitfalls of high school reform.* New York: Teachers College Press.

Lee, V. E., & Smith, J. B. (1997). High school size: Which works best and for whom? *Educational Evaluation and Policy Analysis, 19*(3), 205–227.

———. (1999). Social support and achievement for young adolescents in Chicago: The role of school academic press. *American Educational Research Journal, 36*(4), 907–945.

*Lemov, D. (2010). *Teach like a champion: 49 techniques that put students on the path to college.* San Francisco, CA: Jossey-Bass.

*Lessinger, L. M. (1970). *Every kid a winner: Accountability in education.* New York, NY: Simon and Schuster.

*Levine, A. (2006). Educating school teachers. The education schools project. Retrieved March 5, 2012, from http://www.edschools.org/pdf/Educating_Teachers_Report.pdf.

Linton, R. (1936). *The study of man.* New York, NY: Appleton-Century.

Lortie, D. C. (2002). *Schoolteacher: A sociological study* (2nd ed.). Chicago, IL: University of Chicago Press.

Lucas, T., & Grinberg, J. (2008). Responding to the linguistic reality of mainstream classrooms: Preparing all teachers to teach English language learners. In M. Cochran-Smith, S. Feinman-Nemser, D. J. McIntyre, & K. Demers (Eds.), *Handbook of research on teacher education: Enduring questions in changing contexts* (3rd ed., pp. 606–636). New York, NY: Routledge.

*Lynd, R. S., & Lynd, H. M. (1929). *Middletown: A study in modern American culture.* New York, NY: Harcourt, Brace, & World.

MacDonald, V. M. (2004). *Latino education in the United States: A narrated history from 1513–2000.* New York, NY: Palgrave Macmillan.

*Macintosh, H. K., Gore, L., & Lewis, G. M. (1965). *Educating disadvantaged children in the middle grades.* Washington, DC: Office of Education.

Mangin, M. M. (2009). Literacy coach role implementation: How district context influences reform efforts. *Educational Administration Quarterly, 45*(5), 759–792.

Mangin, M. M., & Stoelinga, S. R. (2011). Peer? Expert? Teacher leaders struggle to gain trust while establishing their expertise. *Journal of Staff Development, 32*(3), 48–51.

Martin, J. (1992). *Cultures in organizations: Three perspectives.* New York, NY: Oxford University Press.

Martinez-Iñigo, D., Totterdell, P., Alcover, C. M., & Holman, D. (2007). Emotional labour and emotional exhaustion: Interpesonal and intrapersonal mechanisms. *Work & Stress, 21*(1), 30–47.

Maslach, C., Jackson, S. E., & Schwab, R. L. (1996). Maslach burnout inventory—educators survey. In C. Maslach, S. E. Jackson, & M. P. Leiter (Eds.), *Maslach burnout inventory manual.* Mountain View, CA: Consulting Psychologists Press, Inc.

*Mathews, J. (2009). *Work hard. Be nice: How two inspired teachers created the most promising schools in America.* Chapel Hill, NC: Algonquin Books of Chapel Hill.

Mawhinney, H.B., & Smrekar, C.E. (1996). Negotiating the institutional constraints in school/community collaborations. *Educational Policy, 10*(4), 480–501.

McDonald, M.A., Bowman, M., & Brayko, K. (2013). Learning to see students: Opportunities to develop relational practices through community-based placements in teacher education. *Techers College Record, 115*(4). doi: http://www.tcrecord.org/library ID Number: 16916

*Meier, D. (2002). *The power of their ideas: Lessons for American from a small school in Harlem* (2nd ed.). Boston, MA: Beacon Press.

Merriam, S. B. (2009). *Qualitative research*. San Francisco, CA: Jossey-Bass.

Mesmer-Magnus, J. R., DeChurch, L. A., & Wax, A. (2012). Moving emotional labor beyond surface and deep acting: A discordance-congruence perspective. *Organizational Psychology Review, 2*(1), 6–53.

*Michie, G. (2009). *Holler if you hear me: The education of a teacher and his students* (2nd ed.). New York, NY: Teachers College Press.

Miles, M. B., & Huberman, A. M. (1994). *Qualitative data analysis: An expanded sourcebook*. Thousand Oaks, CA: Sage Publications.

Miller, P. M. (2011). a critical analysis of the research on student homelessness. *Review of Educational Research, 81*(3), 308–337.

Mintz, S. (2006). *Huck's raft: A history of American childhood*. Cambridge, MA: Belknap Press of Harvard University Press.

Mitra, D. L. (2004). The significance of students: Can increasing student voice in schools lead to gains in youth development? *Teachers College Record, 106*(4), 651–688.

Mohr, N. (2000). Small schools are not miniature large schools: Potential pitfalls and implications for leadership. In M. Klonsky, W. Ayers, & G. H. Lyon (Eds.), *A simple justice: The challenge of small schools* (pp. 139–158). New York, NY: Teachers College Press.

Murphy, J. (2005). *Connecting teacher leadership and school improvement*. Thousand Oaks, CA: Corwin Press.

Naring, G., Briet, M., & Brouwers, A. (2006). Beyond demand-control: Emotional labour and symptoms of burnout in teachers. *Work & Stress, 20*(4), 303–315.

*National Board for Professional Teaching Standards. (2002). What teachers should know and be able to do. Retrieved February 22, 2012, from http://www.nbpts.org/UserFiles/File/what_teachers.pdf.

National Center for Education Statistics. (2009). *Characteristics of the 100 largest public elementary and secondary school districts in the United States: 2006–2007* (No. NCES 2008-339). Washington, DC: Institute of Education Sciences.

*National Commission for Teaching & America' s Future. (1996). *What matters most: Teaching for America's future. Report of the National Commission on Teaching & America's Future*. New York, NY: National Commission on Teaching & America's Future.

*National Commission on Education. (1983). *A nation at risk: The imperative for educational reform*. Retrieved March 5, 2012, from http://www2ed.gov/pubs/NatAtRisk/index.html.

*National Commission on Teacher Education and Professional Standards. (1956). *The professional standards movement in teaching: Progress and projection*. Report of the Parkland Conference, Pacific Lutheran College, Parkland, Washington. Washington, DC: National Education Association of the United States.

———. (1966). *The real world of the beginning teacher*. Washington, DC: National Educational Association.

National Council on the Accreditation of Teacher Education (2010a). The road less traveled: How the developmental sciences can prepare educators to improve student achievement. Washington, DC: Author.

*National Council for Accreditation of Teacher Education. (2010b). Transforming teacher education through clinical practice: A national strategy to prepare effective teachers: Report of the Blue Ribbon Panel on Clinical Preparation and Partnership for Improved Student Learning. Washington, DC: National Council for Accreditation of Teacher Education.

*National Education Association. (1975). Code of ethics of the education profession. Retrieved from http://www.nea.org/aboutnea/code.html.

National Middle School Association. (1995). *This we believe: Developmentally responsive middle level schools*. Columbus, OH: Author.

*National Teacher Corps. (1966). *The national teacher corps:—To reach and teach the children of poverty*. Washington, DC: US Office of Education.

Newmann, F. M. (1981). Reducing student alienation in high schools: Implications of theory. *Harvard Educational Review, 51*(4), 546–564.

Newmann, F. M., Smith, B., Allensworth, E., & Bryk, A. S. (2001). *School instructional program coherence: Benefits and challenges*. Chicago, IL: Chicago Consortium on School Research.

Nieto, S. (2000). A gesture toward justice: Small schools and the promise of equal education. In W. Ayers, M. Klonsky, & G. Lyon (Eds.), *A simple justice: The challenge of small schools*. (pp. 13–17). New York: Teachers College Press.

*Nyquist, E. B., & Hawes, G. R. (1972). *Open education: A sourcebook for parents and teachers*. New York, NY: Bantam Books.

Oplatka, I. (2007). Managing emotions in teaching: Toward an understanding of emotion displays and caring as nonprescribed role elements. *Teachers College Record, 109*(6), 1374–1400.

———. (2011). Emotion management and display in teaching: Some ethical and moral considerations in the era of marketization and commercialization. In P. A. Schutz & M. Zembylas (Eds.), *Advances in teacher emotion research* (pp. 55–71). New York, NY: Springer.

Oxley, D., & McCabe, J. G. (1990). *Restructuring neighborhood high schools: The house plan solution*. New York, NY: Public Education Association and Bank Street College of Education.

Chhandasi, P., Batalova, J., & McHugh, M. (2011). Limited English proficient individuals in the United States: Number, share, growth, and linguistic diversity." Washington, DC: Migration Policy Institute. Retrieved from http://www.migrationinformation.org/integration/LEPdatabrief.pdf

Parsons, T. (1951). *The Social System*. Glencoe, IL: Free Press.

Paternite, C. E., & Johnston, T. (2005). Rationale and strategies for central involvement of educators in effective school-based mental health programs. *Journal of Youth and Adolescence, 34*(1), 41–49.

Payne, C. M. (2008). *So much reform, so little change: The persistence of failure in urban schools*. Cambridge, MA: Harvard Education Press.

Payton, J., Weissberg, R. P., Durlak, J. A., Dymnicki, A. B., Taylor, R. D., Schellinger, K. B., et al. (2008). The positive impact of social and emotional learning for kindergarten to eighth-grade students: Findings from three scientific reviews. Chicago, IL: CASEL.
Pettegrew, L. S., & Wolf, G. E. (1982). Validating measures of teacher stress. *American Educational Research Journal, 19*(3), 373–396.
Phillippo, K. L. (2012). "You're trying to know me": Students from nondominant groups respond to teacher personalism. *Urban Review, 44*(4), 441–467.
Phillippo, K. L., & Kelly, M. S. (2011). Shared language or distant dialects? Opportunities and challenges in connecting school-based mental health services to unique school environments. Paper presented at the 2011 Annual Conference on Advancing School Mental Health.
Phillippo, K. L., & Stone, S. I. (2011). Towards a broader view: A call to integrate knowledge about schools into school social work research. *Children & Schools, 33*(2), 71–81.
———. (in press). Teacher role breadth and its relationship to student-reported teacher support. *High School Journal*.
Piliavin, J. A., Grube, J. A., & Callero, P. L. (2002). Role as resource for action in public service. *Journal of Social Issues, 58*(3), 469–485.
Poliner, R. A., & Lieber, C. M. (2004). The advisory guide: Designing and implementing effective advisory programs in secondary schools. Cambridge, MA: Educators for Social Responsibility.
*Proefriedt, W. A. (1975). *The teacher you choose to be*. New York, NY: Holt, Rinehart and Winston.
Quint, J. (2006). Meeting five critical challenges of high school reform. New York: MDRC.
Rafaeli, A., & Sutton, R. I. (1987). Expression of emotion as part of the work role. *Academy of Management Review, 12*(1), 23–37.
*Raubinger, F. M., Piper, D. L., Rowe, H. G., & West, C. K. (Eds.). (1969). *The development of secondary education*. New York, NY: Macmillan.
*Ravitz, M. (1963). The role of the school in the urban setting. In A. H. Passow (Ed.), *Education in depressed areas*. New York, NY: Teachers College Press.
Raywid, M. A., & Oshiyama, L. (2000). Musings in the wake of Columbine: What can schools do? *Phi Delta Kappan, 81*(6), 444–449.
Reagans, R. (2011). Close encounters: Analyzing how social similarity and propinquity contribute to strong network connections. *Organization Science, 22*(4), 835–849.
Reyers, A., & Matusitz, J. (2012). Emotional regulation at Walt Disney World: An impression management view. *Journal of Workplace Behavioral Health, 27*(3), 139–159.
*Richman, J. M. (1910). A social need of the public school. *Forum, 43*, 161–169.
*Riis, J. (1902). *The battle with the slum*. New York, NY: The Macmillen Company.
Robinson, J. P., & Espelage, D. L. (2011). Inequities in educational and psychological outcomes between LGBTQ and straight students in middle and high school. *Educational Researcher, 40*(7), 315–330.
Robinson, J. P., & Espelage, D. L. (2012). Bullying explains only part of lgbtq-heterosexual risk disparities: Implications for policy and practice. *Educational Researcher, 41*(8), 309–319.

Roeser, R. W., & Midgley, C. (1997). Teachers' views of issues involving students' mental health. *The Elementary School Journal, 98*(2), 115–133.

Rolón-Dow, R. (2005). Critical care: A color(full) analysis of care narratives in the schooling experiences of Puerto Rican girls. *American Educational Research Journal, 42*(1), 77–111.

Roorda, D. L., Koomen, H. M. Y., Spilt, J. L., & Oort, F. J. (2011). The influence of affective teacher-student relationships on students' school engagement and achievement. *Review of Educational Research, 81*(4), 493–529.

Rothstein, R. (2004). *Class and schools: Using social, economic, and educational reform to close the black-white achievement gap.* Washington, DC: Economic Policy Institute.

Rothstein, R. (2012). *Teacher accountability and the Chicago teachers strike.* Retrieved from http://www.epi.org/blog/teacher-accountability-chicago-teachers/.

Rury, J. L. (2008). *Education and social change: Contours in the history of American schooling.* London: Routledge.

Santos, F., & Otterman, S. (2012). City teacher data reports are released. *New York Times.* Retrieved from http://www.nytimes.com/schoolbook/2012/02/24/teacher-data-reports-are-released.

Sarason, S. B. (1996). *Revisiting "The culture of the school and the problem of change."* New York: Teachers College Press.

Schein, E. H. (1992). *Organizational culture and leadership* (2nd ed.). San Francisco, CA: Jossey-Bass.

Sedlak, M. W. (1997). The uneasy alliance of mental health services and the schools: An historical perspective. *American Journal of Orthopsychiatry, 67*(3), 349–362.

Sedlak, M. W. (2008). Competing visions of purpose, practice and policy: The history of teacher certification in the United States. In M. Cochran-Smith, S. Feinman-Nemser, D. J. McIntyre, & K. Demers (Eds.), *Handbook of research on teacher education: Enduring questions in changing contexts* (pp. 855–885). New York, NY: Routledge.

Semel, S. F. (1992). *The Dalton School: The transformation of a progressive school.* New York City: Peter Lang Publishing.

Semel, S. F., & Sadovnik, A. (2008). The contemporary small-school movement: Lessons from the history of progressive education. *Teachers College Record, 110*(9), 1744–1771.

Sewell, W. H. (1992). A theory of structure: Duality, agency and transformation. *American Journal of Sociology, 98*, 1–29.

Sewell, W. H. (2005). *Logics of history: Social theory and social transformation.* Chicago, IL: University of Chicago Press.

Shiller, J. T. (2009). "These are our children!" An examination of relationship-building practices in urban high schools. *The Urban Review, 41*(5), 1573–1960.

Sizer, T. R. (1992). *Horace's compromise: The dilemma of the American high school.* Boston, MA: Houghton Mifflin.

*Slavin, R. E. (1994). "Whenever and wherever we choose": The replication of Success for All. *Phi Delta Kappan, 75*(8), 639–640, 642–647.

Smylie, M. A. (1992). Teacher participation in school decision making: Assessing willingness to participate. *Educational Evaluation and Policy Analysis, 14*(1), 53–67.

Smylie, M. A., & Denny, J. W. (1990). Teacher leadership: Tensions and ambiguities in organizational perspective. *Educational Administration Quarterly, 26*(3), 235–259.

Song, J. (2010). Teachers blast L.A. Times for releasing effectiveness rankings. *Los Angeles Times*. Retrieved from http://articles.latimes.com/2010/aug/30/local/la-me-teacher-react-20100830.

*Special Studies Project Panel. (1958). *The pursuit of excellence: Education and the future of America*. Garden City, NY: Doubleday.

Spillane, J. P. (2004). *Standards deviation: How schools misunderstand education policy*. Cambridge, MA: Harvard University Press.

Spillane, J. P., Pairse, L. M., & Sherer, J. Z. (2011). Organizational routines as coupling mechanisms: Policy, school administration, and the technical core. *American Educational Research Journal, 48*(3), 586–619.

Spindler, G., & Spindler, L. (1987). *Interpretive ethnography of education: At home and abroad*. Hillsdale, NJ: Erlbaum Associates.

Sporte, S. E., & de la Torre, M. (2010). *Chicago High School redesign initiative: Schools, students and outcomes*. Chicago, IL: Chicago Consortium on School Research.

Stanton-Salazar, R. D. (1997). A social capital framework for understanding the socialization of racial minority children and youths. *Harvard Educational Review, 67*(1), 1–40.

Stanton-Salazar, R.D. (2011). A social capital framework for the study of institutional agents and their role in the empowerment of low-status students and youth. *Youth & Society, 43*(3), 1066–1109.

Strike, K. A. (2010). *Small schools and strong communities: a third way of school reform*. New York, NY: Teachers College Press.

Swain, K. D., Nordness, P. D., & Leader-Janssen, E. M. (2012). Changes in preservice teacher attitudes toward inclusion. *Preventing School Failure: Alternative Education for Children and Youth, 56*(2), 75–81.

Swidler, A. (1979). *Organization without authority: Dilemmas of social control in free schools*. Cambridge, MA: Harvard University Press.

*Task Force on Teaching as a Profession. (1986). *A nation prepared: Teachers for the 21st century*. New York, NY: Carnegie Forum on Education and the Economy.

Taylor, S. J., & Bogdan, R. (1998). *Introduction to qualitative research methods* (3rd ed.). New York: John Wiley and Sons.

Thomas, E., & Wingert, P. (2010, March 6). Why we must fire bad teachers. *Newsweek*.

Thompson, A. (1998). Not the color purple: Black feminist lessons for educational caring. *Harvard Educational Review, 68*(4), 522–554.

Tocci, C., & Allen, D. (N.D.). *Key dimensions in advisory programs* (No. 2). New York, NY: National Center for the Restructuring Education, Schools and Teaching.

*Tompkins, A. (1894). *The philosophy of teaching*. Boston, MA: Gin & Company.

Tsang, K. K. (2011). Emotional labor of teaching. *Educational Research, 2*(8), 1312–1316.

Tschannen-Moran, M., Woolfolk Hoy, A., & Hoy, W. K. (1998). Teacher efficacy: Its meaning and measure. *Review of Educational Research, 68*(2), 202–248.

Turner, R. H. (1990). Role change. *Annual Review of Sociology, 16*, 87–110.
Tyack, D. B. (1974). *The one best system: A history of American urban education*. Cambridge, MA: Harvard University Press.
Tyack, D. B., & Cuban, L. (1995). *Tinkering toward utopia: A century of public school reform*. Cambridge, MA: Harvard University Press.
*US Department of Education. (2001). Title 1—Improving the academic achievement of the disadvantaged. Retrieved February 22, 2012, from http://www2.ed.gov/policy/elsec/leg/esea02/pg1.html.
———. (2006). *The secretary's fifth annual report on teacher quality: A highly qualified teacher in every classroom*. Washington, DC: US Department of Education, Office of Postsecondary Education.
———. (2009). Race to the top executive summary. Retrieved February 5, 2012, from http://www2.ed.gov/programs/racetothetop/executive-summary.pdf.
———. (2010). *ESEA reauthorization, a blueprint for reform*. Washington, DC: US Department of Education.
US Department of Education. (2011). Our future, our teachers: The Obama admnistration's plan for teacher education reform and improvement. Washington, DC: US Department of Education.
*US National Commission on Excellence in Education. (1983). *Nation at risk: The imperative for educational reform*. Retrieved March 5, 2012, from http://www2.ed.gov/pubs/NatAtRisk/risk.html.
*US Office of Education (1948). *Life adjustment education for every youth*. Washington, DC: Federal Security Agency, Office of Education, Division of Secondary Education, and Division of Vocational Education.
Valenzuela, A. (1999). *Subtractive schooling: U.S. Mexican youth and the politics of caring*. Albany, NY: State University of New York Press.
Valli, L., & Buese, D. (2007). The changing roles of teachers in an era of high-stakes accountability. *American Educational Research Journal, 44*(3), 519–558.
Valli, L., Croninger, R. G., Chambliss, M. H., Graever, A. O., & Buese, D. (2008). *Test driven: High-stakes accountability in elementary schools*. New York, NY: Teachers College Press.
Vasudeva, A., Darling-Hammond, L., Newton, S., & Montgomery, K. (2009). *Oakland Unified School District new small schools initiative evaluation*. Stanford, CA: School Redesign Network at Stanford University.
Villegas, A. M., & Lucas, T. (2011). Preparing classroom teachers for English language learners: The policy context. In T. Lucas (Ed.), *Teacher preparation for linguistically diverse classrooms* (pp. 35–52). New York, NY: Routledge.
Walker, C., & Stone, K. (2011). Preparing teachers to reach English language learners: Pre-service and in-service initiatives. In T. Lucas (Ed.), *Teacher preparation for linguistically diverse classrooms* (pp. 127–142). New York, NY: Routledge.
Waller, W. (1932). *The sociology of teaching*. New York, NY: Wiley.
*Walsh, K. (2006). Teacher education: Coming up empty. *Fwd: Arresting Insights in Education, 3*(1).
Ware, F. (2006). Warm demander pedagogy: Culturally responsive teaching that supports a culture of achievement for African American students. *Urban Education, 41*(4), 427–456.

Warikoo, N. (2004). Race and the teacher-student relationship: interpersonal connections between West Indian students and their teachers in a New York City high school. *Race, Ethnicity and Education, 7*(2), 135–147.

Waxman, R. P., Weist, M. D., & Benson, D. M. (1999). Towards collaboration in the growing education-mental health interface. *Clinical Psychology Review, 19*(2), 239–253.

*Weiner, L. (2006). *Urban teaching: The essentials.* New York, NY: Teachers College Press.

Weiss, R. (1994). *Learning from strangers: The art of qualitative interview studies.* New York: The Free Press.

Werblow, J., & Duesbery, L. (2009). The impact of high school size on math achievement and dropout rate. *High School Journal, 92*(3), 14–23.

Weston, K. J., Anderson-Butcher, D., & Burke, R. W. (2008). Developing a comprehensive curriculum framework for teacher preparation in expanded school mental health. *Advances in School Mental Health Promotion, 2*(4), 25–41.

*White, W. A. (1927). *The mental hygiene of childhood.* Boston, MA: Little, Brown, and Company.

Whitehurst, G. J., & Chingos, M. M. (2011). *Class size: What research says and what it means for state policy.* Washington, DC: Brown Center on Education Policy, Brookings Institution.

Winograd, K. (2003). The functions of teacher emotions: The good, the bad and the ugly. *Teachers College Record, 105*(9), 1641–1673.

*Wong, H., & Wong, R. (2005). *The first days of school: How to be an effective teacher.* Mountain View, CA: Harry K. Wong Publications.

Woolley, M. E., & Bowen, G. L. (2007). In the context of risk: Supportive adults and the school engagement of middle school students. *Family Relations, 56*(1), 92–104.

Yin, R. K. (2009). *Case study research: Design and methods* (4th ed.). Thousand Oaks, CA: Sage Publications.

York-Barr, J., Sommerness, J., & Hur, J. (2008). Teacher leadership. In T. Good (Ed.), *21st century education: A reference handbook* (Vol. 1) (pp. 12–20). Thousand Oaks, CA: Sage.

Zeichner, K. (2010). Rethinking the connections between campus courses and field experiences in college- and university-based teacher education. *Journal of Teacher Education, 61*(1–2), 89–99.

Zembylas, M. (2002). "Structures of feeling" in curriculum and teaching: Theorizing the emotional rules. *Educational Theory, 52*(2), 187–208.

Index

Advisor role
  gender and, 79–80, 98–99
  novice teachers and, 102–106, 113, 116, 124–127, 136–137, 144–145, 153
  proposed areas of competency for, 112, 154–156
  race and ethnicity and, 79–80, 97–98, 101
  school structural support of, 44–63, 86–88, 103, 112–113, 126–127, 150–154
  structure of, *see* Role structure, advisor
  teacher age and, 94–95
  teacher enactment of, examples, 1–2, 6–8, 41–42, 65–66, 68–79, 83–85, 93–100, 102–112, 116–118, 120–127, 129–135
  teacher interpretation of, 67–80
    academic interpretation, 73–75
    life skills interpretation, 77–78
    social-emotional support interpretation, 75–77
  teacher learning in preparation for, 13, 95–96, 138, 153
  teacher mutual collaboration and, 57–59, 155
  teacher schemas (ideas) that informed, 83–93, 101–113, 123–124, 127–128
  teachers' minimal implementation of, 78–79
  teachers' personal resources that informed enactment of, 6–7, 50–51, 57, 83–88, 93–100
  combined with advisor role schemas, 101–113
  influence of prior professional experience upon, 95
  relational skills, 99–100
  social support, 96–97
Advisory class
  activities done during, 67–79, 81
  curriculum for, 49–52, 68–72, 89, 107, 152–153
  time for, 48–50
Advisory programs
  descriptions of, 18
  history of, 10–12
  need for structural support of, *see* Advisor role, school structural support of
Age of advisor, *see* Advisor role, teacher age and
Allensworth, Elaine, 44, 47
Antrop-González, Rene, 5, 79
Anderson-Butcher, Dawn, 16, 137, 158, 159, 162
Ayers, William, 11, 13, 34, 35

Bestor, Arthur, 29, 30
Bidwell, Charles, 9, 16, 24, 28
Boundaries on advisor role, 53, 89–93, 108, 111, 128, 131–139, 162–163
  and teacher responses to emotional display rules, 135

Bowen, Gary, 5
Bryk, Anthony, 9, 41, 47
Buese, Daria, 3, 41, 118
Burke, Robert, 16, 137, 158, 159, 162
Burnout, 104, 119–120, 124–128, 131, 135–137, 144, 150, 171, 173

Carnegie Council on Adolescent Development, 10
Coburn, Cynthia, 44, 85
Cohen, David, 44, 47
Comer, James, 33, 36
Cotton, Kathleen, 10, 34, 35
Covello, Leonard, 32, 157
Crosnoe, Robert, 5, 10, 44
Cuban, Larry, 2, 12, 147, 149, 163

Darling-Hammond, Linda, 6, 11, 148, 149
DeJésus, Anthony, 5, 79
Depersonalization, 119–120, 124, 126
Diefendorff, James, 129, 131, 140

EDRs, *see* Emotional display rules
Efficacy, teachers' perception of own in advisor role, 104, 119–124, 127–128, 134–136, 139, 171, 173
ELLs, *see* English Language Learners
Elmore, Richard, 47, 62
Emotional display rules (EDRs)
 defined, 116, 129
 examples at participating schools, 129–130
 research on, 128–129, 131, 139
 school definition of, 116, 129–130, 138
 teacher autonomy in responding to, 139–140
 teacher responses to, 130–135
 teachers defining boundaries in response to, 131–135, 139
Emotional Exhaustion, 119–120, 124–125, 136

Emotional labor
 advisor role as, 128
 defined, 17, 115
 individual characteristics that inform performance of, 140
 research on, 129–131, 139–140
 teaching as, 129
English language learners (ELLs), generalist teachers teaching, 3, 13–14, 39, 148–149
Ethnicity of advisor, *see* Advisor role, race and ethnicity and
Evenden, Edward, 29
Expanded teacher roles
 contemporary context of, 2–3, 9–12, 146–149
 defined, 3
 examples of (besides advisor role), 3, 13–15, 38–39, 115, 148–149
 historic context of, 8–9
 multiple dimensions of, 14–15
 schools' organizational support of, 25, 38–39, 63, 111–113, 147–150
 and teacher education 14–15, 147–150
External alignment of advisor role structures, *see* Role structure, alignment of advisor role structural elements and other school structures (external alignment)

Gender of advisor, *see* Advisor role, gender and
Giddens, Anthony, 43, 46, 62, 86, 113
Grant, Gerald, 9
Grossman, Pamela, 13, 24, 99, 147, 162

Hargreaves, Andrew, 139
History of advisory, *see* Advisory programs, history of
Hochschild, Arlie, 17, 130, 139, 140
Hoffman, Marvin, 10

House structure within schools, 6, 10, 42, 56–59, 61, 80–81, 97, 143
Hurn, Christopher, 9

Ingersoll, Richard, 4, 41, 44, 136
Internal alignment of advisor role structures, *see* Role structure, alignment among advisor role structural elements (internal alignment)

Job Satisfaction, 119–120, 122–124, 127–128, 135, 144, 171, 173
Johnson, Susan Moore, 6, 15, 41, 55, 63

Klonsky, Michael, 13, 34, 35
Kohl, Herbert, 9, 32
Koller, James, 13, 24, 147
Kumashiro, Kevin, 2

Labaree, David, 16, 23, 25, 26, 28
Lortie, Dan, 14, 16, 24, 28

Meier, Deborah, 34, 35
Michie, Gregory, 9, 31
Murphy, Joseph 14

Narrow teacher roles, factors that reinforce in U.S. schools, 13–15, 146–148
Nieto, Sonia, 11
Novice teachers and advisor role, *see* Advisor role, novice teachers and

Oplatka, Izhar, 115, 116, 139

Paternite, Carl, 137, 164
Payne, Charles, 6, 80

Quadrants illustrating advisor role resource and schema combinations
  defined, 101–102
  examples of teachers belonging to each quadrant, 102–111

Race of advisor, *see* Advisor role, race and ethnicity and
Relational practices and skills, teachers', 13, 99–100, 107, 112, 154–155, 161
Resources, *see* Advisor role, teachers' personal resources that informed enactment of; School-level structures, resources, as part of school structures
Responses to advisor role, teachers', 115–135
  differences between schools, 119–123
  differences between teachers, 123–128
Role overload and role load perception, 14, 104, 119–120, 122–126, 135–137, 139, 145–146, 160, 171, 173
Role structure, advisor, 41–63
  alignment among advisor role structural elements (internal alignment), 53–57, 60–62
  alignment of advisor role structural elements and other school structures (external alignment), 57–62, 153–154
  elements (defined), 43–46, 86
    cultural elements, 45
    formalized procedures, 45–46
    resources, 43–44
    schemas, 44–46
  evidence of elements at research sites, 47–53
Role theory, 82, 144

Sarason, Seymour, 9, 45
Schein, Edgar, 45

Schemas, *see* Advisor role, teacher schemas that informed; Role structure, advisor, elements; School-level structures, schemas as part of

School-based mental health services
  relationship to advisor role structure, 58–61, 63, 152–153
  relationship to teacher practice, 24–25, 33–35, 157–158, 163–165
  at research sites, 19, 54, 59–60, 122
  in small schools, *see* Small schools, school-based mental health services in
  as source for teacher consultation and professional learning, 12, 51, 59–60, 67–68, 138, 155, 164–165

School-level structures
  alignment of, defined, 46–47
  cultural dimensions, as element of structures 45–46, 86
  defined, 43–46, 86
  and expanded teacher roles, 63
  formalized procedures, as element of structures 44–45, 86
  resources, as element of school structures, 44, 86
  schemas, as part of 43–44, 86

School organizational culture, 5, 45–46, 56–57
School sites, description of, 18–19
Semel, Susan, 10, 11
Sense of reduced accomplishment, 119–120, 124–125
Sewell, William Jr., 43, 45, 46, 62, 86, 93, 101, 109, 113
Sizer, Theodore, 10, 34, 35
Small schools
  history of, 11
  model, description of, 12–13
  research on, 5–6
  school-based mental health services in, 11
  student-teacher relationships in, 11–13
  teacher social-emotional support role in 34–35

Smylie, Mark, 14
Social-emotional support, *see* Teachers and the social-emotional support of students
Special education student inclusion and teachers, 115, 147
Spillane, James, 24, 45, 85
Strike, Kenneth, 13, 34
Structuration theory, 43–44, 86, 133
Student-teacher relationships
  and the conditions of teaching, 3, 23–25
  research on, 5
  and school context, 5, 8–13, 23–24
  schools' support of, 15
  and small schools, 12–13
  and teacher learning, 13

Teacher attrition, *see* Teacher turnover
Teacher education
  and advisor role, *see* Advisor role, teacher learning in preparation for
  reinforcement of narrow teacher roles 13, 147
  and support for teachers' social-emotional support role, 13, 24, 29, 38
Teacher leadership, as an expanded teacher role, 14, 147
Teacher roles, evolution of in U.S. schools, 8–12
Teacher teams, influence on advisor role enactment, 6, 42, 56–57, 59–63, 70–71, 75–76, 97, 103, 108, 113, 153–154
Teacher turnover, 104, 119–120, 123, 135–137

Teachers and the social-emotional support of students
conceptualizations of in K-12 education literature, 12–13, 29–39
dimensions of teachers' responsibilities, as identified in review of K-12 education literature, 28–29
expectations about at research sites, 75, 122–123, 128–130
impact of social-emotional support expectations on teacher responses to advisor role, 119–123
mixed messages about, 36–39
opposition to, 29–30, 74–75
proposed competencies, 51, 59–60, 138, 158–165
support from school-based mental health providers for, 164–165
teacher learning and preparation for, 95–96, 138, 160–162, 164–165
teacher strain related to, 105–106, 119–123
teachers' reluctance about, 74–75, 91–92, 95, 130–131, 158
unclear expectations about, as identified in review of K-12 education literature, 32–33, 35–36
Tyack, David, 9, 12, 26, 30, 147, 149, 163

Valenzuela, Angela, 5, 10, 24, 80
Valli, Linda, 3, 41, 118

Waller, Willard, 16, 23, 24, 28
Ware, Franita, 6
Weston, Karen 16, 137, 158, 159, 162
Woolley, Michael, 5

GPSR Compliance

The European Union's (EU) General Product Safety Regulation (GPSR) is a set of rules that requires consumer products to be safe and our obligations to ensure this.

If you have any concerns about our products, you can contact us on

ProductSafety@springernature.com

In case Publisher is established outside the EU, the EU authorized representative is:

Springer Nature Customer Service Center GmbH
Europaplatz 3
69115 Heidelberg, Germany

www.ingramcontent.com/pod-product-compliance
Lightning Source LLC
LaVergne TN
LVHW051912060526
838200LV00004B/109